Radical as Reality

Radical as Reality

*Form and Freedom in
American Poetry*

Peter Campion

THE UNIVERSITY OF CHICAGO PRESS
Chicago & London

The University of Chicago Press, Chicago 60637
The University of Chicago Press, Ltd., London
© 2019 by The University of Chicago
Published 2019
Printed in the United States of America

28 27 26 25 24 23 22 21 20 19   1 2 3 4 5

ISBN-13: 978-0-226-66323-4 (cloth)
ISBN-13: 978-0-226-66337-1 (paper)
ISBN-13: 978-0-226-66340-1 (e-book)
DOI: https://doi.org/10.7208/chicago/9780226663401.001.0001

Library of Congress Cataloging-in-Publication Data

Names: Campion, Peter, 1976– author.
Title: Radical as reality : form and freedom in American poetry /
    Peter Campion.
Description: Chicago : University of Chicago Press, 2019. |
    Includes bibliographical references and index.
Identifiers: LCCN 2019024360 | ISBN 9780226663234 (cloth) |
    ISBN 9780226663371 (paperback) | ISBN 9780226663401 (ebook)
Subjects: LCSH: American poetry—History and criticism. | Liberty
    in literature.
Classification: LCC PS303 .C36 2019 | DDC 811.009—dc23
LC record available at https://lccn.loc.gov/2019024360

♾ This paper meets the requirements of ANSI/NISO Z39.48–1992
(Permanence of Paper).

When Lenin was in exile in Zurich during the First World War, before the sealed train brought him back to Russia in 1917, he used to visit a restaurant frequented by Bohemian types, Dada poets and painters, and low-lifers of one sort or another. A young Romanian poet called Marcu wrote an account (to be found in Robert Motherwell's *Dada Documents*) of a chat he had with Lenin there....

"How can you expect to foster hatred of this war," I asked, "if you are not in principle against all wars? I thought that as a Bolshevik you were really a radical thinker and refused to make any compromise with the idea of war....

Lenin listened attentively, his head bent toward me. He moved his chair closer to mine. He must have wondered whether to continue to talk to this boy or not. I, somewhat awkwardly, remained silent.

"Your determination to rely on yourselves," Lenin finally replied, "is very important. Every man must rely on himself. Yet he should also listen to what informed people have to say. I don't know how radical you are, or how radical I am. I am certainly not radical enough. One can never be radical enough; that is, one must always try to be as radical as reality itself."

ALEXANDER COCKBURN
The Golden Age Is in Us (1996, 225)

Contents

Introduction: Radical as Reality 1

PART ONE

Frost and Stevens at the Casa Marina—9
A Dream We Dreamed Each Separately—28
John Berryman's Acoustics—71
James Wright's Classicism—85
Palpable Fact: James Schuyler and Immediacy—103

PART TWO

Biographical Form: Five Poets—113
Mah Wallah-Woe—154
Larry Levis—166

PART THREE

Verse Chronicle: Poems of Force—179
"The Wolf, the Snake, the Hog,
Not Wanting in Me": Poetry and Resistance—207
Free within Ourselves—217
Sincerity and Its Discontents—226

Acknowledgments 249
Works Cited 251
Index of Names 259

Introduction:
Radical as Reality

Readers might detect something strange in my naming a book about American poetry after a remark of Vladimir Lenin's. Admittedly, my first encounter with the word *radical* came in adolescence, when friends and I applied it to anything that thrilled us—bootleg concert tapes, skateboard tricks, celebrities—not knowing we were emulating Californian surf culture. I hope that spirit survives here: I want to identify what in modern poetry fills me with awe, what feels most surprising and inevitable, built to endure. But that story of the poet and the revolutionary also offers a serious parable about modernity. The encounter between Valeriu Marcu and Lenin, resulting in the declaration that the artist and the political actor share an ambition to create something as "radical as reality itself," suggests not only how political movements in the years ahead would often adopt aesthetic dimensions, but also how modern art would emerge. If such a parable carries ominous undertones, dark hints of the nightmares those dreams could become, I still catch a canny hopefulness in that statement, asking us to consider how moments of wonder, liberating moments, might be sustained as made things.

This book is about such making as it occurs in American poetry. But geographic and generic borders, even identities, are seldom secure in the writing considered here. Poets the world over attempt to make art from the tensions between form and freedom, to reconcile social conventions with expressive liberties. In American poetry, though, the process proves unique for its instability. The United

States is a famously new and restless nation, "the land of the free." At the same time, uneasy about its newness, its formation from continuing waves of immigration, its history as slave republic, and its growth into a military and economic Goliath, Americans tend to obsess over what the Right considers "heritage" and the Left an affirmation of identity—notions no less powerful for being, most often, recent inventions. We all construct the future from the past, whether well or poorly. The conviction sponsoring this book is that the best artists not only receive but comprehend and adapt what comes before them. They reinterpret the history of their art and history itself, and this makes their work "radical as reality."

Such acts of transformation remain both smaller and larger than writing political poetry: a single syllable—the word *we*—suggests one of the central concerns addressed in this book. To be alert in America, as in its poetry, means to be troubled by this pronoun. Among overlapping affiliations, *we* can turn into a homogenous, received form, prohibiting difference and self-determination. Remember the famous E. Nelson Bridwell cartoon from *Mad*: Tonto turns on the Lone Ranger with his immortal rejoinder "What do you mean *we*?" The punch line remains sovereign, and still, the need to be a "we" must be hard-wired, fundamental to love and justice.

This same tension between public and private selves, including nervousness about speaking for others and having others speak for us, as well as the simultaneous need for others, pops up all over American poetry. Take a poem that might at first seem merely whimsical or tongue in cheek—Emily Dickinson's poem #288 (1960):

I'm Nobody! Who are you?
Are you—Nobody—too?
Then there's a pair of us!
Don't tell! They'd advertise—you know!

How dreary—to be—Somebody!
How public—like a frog—
To tell one's name—the livelong June—
To an admiring bog!

It's worth attempting to read this as the driest formalist might, without any appeal to history or politics. What becomes clear? These two quatrains dramatize the process of any two people becoming a pair, and yet the partnership feels as much like subtraction as addition—a call to escape the group. Will escape be possible? Hard to tell. All eight lines keep to the initial moment of exchange. The bog-like public hasn't yet receded. The addressee seems to sign up with the speaker between lines 2 and 3, but he or she's never heard from, making it possible that the speaker's talking past, while buttonholing, this potential lover or confidant. For him or her, as well as the reader, the speaker's invitation may feel genuine, alluring, or not.

In the verse form, too, singular expression and shared knowledge prove mutually entailing tensions. Each quatrain contains three lines of trimeter and one of tetrameter, but the position of this elongated line shifts in the second, so that even with two lines, the minimum for any repetition, Dickinson stages a little drama of disguise and recognition. End rhyme occurs twice as well, at the very beginning and the conclusion, making three-quarters of the poem unfold as naturalistic speech, a seeming departure until "bog" fulfills the convention of rhyme and, at the same moment, casts aspersions on the whole world of convention.

Even to read the poem like this, with an admittedly pinched attention to its form, means to understand it as a drama of ambiguous allegiances and unstable identities, cast in language that intends at turns to emancipate and dominate.

So what to make of the fact that Dickinson wrote poem #288 in 1861, during the beginning of the American Civil War? Her father, Edward Dickinson, was a former United States congressman, an antislavery Whig who voted against the Kansas-Nebraska Act. Her close confidant Thomas W. Higginson was a staunch abolitionist. Less than ten miles from the Dickinson home, across the Connecticut River in Northampton, the Hill-Ross farm was a major station on the Underground Railroad, and in 1861, with war breaking out, the flow of escapees through central Massachusetts was becoming greater than ever.

Poems are not secret analogs of their historical situations; the frog who's become a "Somebody" to his admiring public is no stand-in for Abraham Lincoln or Jefferson Davis. Dickinson did write a few overtly topical poems during the war, and this isn't one of them. But its historical situation seems to me an undeniable atmosphere of the poem, soaked into the boards: after all, this lyric presents a secretive flight to freedom conducted in fear of exposure by those who "advertise," as well as a disputed claim to sovereign rule. Even Dickinson's formal abstraction—including her obliquity toward the same public sphere her speaker invokes only to condemn—reveals not only the poet's ancient desire to transcend history but also the desire, just as inveterate, to collect and transform historical and social energies.

Some of the questions implicit in Dickinson's poem prove central to this book. Is freedom inherently divisive? How can a free society prevent not only secessions and rebellions but also its own tyrannical forms of domination? How does an individual recognize and experience freedom? What do we mean by that word anyhow?

I wrote these essays in the fifteen years between 2001 and 2016. During that time, "freedom" was often invoked to justify wars—extending today across at least six countries and incurring vicious reprisals in the form of terror. "Freedom" was also used to cloak an arrogation of wealth so massive, and by an elite so small, that any medieval despot catapulted into the present day would burst into fits of jealousy.

Such conditions inform my understanding of the word. But *freedom* has carried dark connotations for a long time now. I have in mind the tendency D. H. Lawrence identified in *Studies in Classic American Literature* (1968): from the Puritan migration onward, American ambition was not merely what it claimed, the progress toward freedom, but a darker inclination "neither free nor easy" (5), an individualistic, restless, often violent force. Unlike Lawrence's prose, Dickinson's poem suggests but doesn't argue this claim. Instead the poem makes a figure, enacting that argument and its encompassing contrary, the invitation to true freedom.

What *is* true freedom? Different poets answer differently, and most tend not so much to answer as propose, compelling their readers to entertain a freedom that would realize cost, risk, ambiguity, and consequence. Such freedom implies a dialectical relation with form—a process that pervades the everyday: what shapes do

4

we want to give our lives, how much can we choose those shapes, and what do we mean by *we*—these questions contain radical potential not because they're far out, novel, or extreme but because they are embedded, kneaded into common experience. I subscribe to the old notion that to be radical is to grasp things by the root. The poets whose work most compels me understand the past, take hold of those forces that determine the present, and transform them in their art.

These essays unfold in rough chronological order, from early American Modernism to the present. The opening section begins with two longer essays, the first an investigation of the divergent ways that Wallace Stevens and Robert Frost made poems out of the tensions between personal and communal experience, and the second an exploration of how four American Modernist poets reinvented their art form by combining epic and lyric precedents. The shorter essays following these attend to the specific achievements of individual poets who similarly negotiated the pull between convention and individual expression, abstract formal energies and the thick texture of social experience. The second section starts with another essay about the reinvention of form—specifically the integration of the conventions of biography with poetic structures—in the work of Robert Lowell and four poets from the generation following his. That essay precedes two shorter considerations of major poets from the same, later generation. The third section contains four essays: the first three examine how American poets contend with such forces as war and racial tension; the final, while considering contemporary examples, addresses the historical energies informing an often troubled term, *sincerity*.

When I began as a critic, reviewing books and gallery shows for magazines and newspapers, I shied away from principles or prescriptions about what makes art worthwhile. After all, wasn't the point to be surprised? But I also felt powerful convictions: judgment seemed more than a matter of unaccountable personal preference. My situation was something like Justice Potter Stewart's when, attempting to define obscenity, he wrote, "I know it when I see it." Twenty years after starting out as a critic, when someone asks, I resort to retelling the story about Marcu and Lenin—art should be "as radical as reality itself." I intend the essays collected here to explain how such an ambition has been realized in modern and contemporary American poetry, developing through the counterpoint between form and freedom. Most of the poets considered here I admire a great deal, and the few with whom I quarrel have already earned my respect. But conflict can be helpful, especially when it locates pressure points in the development of the art. For this reason, the first essay begins with a fight between poets—a fight about poetic freedom and the actual ways that modern Americans live.

Part One

Frost and Stevens
at the Casa Marina

In February 1940, at the Casa Marina on Key West, Robert Frost, a guest at the hotel, invited Wallace Stevens over for the afternoon. The two knew each other from as far back as 1897, when both enrolled as nondegree students at Harvard. In fact, they had dined together in Key West once before, in 1935, and things seemed to go well enough; writing to a friend, Stevens said how much he enjoyed introducing Frost to conch chowder and sapodilla, a Caribbean pearlike fruit with big black seeds. Not long after their dinner, Stevens sent Frost a Latin dictionary as a gift. But sometime during this 1940 visit, the two poets began to make fun of each other. Stevens said, "The trouble with you, Robert, is that you're too academic." Frost countered that Stevens was "too executive." Stevens said, "But you write about ... subjects." Frost came back again: "And you, Wallace, you write about bric-a-brac." Accounts diverge, and some have the two men pummeling each other on the sand.

Even as apocrypha, the sparring match makes a memorable image. Frost and Stevens stand as convenient opposites. Frost is the traditionalist, Stevens the self-consciously modern artist. One renders established topics in plain language, the other jumbles or even ignores the world as conventionally understood. On Frost's side stands the democratic yet conservative demand that art remain not only representational but also representative: the American poet should delight and instruct, should speak for, to, and about the people. On Stevens's side, the avant-garde withdraws from all that earnest pedestrian stuff: should American poets accept any public responsibility—different from that of poets in, say, Bali or Sweden—this would be to discover new worlds of the imagination.

Like most effective provocations, "subjects" and "bric-a-brac" bear powerful colorings of truth. Reading Stevens often means following end runs around conventional meaning. Stevens tends to introduce what at first read like propositions of argument, then bend into associative reasoning. There are often moments of sheer linguistic play (Stevens 1997):

> Chieftan Iffucan of Azcan in tan and henna hackles halt (60)

or

> In Hydapsia by Howzen
> Lived a lady, Lady Lowzen (243)

or

> Play the present, its hoo-hoo-hoo
> Its shoo-shoo-shoo, its ric-a-nic. (107)

Such lines sound like private parodic reverie—the kind of abstract doodling Frost meant by "bric-a-brac."

For his part, Frost sometimes let popular appeal exceed imagination. Teasing him about his academic "subjects," Stevens might have been thinking of "Not of School Age" (1995), a recent lyric ending with these two quatrains about a patriotic preschooler:

> He was too young to go,
> Not over four or so.
> Well, would I please go to school,
> And the big flag they had—you know
>
> The big flag, the red—white—
> And blue flag, the great sight—
> He bet it was out today,
> And would I see if he was right. (333)

There's evidence enough in both poets to support the image of them as the populist and the aesthete.

But that last Stevens quotation comes from "Mozart, 1935." Written, as its title shows, after the ascent of fascism in Germany and

Italy, and during the escalation toward the Spanish Civil War, this poem addresses the ability of art both to resist and to render political catastrophe—to "play the present." Stevens not only has subjects, he has public subjects. And "Not of School Age" hardly represents a body of work that stands as a grand achievement, even while preceding and outdoing all tired cant about "subversion." Frost may find his dramas and meditations in the familiar sphere of the home, the farm, the nearby woods, and his prosody in the English metrical tradition, but he works continually to unsettle habits of mind and feeling. His poems often leave the reader confronting fissures in the very surface of assumed reality: a neighbor carrying stones looks for a second like a caveman, the headboard of a mother's bed hides the attic where the bones of her lover crumble, a picturesque winter landscape opens onto vertiginous "desert places." Even when they're not secretly terrifying as Lionel Trilling once claimed, Frost's poems tend to be estranging: they lead us to an impasse, bewildering, wondrous, or both, where our imagination and intellect must begin anew.

But this lore about the fight in Key West distills more than differences in style: it suggests tensions about the assumptions and commitments behind style. Just as provocative as "subjects" and "bric-a-brac" would have been "academic" and "executive." The words contain jokes about the way the poets, both now in their sixties, earned their bread: Stevens as a vice president at the Hartford, and Frost as the recipient of writer-in-residence positions at colleges and universities—he'd just spent fall term of 1939 at Harvard. If "academic" and "executive" were good-natured jabs, they carried sharp edges, implying a particular social sin, authority gained not from merit but from institutions. The academicians were those mere success stories, the stifling forebears of the School of Paris painters, whom Stevens loved. Frost's most recent book, *A Further Range*, may have been a Book of the Month Club selection in 1936, assuring sales above fifty thousand. His publisher, Holt, may have given him a monthly allowance for life. But couldn't these prove signs of irrelevance to the genuine spirit of modern art? Couldn't such a poet end up being Robert Southey in the eyes of Byron?

And if Frost was such a democratic populist, what about this academic business? Academics are not known for summoning the spirit of the tribe. In fact, the critics jumped on *A Further Range* precisely because of what they saw as Frost's tepid treatment of public life. Dudley Fitts, the excellent translator of poems from the *Greek Anthology* (1938), wrote in *New England Quarterly* that it was a "strange thing that Robert Frost, pondering the problems of a sick society, should suddenly become ineffectual" (1936). In *New Masses*, a magazine its editor Michael Gold wanted "read by lumberjacks, hobos, miners . . . ," a magazine supporting Stalin through the purges and show trials of the 1930s, Rolfe Humphries, himself a fine translator of Ovid, claimed that Frost's "excursion into the field of political didactic" was "unbecoming" (1936). R. P. Blackmur, the most formidable of Frost's critics, argued in *The Nation* (1936) that Frost courted his political subjects only to evade them: "as bad religious poetry versifies the need of an attitude toward God, bad social poetry versifies the need of an attitude toward society" (818). And hadn't Blackmur himself given Wallace Stevens a tremendous boost with his 1935 essay in *Hound and Horn*, "Examples of Wallace Stevens"?

Frost got his digs in too. "Executive" spelled elitism, perennial bane of all avant-gardes. Frost was repeating a charge Blackmur defended Stevens against, one the poet knew all too well—that he was minor, an aesthete, his work a rarefied cabinet of curios. Frost may have meant that for all the presumptive freedom of Stevens's imaginative flights, there was something programmatic, overly elevated, bloodless in his poems. "Executive" may have hinted at moral and social failure bound up in Stevens's aesthetics, an asymmetry in the exchange between writer and reader—executives tending to rig tables in their favor. But if so, this was a charge Blackmur leveled against Frost himself, using an economic metaphor to explain that Frost's poems of the 1930s were not "something others may use on approximately the same level as the poet did" (1936).

Perhaps "subjects" and "bric-a-brac" as well as "academic" and "executive" were only good-natured jokes. Where's the hard evidence of a fight? A photograph exists from that day. The two poets are sitting together on a low wall outside the Casa Marina. Stevens wears a white jacket, Frost a darker one. Behind Frost's shoulder, a potted palm tree spreads its fronds. Behind Stevens, a Spanish Revival–style arcade tapers to the edge of the picture. Auden's "low dishonest decade" has just ended. It's a sunny afternoon. These poets hardly appear hungry for vengeance.

Still, even as good jokes, their words have the edginess of fighting terms. They carry assumptions about history, politics, and the conduct of everyday life, along with propositions about what modern poetry can be and do. This is not a matter of either man's views as such, but of how each gave form to historical energy. Out of the tension between communal contingencies and individual aspirations, Frost and Stevens wrote their best poems.

"The American Sublime" and "Large Red Man Reading"

To understand such form-finding it may be helpful to look at a motif both poets employ, one not specifically political but having to do with the inheritance and adaptation of the past. I have in mind the theme of Christian ritual, centering around Communion, or Eucharist, as it appears in both the imagery and fundamental action of certain poems. Neither Frost nor Stevens was a Christian poet like late Eliot or early Lowell. In fact, their distance from religious convention is what makes their allusions to the ritual so interesting. *Communion* implies fellowship, like its cognate *community*. It also calls to mind the concept of transubstantiation, in which bread and wine become divine substance. To invoke the ritual in a secular poem is then to ask: as modern men and women, living without overriding doctrines, what kind of shared bonds can we expect, what kind of community? At the same time, can we transcend our contingent selves? Can lyric poetry, an art deriving from ritual speech, offer what once came from religion?

For Stevens more than Frost, religion, its loss and possible replacement through art, was a perennial occupation. In a 1951 essay titled "Two or Three Ideas" (1997) he claimed, "In an age of disbelief, or, what is the same thing, in a time that is largely humanistic, it is for the poet to supply the satisfactions of belief, in his measure and in his style" (841). While Stevens might appear more modern than Frost, he remains unique among his contemporaries for devotion to this essentially nineteenth-century theme. Those sentences from "Two or Three Ideas" could read as summations of such admittedly different poets as Charles Baudelaire and Matthew Arnold.

But neither would have taken the forward-looking stance Stevens does in his poetry. This attitude—his most profound inheritance from Whitman—suggests what's so American about Stevens, his assumption, even in the austere late poems, that he's taking part in an urgent new endeavor.

This endeavor comes with challenges. Consider a lyric from the mid-1930s, "The American Sublime" (1997), in which Stevens imagines a form of ritual communion, a seemingly failed one. Here are the two stanzas with which the poem ends:

> But how does one feel?
> One grows used to the weather,
> The landscape and that;
> And the sublime comes down
> To the spirit itself,
>
> The spirit and space,
> The empty spirit
> In vacant space.
> What wine does one drink?
> What bread does one eat? (106)

Maybe the uncertainty conveyed by those question marks suggests the perpetual possibility offered by the nonreligion Stevens envisions—one remembers how in "Sunday Morning" the poet imagines modern celebrants chanting to the sun "not as a god but as a god might be." But here any open-ended "might be" proves tinged with disappointment. By reducing ritual to bare essentials, "spirit and space," Stevens conjures a sublime that's neither grandiose nor transcendent. In fact it feels a lot like isolation, and the suspicion that the poet can't "supply the satisfactions of belief" still lingers. The material world won't allow such belief. The poet's surroundings are "empty" and "vacant," and the sacraments that would link matter and spirit turn out to be missing: "What wine does one drink? / What bread does one eat?" "One" acts here both as the general third-person pronoun and the number 1—the impossibility of ritual derives not only from a lack of established sacraments but also of the plurality to establish them: "one" alone cannot have ritual.

And it's not just the material world that proves deficient but *American* public life, this society that appears a homogenous swarm of "ones." Consider the opening two stanzas:

How does one stand
To behold the sublime,
To confront the mockers,
The mickey mockers
And plated pairs?

When General Jackson
Posed for his statue
He knew how one feels.
Shall a man go barefoot
Blinking and blank? (106)

More than a hint of resentment laces those lines about the "mickey mockers" and "plated pairs." This semi-abstract caricature spoofs the vulgarity of middle-class couples — "plated pairs" being a mercantile term for earrings: if the husband appears a hostile skeptic, the wife's a cutout from a newspaper ad. From the poet's point of view, such deflationary realists and the practical-minded, materialistic, irreverent society for which they stand hold a dismaying advantage over the individual imagination.

This theme, the leveling numbness of modern mass culture, appears often in Stevens. The mickey mockers and plated pairs may, for example, be the daytime incarnation of the people asleep in their houses in "Disillusionment of Ten o'Clock," the people who "are not going / To dream of baboons and periwinkles," and may be relatives of those invisible inhabitants who haunt "Loneliness in Jersey City" where "there's nothing whatever to see / Except Polacks that pass in their motors" (1997, 52, 191).

But Frost was wrong when he implied Stevens was an "executive" elitist. I mean that Stevens isn't given to the Old World equation of high culture with class distinction. Integral to the larger *commedia* in which they participate, these caricatures appear as Stevens's reality principle. Even as they frustrate his desire for grandiosity, he trusts them. He must account for them.

Take the figure of grand scale he employs in "The American Sublime," the image of Andrew Jackson posing for his statue. The poet alludes to Clark Mills's statue standing across from the White House in Lafayette Square, a monument whose incongruity he'll discuss again in his essay "The Noble Rider and the Sounds of Words" (1997): "One looks at this work of Clark Mills and thinks of the remark of Bertrand Russell that to acquire immunity to eloquence is of the utmost importance to a democracy" (648). In his poem, as in his essay, Stevens is worried by a modern American prejudice against the artistic imagination. But in the poem he countenances "immunity to eloquence" and does so with humor many critics miss. Mills's monument is doomed to be ridiculous by the incongruity of New World realities and Old World ideals. And Jackson himself is the embodiment of that contradiction. If any American president *could* be cast in the manner of the Renaissance military statues Stevens claims to favor over the work of Clark Mills, it would be Andrew Jackson. The leader of the Seminole Campaign had an imperial reputation. He was a post-Napoleonic, Romantic hero of cultural imagination. At the same time he was the original populist, the leader of the "Jackson Democrats," famous for their nativistic belief in what Richard Hofstadter once called "the superiority of the inborn, intuitive, folkish wisdom" (1963, 154–55). The man's very behavior was a contradiction: the great British historian George Dangerfield writes of Jackson that "he was all tenderness on the one hand, and all savagery on the other" (1965, 43). As statuary, such a moving, two-sided target presents a problem: however he's cast, he'll appear ridiculous to anyone who knows the other side of him—and everyone does. The image of his heroic pose is physically funny too: even schoolchildren in Stevens's day knew that Andrew Jackson was emaciated. But most comical of all, the narrator of "The American Sublime" *relates* to Jackson:

When General Jackson
Posed for his statue
He knew how one feels. (106)

Here, "one" becomes the implied first person, the frustrated aspirant who, in his grandiose self-pity, identifies with no less a figure than the seventh president of the United States. Stevens knew his despair about what he once called the "slime of men in crowds" was worth both expressing and mediating with humor. And this is what's so ingenious about "The American Sublime": the "low" tone of social comedy tempers and democratizes the gorgeous feeling of longing that remains, even as the poet declares failure in the last lines.

But some of Stevens's most affecting poetry comes when he countenances what resists his desire for the sublime or grandiose and still manages to fulfill that desire. In such poems, Stevens incorporates or preempts Frost's criticism of his tendency toward the "executive." I have in mind his final two collections, *The Auroras of Autumn* (1950) and *The Rock* (1954), as well as much of his late uncollected work.

Consider a poem that attempts to describe and enact a modern ritual of communion, "Large Red Man Reading" (1997). The poem opens by recounting a kind of cosmic poetry reading:

There were ghosts who returned to earth to hear his phrases,
As he sat there reading, aloud, the great blue tabulae.
They were those from the wilderness of stars that had expected more.
(365)

The ghosts in this poem, the mysterious host of souls who attend upon the priestly figure of the reader, are "those who wanted more." But in a reversal of expectations, wanting more doesn't translate into a desire for the absolute or ascension out of nature. Instead these beings descend *into* reality:

There were those that returned to hear him read from the poem of life,
Of the pans above the stove, the pots on the table, the tulips among
them.
They were those who would have wept to step barefoot into reality,

That would have wept and been happy, have shivered in the frost
And cried out to feel it again, have run fingers over leaves
And against the most coiled thorn, have seized on what was ugly

And laughed, as he sat there reading, from out of the purple tabulae,
The outlines of being and its expressings, the syllables of its law:
Poesis, poesis, the literal characters, the vatic lines,

Which in those ears and in those thin, those spended hearts,
Took on color, took on shape and the size of things as they are
And spoke the feeling for them, which was what they lacked.

In the earlier poem as well, Stevens declares, with an idiomatic turn
to underline his meaning, that the sublime "comes down." But in
"Large Red Man Reading" this descent sheds all bewilderment and
disappointment. Even when the returning spirits experience pain
and ugliness, all they do is laugh.

Stevens's celestial comedy has at its core the tension between
modern, democratic everyday life on the one hand and the individual's desire for something greater on the other. The elevation he
sought in "The American Sublime" appears here in the biblical ring
of the anaphora, the repetition of the Greek "*poesis poesis poesis,*" the
reference to poetry as "vatic lines," and the Virgilian image of souls
seeking rebirth. But transcendent experience leads to the ordinary
world of "the pans above the stove," just as Stevens finds lyric intensity not in spite of the mundane but in it—as with Whitman's
vision of a muse "install'd with the kitchen ware" (1982, 343). Most
important, the framing of the poem in the third person and the
past tense creates a slight but crucial distance from the transcendent experience, making the address of this poem the opposite of
"The American Sublime." Here the poet returns to the quotidian
public sphere to relate the wonder of the individual large red man
reading—a reading that's itself an earthly communion—and not
to seek transcendence apart from the public that exasperates him.
Tempering grandiosity with simplicity, Stevens achieves a powerful
synthesis, an immanence that remains impatient with immanence,
striving as it does toward transformation.

"The Black Cottage" and "Directive"

Stevens's desire for poetry to inhabit the void left by religion was not one Frost seems to have shared. Stevens himself was, at least as an adult, no practicing Christian, and even enjoyed humor at the expense of traditional piety, as in such early poems as "A High-Toned Old Christian Woman." But his parodies don't belie his desire to make his art, as he puts it in one poem, "out of the old cathedrals, empty and grandiose." He would seldom take the tone of the no-nonsense empirical American. Frost often would, once treating the very subject of the communion motif in modern poetry with such irony, quipping in a letter that "T. S. Eliot and I like to play, but I like to play Euchre, while he likes to play Eucharist" (1963, 321).

But the problems and desires that the communion motif present in Stevens (and in Eliot) are crucial to Frost as well. Like the Stevens of "Large Red Man Reading," Frost seeks moments not of transcendence so much as of immanence, moments when human imagination and the sheer material of the natural world intermingle. This desire meets a strong counterforce: Frost often works against the urge to see nature through the lens of human subjectivity. He sometimes portrays that tendency as sentimentality, the idle fantasies of those "not versed in country things." At other times the personification of nature appears a dangerous symptom of madness—consider how the protagonist of "The Hill Wife" expresses her own unquiet mind through her perceptions of the birds and trees surrounding her home. Still, what images of fulfilled desire appear in Frost arise when reality and imagination have convincingly meshed, offering the poet and reader a "satisfaction of belief." At the end of "West-Running Brook," such merging comes as close to the ecstatic as possible in Frost. More typically, in the early lyric "Mowing" the poet claims of the rural labor he celebrates that "it was no dream of the gift of idle hours, / Or easy gold at the hand of fay or elf," and yet "dream" recurs in his description of the true satisfaction of mowing: "The fact is the sweetest dream that labor knows" (1995, 26). Imagination can prove illusory but remains a necessary element of material reality.

It was an obsession with the relation between imagination and material reality that led Frost to develop his seriousness as a thinker. His path wended through the work of William James, the teacher Frost wanted most to study with when he went to Cambridge in 1897. Although James turned out to be on leave that year, Frost adhered to *Will to Believe*, then *Pragmatism*, which in 1912 he taught at the New Hampshire State Normal School, a teachers' college in Plymouth, New Hampshire. "Truth is made," James wrote in the sixth lecture of *Pragmatism*, "just as health, wealth and strength are made, in the course of experience" (1987, 581). James believed truth was useful and therefore variable. "If I am lost in the woods and starved," begins his classic analogy from that same lecture, "and find what looks like a cow-path, it is of the utmost importance that I should think of a human habitation at the end of it," but some other time the house may be "practically irrelevant, and had better remain latent" (574). Because of this variability, James writes, "the advantage of having a general stock of *extra* truths, of ideas that shall be true of merely possible situations, is obvious" (575). The influence of these arguments upon Frost has been elaborated by scholars such as Richard Poirier and Frank Lentricchia, but I want to look at two poems remarkable not only for staging a pragmatic negotiation of competing realities but also for doing so in the context of an encounter with older Christian beliefs. What's more, these poems contain a parallel drama of faith and doubt about the prospects for democratic society.

Frost wrote "The Black Cottage" in 1905, ten years before it was published in *North of Boston*. Its narrator relates a story told by his minister friend after the two chanced upon the ramshackle home of a deceased Civil War widow, once a member of the minister's congregation. The widow used to present the minister with a conundrum: when he wanted to slightly alter the liturgy, taking out the words "descended into Hades" to reflect the ethos of his "liberal youth," her presence in the pews prevented him. Surprisingly, the minister turns out to be a Jamesian pragmatist. Even as he defends sticking to possibly outdated phrases, he appeals to the multiplicity of truth:

    ... why abandon a belief
Merely because it ceases to be true?
Cling to it long enough, and not a doubt
It will turn true again, for so it goes. (1995, 61)

This belief in varying truths also informs the minister's portrayal of the widow herself. She stands as an emblem of loss, and her hopefulness rests upon this loss's having meaning, as sacrifice. The minister wants to believe, and also doubts, that transformation:

Her giving somehow touched the principle
That all men are created free and equal.
And to hear her quaint phrases—so removed
From the world's view today of all those things.
That's a hard mystery of Jefferson's.
What did he mean? Of course the easy way
Is to decide it simply isn't true.
It may not be. I heard a fellow say so.
But never mind, the Welshman got it planted
Where it will trouble us a thousand years.
Each age will have to reconsider it. (60)

The variability behind the minister's resolve, his needing to *choose* to believe in the widow's hope, as in the future of the democratic experiment, leads to bewilderment by the end of the poem. The minister tells his fantasy of being a "monarch of desert land" dedicated to "the truths we keep coming back and back to." But Frost pops this dreamy bubble by having the wish fulfillment get carried away. The minister meanders into a vainglorious image of a desert wind that will "retard mid-waste my cowering caravans." And there the story itself stops midsentence when, caught off guard, he discovers bees in the wall of the widow's cottage.

With this framing, Frost carves a dark turn into the very Jamesian pragmatism that compels him. The minister's philosophical "will to believe" seems like self-absorption, his acknowledgment of the variability of truth, permission for ponderous tangents, tinged with more than a little self-aggrandizement. The critique applies not only to pragmatism but also to its roots in Emersonian self-reliance and, further back, in New England Puritanism. It's a criticism familiar from Hawthorne and Melville, as well as Frost's immediate precursor Edwin Arlington Robinson. Behind the surface of American optimism, such narratives tell us, lie loneliness and dark melancholy. Behind the belief in progress and public-spirited democracy lies the original contradiction of predestination and individual election: as Max Weber held in his *Protestant Work Ethic and the Spirit of Capitalism* (1905), the urge to reveal election empowers a capitalist class bent upon individual gain and exploitation, and satisfies simultaneous pretensions to moral authority. Strong strains of this tendency appear not only in American life but also in literature: Benjamin Franklin's moralistic prose, with its smug, homespun apothegms, provides Weber with his prime example.

In Frost the critique becomes subtler, more playful. The minister, for example, may exhibit a Franklinian blend of practicality and hauteur, but he's neither absurd nor blameworthy. Still, the shadow the poet throws across him, suggesting his character flaws reveal defects in national character, provides only one of many instances in Frost of testing and troubling the same pragmatism he admires. In fact, the very structures of his poems can be read this way. If we ask of pragmatism how it can be sustained when the constant need to select from a "stock of extra truths" exhausts the chooser, we get the premise of "The Wood Pile," in which the poet finds a cord of maple logs someone has split, piled, and then mysteriously abandoned to the "slow smokeless burning of decay" (1995, 101). We have as well the situation of "The Census Taker," in which a traveling census taker comes to an abandoned logging tract where industry has left the land "an emptiness flayed to the very stone" (164). Asking what happens when the individual, making truth in the course of experience, can't tell where his subjectivity stops and the world begins, we have the occasion of "The Most of It" and "For Once, Then, Something." Asking what happens when as few as two individual truth-makers attempt to make collective truth, we end up with Frost's darker marriage poems, "The Fear," "The Hill Wife," and "Home Burial," the latter of which directly precedes "The Black Cottage" in *North of Boston*.

Frost seldom solves such contradictions. Instead his poems provide forms in which contradictions have room to move. Stevens, even when he abandons Imagination as an ultimate good, still summons and faces "desire beyond an object to desire" as a godlike force (1997, 311). Frost has no such absolute to which he can appeal. Doubting Jamesian pragmatism, he comes around again to express pragmatism's fundamental emphasis upon freedom and choice. Two roads are always diverging for him, and, not without his remarkable skill for doublespeak, he's always taking both.

For a poet, the risk of this extreme ambiguity turns out to be the loss of the intention and intensity of ritual action. Garrulity, mere charm, as well as those plain-style longueurs that sometimes dilute Wordsworth, can step in where necessity fears to tread. It's characteristic of Frost's genius that in dozens of his best poems he balances against such risks by pitching his poems from crucial occasions, with the idiomatic clarity and vibrant "sentence sounds" of his democratic realism.

But in at least one of his best poems he creates that balance by reimagining ritual action. The one in which Frost does in fact "play Eucharist" is "Directive." It's become an anthology piece, famous for its opening and closing lines—"Back out of all this now too much for us" and "Drink and be whole again beyond confusion"—perhaps because in the middle of the poem Frost intends to get us lost. In fact, it doesn't take more than nine lines for the ruse to begin:

> Back out of all this now too much for us,
> Back in a time made simple by the loss
> Of detail, burned, dissolved, and broken off
> Like graveyard marble sculpture in the weather,
> There is a house that is no more a house
> Upon a farm that is no more a farm
> And in a town that is no more a town.
> The road there, if you'll let a guide direct you
> Who only has at heart your getting lost ... (1995, 341)

Frost himself is the guide "who only has at heart your getting lost," the guide who believes you have to be "lost enough to find yourself." And the middle of the poem overflows with images, turns of phrase, and embedded mini-narratives that are nothing if not weird. Frost conjures, for example, the personified glacier "that braced his feet against the Arctic Pole," thereby asking us, from out of his seemingly simple vernacular, to consider geography as allegorical and anatomical—as in depictions of Zephyrus or Boreas on a medieval or Renaissance map. The woods, encroaching upon the ghost town, also appear personified: they become overly excited welcomers, the children of our hosts. And yet the tone with which the poet offers these images sounds almost facetious. Are there really sympathetic otherworldly presences here? Do the guide's flights of fancy point to such presences, or only the willfulness required to populate this deserted, inhospitable place with merely imagined mysteries? Two similes near the end of the middle section point to a continual process of diminution and disappearance. The former house is "closing like a dent in dough" and the former field "now left's no bigger than a harness gall" (342)—a harness gall being the little swath of scar tissue left by the harness on a horse's hide.

These comparisons are off kilter, hallucinatory in the manner of a book Frost often mentioned with admiration, *Alice in Wonderland*. The feeling of being turned around and dizzied may lead the reader to question the sincerity of the improvised Communion at the end. In fact, that ending's replete with ironies:

> I have kept hidden in the instep arch
> Of an old cedar at the waterside
> A broken drinking goblet like the Grail
> Under a spell so the wrong ones can't find it,
> So can't get saved, as Saint Mark says they mustn't.
> (I stole the goblet from the children's playhouse.)
> Here are your waters and your watering place.
> Drink and be whole again beyond confusion. (342)

Even as an impromptu ritual, these lines are nearly parodic. The reference from the Gospel of Mark turns out to be one of those awkwardly dark ones that the young, liberal milieu of the minister from "The Black Cottage" would have found objectionable. The grail itself is the cup stolen from the children's playhouse, now stashed beneath a cedar tree. Has the journey of the poem toward resolution all been stagecraft? We may begin to question even the seemingly inviting opening:

Back out of all this now too much for us,
Back in a time made simple by the loss
Of detail, burned, dissolved, and broken off
Like graveyard marble sculpture in the weather,
There is a house that is no more a house
Upon a farm that is no more a farm
And in a town that is no more a town.

What "this" has become too much for us? It could be modern urban life, from which we're returning. It could be historical trauma — Frost wrote "Directive" in 1945. It could also be age, or weariness, or any possible confusion whatsoever. Even if the vagueness itself doesn't dampen the intensity of our setting forth, Frost's tone takes an ironic turn in the second and third lines: the idealized simplicity appears the result of abandonment. The middle of the poem would now seem to reveal little more than "mumbo-jumbo" or "smells and bells," leading to a ritual no more than dramaturgy.

But irony and sincerity are less opposites here than one internal contrary driving the entire poem. As in "The Black Cottage," Frost uses irony to evoke the bewildering sense of total provisionality, the shadow side of his own pragmatism. From the beginning of the poem to the ceremony of renewal at the end, we participate in the creation of individual and communal reality through a succession of choices. First, what do we invest in the vague "this" of the opening line? And then, how much do we trust our guide? But the earnest feeling of necessity, the promise that we will find some "stay against confusion," depends upon our being able to doubt as well as trust the guide's "executive" command of ritual action. Such an ambiguity proves neither evasion nor denial but a spiritual and democratic commitment that the minister of "The Black Cottage" could only ponder from his fanciful distance. To read "Directive" is to entertain the possibility that we're participating in make-believe. But make-believe is no idle task for a pragmatist, whose trust in individual will and choice replaces belief in religion. The poet here becomes an authority whose power depends upon allowing us to doubt his authority. Precisely because the ending of the poem has been so thoroughly surrounded with preemptive irony, its promise may be trusted: "Drink and be whole again beyond confusion."

The old story of the fight between Frost and Stevens is remarkable not only for the differences between "subjects" and "bric-a-brac," "academic" and "executive," but also the shared assumptions those terms reveal about modernity. Beneath the gibes about institutions, Frost and Stevens both seem to prize individual freedom above collective constraints. They both value life above literature, or else demand literature that will. Both are concerned with the vitality of poems and wary of writing that leaches it, either by replacing aesthetic feeling with worn-out forms of expression or by abandoning collective forms entirely. Both want originality, and style reveals originality—the unique traits of the writer's imagination.

At the same time, they seem to disagree about how *originality* depends upon its cognate *origin*. Stevens begins with his belief in an absolute, for which he invents various synonyms, none more obvious than "Imagination," and this absolute remains both origin and destination. Faith in it leads him to a formal originality that requires trust in imagination over convention. But everything we take as convention, common understanding, everyday life, then becomes the irrepressible excess he must assimilate back into his poems. Parodic and satirical early on, in the late poems this act of recovery becomes his insistence upon "the plain sense of things," a fidelity inseparable from radical freedom, sublime transport that would earlier have appeared its opposite.

Frost has a no less contradictory relationship with origins and originality, social forms and personal freedoms. A certain level of convention appears throughout his poetry. But he's never one to mistake precedent for truth: his inclination toward traditional meters, for example, comes not from a reverence for paternal standards, such as that of the neighbor in "Mending Wall" who "will not go behind his father's saying," but a sense that commonly accepted norms such as the regular beat of the meter will allow him to convey, by relief, all the irregularity of accent in living speech and life. From the very first poem of his first book, "Into My Own," his trust in collective identity depends upon *in*dependence, and vice versa. The Pan-like speaker who claims "I do not see why I should e'er turn back" will follow with "Or those should not set forth upon my track." As the allusion to Jefferson in "The Black Cottage" suggests, the modern challenge of making independence a public virtue proves considerable. When the same figure of leading and following recurs in "Directive," as improvised pilgrimage through the abandoned remnants of community, the reader has just one other voice to trust, or not.

That afternoon in 1940, Frost and Stevens may have said very little to each other. Along with the photograph, only the anecdote of their quick exchange remains. But the poets made of this exchange something like a riddle, offering two ways to imagine a modern poem that celebrates and enjoins freedom even as it depends upon historical and political contradictions. Treading the line between joke and insult, they were true to their fundamental imperative as poets: to make their words survive.

Later in the evening they must have been just two people again, alive in the present, where no achievement can be assumed permanent. Two hardworking men, neither of them young, both trying to get some rest. They tend to grouse about Roosevelt, though neither will vote this year for Wendell Wilkie. Frost spent some time in Massachusetts General Hospital in the fall of 1939—blaming his nervous condition on a medicine he took for cystitis, and telling a friend in a letter, "I went crazy with it one night alone and broke chairs ad lib" (1964, 487). The story Ernest Hemingway has spread about his fistfight with Stevens in Key West a few years back may or may not be true, but it has a subtext: Stevens likes to drink, and his time down south allows it.

So here they are. It's not yet the South Florida of John Huston's *Key Largo*, with Humphrey Bogart and Lauren Bacall pitted against Edward G. Robinson's mafioso, though it's hardly a secret that the Casa Marina's owned, as it will be until the 1960s, by the Cosa Nostra, controlled from New York to Havana by Meyer Lansky and Charles "Lucky" Luciano. The keys are still a wild, faraway place. But the international uneasiness of the moment can be felt here too. After two decades of peace so seemingly permanent that the country began to scrap its fleets—and was even selling war material to the Japanese until a few months back—the naval base at Key West has grown busy again. Before the year's up, the Casa Marina will be converted into a barracks.

A Dream We Dreamed
Each Separately

What does it mean to be modern? What makes modern poetry modern? Answers to such obdurate and airy questions fill whole libraries and still feel provisional—because modernity for us is water to the fish: we're immersed in this developing thing we're attempting to map. Admitting so may be the only way to begin. At least that's what makes Hannah Arendt's account of modernity so powerful. In the essays from the 1950s she collected as *Between Past and Future* (1958), Arendt described modern humankind as having "decided never to leave what Plato called 'the cave' of everyday human affairs" (39). The shift from reason toward action she identified in the great nineteenth-century thinkers, Kierkegaard, Nietzsche, and Marx, foreshadowed a larger fissure in the twentieth century, when secularism, mechanization, and political catastrophe pulled human experience away from old ideals and down into embedded contingent struggle.

This description of Arendt's feels apt to me not only because her thinking affected contemporaneous poets—Auden after he moved to New York and, later, Lowell—but also because, explaining the modern condition, she returned to Plato's old question of poetry and the state, revealing hopes and fears about modernity similar to those of American poets. During the first decades of the twentieth century, the problem for American poetry was also one of contingency. Poets looked for the necessary, unprecedented shapes their subjects demanded, essential or abstract forms now aspiring to the power of absolute spiritual reality lost during the break of modernity from the past. At the same time, poets found in contingency itself a new aesthetic freedom. Think of the gusto with which they adapted advertising slogans, accounting ledgers, chatter overheard in barrooms. The field of the page lay wide open — cause for bewilderment as well as celebration: Frost's and Stevens's spat over "subjects" and "bric-a-brac" provides only one example of a pervasive uneasiness about what twentieth-century poems could be, what would make them necessary and enduring, how they could be recognized and shared.

In Arendt's estimation, poets gained from the anti-Platonic development of modern thought, the return of philosophy to everyday human affairs. She portrays a shift from the *academia* to the *polis*, where poetry has drawn its power since the time of Homeric epic, when Greek aspiration toward immortality led not to abstract reason but to shared history, the memory of word and deed preserved through cycles of human generation.

This essay treats the work of four American Modernists whose engagement with their age led them to adapt that same tradition. In different ways, these poets wrote "poems containing history" — Ezra Pound's definition of epic seems fitting in its laconic vagueness, since the reinvention I have in mind is not limited even to long poems, much less those bearing the label "Modernist epic." Even in such works, these poets depended upon lyric resources, especially to convey wonder — "an emotional and intellectual complex in an instant of time" was Pound's definition of the image, one relevant well beyond the firefly vogue of imag*ism* (1968, 3). Along with old claims to beauty and truth, these poets placed a premium on wonder because they faced the situation Arendt identified, one in which "the ubiquitous functionalization of modern society" deprived collective life of "one of its most elementary characteristics — the instilling of wonder at that which is" (Arendt, 1958, 39). For these poets, modernism was often the pitched foe of modernity: the chance for their art to prove empancipatory lay not only in overcoming old forms but also in promising a return to original vitality. The Modernist fascination with recovering premodern, "synchronic" time was not limited to T. S. Eliot's reinterpretation of grail mythology and ancient fertility rites: Walter Benjamin's readings of Baudelaire and Proust, and Henri Lefebvre's notion of "festival" time offer prime examples of this tendency among thinkers on the Left. Among Modernist poets, even those who expressed delight with modernity, such as Williams and Crane, also voiced the desire to recover some more germane form of collective experience. And still, recovery itself was never enough. The challenge was to receive, understand, and adapt the past in order to make radically unprecedented art.

Ezra Pound

Pound's "Hugh Selwyn Mauberley (Contacts and Life)" here becomes the Modernist poem par excellence. The poem reads like a bildungsroman running downhill: instead of finding his eventual true form, the modern protagonist collapses into dissipation. The *literary* form of this lyric narrative, on the other hand, proves built to last, announcing its newness while deriving its energy from shared history.

Mauberley, the young American man of letters "born in a half savage country," finds himself in the cultural center of London, where he's torn between his "obscure reveries of the inward gaze" that most often settles on bygone eras of aesthetic splendor, and the competitive race of all "the age demanded"—in literature and in a daily life with its own savageries. As the poem progresses, Pound seeks originality by chiseling down the English rhymed quatrain, aesthetic liberty mirroring his anger at a society that enabled World War I:

> frankness as never before,
> disillusions as never told in the old days,
> hysterias, trench confessions,
> laughter out of dead bellies. (1990, 188)

At the same time Pound depends upon collective forms of understanding, the quatrain among them. He "makes it new" through a series of allusions, attempting to pilot high culture and the avant-garde past the rough shores of vulgar mercantilism. "No one knows at sight a masterpiece," the Edwardian author Mr. Nixon (based, somewhat unfairly, on the novelist Arnold Bennett) advises from his yacht. "And give up verse, my boy, / There's nothing in it" (190). To Mauberley, Mr. Nixon's success appears loathsome, coming from a class that dealt arms both ways in the "Great War." But Nixon's advice touches a genuine fear: that art will dissolve in the same deliquescent Romanticism that Pound encountered at the end of the nineteenth century; that public life will become a multiplicity of private lives, and private lives, solipsistic isolation, loneliness in apparitional crowds. Such a fate awaits Pound's antihero. "The stylist has taken shelter," Mauberley observes, on a poetic journey that ends with his epitaph—like Gauguin, a modern Crusoe: "Then on an oar read this: // I was / And no more exist; / Here drifted / An hedonist" (201).

After "Mauberley," Pound's poetry leads to a journey more ambitious than the hedonist's. The poet, still often refracted through his personae, turns out a less passive actor than Mauberley—much more confident in his attempt to forge a Modernist alternative to modernity. As the eventual form of *The Cantos* unfolds, Pound proves just as dependent upon figures of personal and social failure, tragically so. He once described his ambition in writing *Cantos* as his long endeavor "to write an epic that begins 'In the Dark Forest,' crosses the purgatory of human error, and ends in the light." As many have pointed out, the holistic neatness of that statement contrasts with the eventual shape of the poem. "I cannot make it cohere," Pound would come to write in Canto CXVI (1995, 816). But as with "Mauberley," it's important to distinguish between moral and aesthetic failure. In fact, the suspicion that this new epic form will not cohere appears at the very beginning of the poem, too, when the poet is at his most ambitious. Pound starts off Odyssean and heroic in Canto I, then abruptly turns Ovidian and anarchic in Canto II. That contrary presents prominent themes: involving tales of Italian warlords, the Sung Dynasty, and John Adams, Pound's Homeric ambition "to build the city of Dioce, whose terraces are the color of stars," continues to the end, as do passages of love, violation, irreparable change, and banishment. Such an explanation perhaps makes the thematic pairing, not to mention the segue from Greek to Roman literary sources, sound too neat (1995, 445). In fact these passages feel jagged, even ominous: Pound leaves Odysseus in the underworld in Canto I and ends the Ovidian passage with a warning delivered to Pentheus, king of Thebes—a warning the king will legendarily leave unheeded, causing his death.

There are also important interruptions within these two sections themselves. Before the close of the first canto, we hear the poet cutting himself off, cursing, taking stock of the Renaissance Latin translation of Homer he's just rendered into English. Classical splendor returns as Pound translates a fragment depicting Aphrodite holding the golden bough. But by the beginning of the second canto, we're back to the contemporary poet's grumbling, this time about his great predecessor Robert Browning, before the register rises once more with the tale of Bacchus's metamorphoses into a leopard onboard a ship to Thebes. The feeling that these parts do not cohere indicates no failure of the poem but reveals Pound's genius for inventing a new form that would contain not only history but also the individual consciousness making something from that history, a form whose layering of fragment on fragment in fact does more than "contain"—it also shows an expansive force breaking past its own boundaries.

Pound's moral failure *did* stain his art. None of those competing tendencies, neither the Homeric nor the Ovidian, the Apollonian nor the Dionysian, the epic nor the lyric, the literary nor the demotic, correlates with the poet's turn toward fascism so much as all of them intertwined: the nihilistic power of Pound's fascism comes from a desperate and fundamental rage to demolish the culture in which he finds himself, and to remake it from a legacy he himself selects. This corresponds with an aesthetic gift for eliciting wonder: Pound creates a language out of fragments, so that he may speak with the clarity of Hemingway, even as the content of his lines and sentences, spanning time and geography in the service of the precise selection of tone and reference, makes his poetry a historico-linguistic cornucopia. Unsettling though it may be, the best of the late cantos come not despite Pound's political arrogance but from its same source.

Consider a passage from LXXVI, the third of the *Pisan Cantos*, those written when Pound was imprisoned by the American army in Pisa. These lines move between the heights of heroic, rage-filled ambition and a chastened refuge in mundane observation, jokes and memories, both personal and cultural:

As a lone ant from a broken ant-hill
from the wreckage of Europe, ego scriptor,
    The rain has fallen, the wind coming down
    out of the mountain
    Lucca, Forti dei Marmi, Berchtold after the other one . . .
parts reassembled.
    . . . and within the crystal, went up swift as Thetis
in colour rose-blue before sunset
and carmine and amber,

spiriti questi? personae?
             tangibility by no means *atasal*
             but the crystal can be weighed by the hand
formal and passing within the sphere: Thetis,
Maya, Aphrodite,

                 no overstroke
    no dolphin faster in moving
    nor the flying azure of the wing'd fish under Zoagli
    when he comes out into the air, living arrow.
and the clouds over the Pisan meadows
        are indubitably as fine as any to be seen
    from the peninsula
        oi Barbaroi have not destroyed them
        as they have Sigismundo's Temple
Divae Ixottae (and as to her effigy that was in Pisa?)
Ladder at swing jump as for a descent from the cross
O white-chested martin, God damn it,
        as no one will carry a message,
    say to La Cara: amo. (1995, 478–79)

One of the wonders of reading Pound comes from following the affective contours of such lines, even before catching all the allusions: this section begins with a stentorian proclamation, one wearing its own mock-heroic undermining—"As a lone ant from a broken ant hill"—then moves through an address to the gods associated with the Pisan countryside, as seen from the poet's prison cell, only to meet frustration again, and finally to reach a lover's address.

Still, the particular allusions are crucial. One of the two most prominent here is "Berchtold. . . . after the other one / parts reassembled." "Berchtold" is Leopold Graf von Berchtold, the Viennese foreign minister who secretly bargained with the Russians to allow the Austro-Hungarian annexation of Bosnia and Herzegovina, a piece of diplomatic treachery the poet identifies as the cause of World War I. The "parts reassembled" are the metaphorical and literal components of a profitable war machine, one that reshaped itself for a second world war, one whose machinery now included the sheets of airplane metal out of which Pound's cell was built on the American base in Pisa. A dark pedal tone, this reference to Count Berchtold lingers over the descriptive lines that follow, so that "the rain has fallen, the wind coming down / out of the mountain," the more grandiose "in colour rose-blue before sunset," as well as the "flying azure of the wing'd fish under Zoagli," grow into much more than pretty moments: they carry the force of testimony.

The second central figure here is "Divae Ixottae," Divine Isotta, mistress of Sigismundo Malatesta, the quattrocento warlord and recurring protagonist of *Cantos*. Malatesta had a temple built in Isotta's honor in Rimini and commissioned an effigy of her in Pisa. In Pound's rendering the union of art and political power in Italy during the first half of the fifteenth century presents an ideal: Pound sees early Italian Renaissance art as a culmination of historical and aesthetic potential, one preceding the corruption of nascent capitalism. As with Yeats, who at least had the semi-plausible claim of his ancestry, Pound's romance with feudalism was a bulwark against the malevolent and leveling power of modernity. As with Yeats again, there's something in this romance that's hard to dismiss, even for a reader who finds the valorization of feudalism silly at best. (Sigismundo Malatesta, "The Wolf of Rimini," was a sociopath who killed Italian villagers for sport.) I have in mind the promise of continuity between the aesthetic, personal, and historical—showing here in the movement from deities to idealized human figures of legend, and then to the imprisoned poet's own beloved.

The disaster of Pound's politics is impossible to separate from this same achievement: the hateful lines in his jeremiads against Anglo-American capitalism, "the yidd is a stimulant, and the goyim are cattle in gt / proportion and go saleable to slaughter," arrive only a few pages earlier in Canto LXXIV, written while he was imprisoned for broadcasting much worse on Italian radio (1995, 459). This anti-Semitism has the characteristic of a fetish, a tic, the displacement of an overwhelming emotion, anger, onto a self-perpetuating Möbius strip of near-murderous outbursts: Jews are scapegoats for Pound's rage against the barbarism that he—himself a wanderer without a nation—displays in the pseudo-sacrificial act of scapegoating.

What the gorgeous and bilious passages have in common is a belief in continuity between all of history and the modern artist who would excavate the future. Far from being either an irrelevant matter of gossip or a sign of Pound's aesthetic failure, the flaw turns out to be central. His best poetry and his most rotten derive from the same ambition: to give new form to anti-imperial political force, in a form that merges epic and lyric, and in lines resembling both carvings in marble and streams of consciousness. This is why he remains crucial. Taking a big turn to the left, all the strongest American poets to follow reckon with Pound not only as a vexed figure of political history or as an ingenious maker, but as both.

William Carlos Williams

There are many ways to map the mountain range of American Modernist poetry, but no disputing that William Carlos Williams's poetry accounts for some of the most vigorous and surprising territory, offering the thick texture of lived history without succumbing to ideological limitations. This is not to bestow some preposterous badge of merit in literary ethics. I mean instead to acknowledge something for which Williams has never received enough credit, his strength as a historical and political thinker. To understand both the ambition and the worldliness with which Williams matches his U Penn classmate Ezra Pound, consider a poem that may seem to reveal Williams's *merely* local tendency, the 1927 lyric "Young Sycamore" (1986, 266):

I must tell you
this young tree
whose round and firm trunk
between the wet

pavement and the gutter
(where water
is trickling) rises
bodily

into the air with
one undulant
thrust half its height—
and then

dividing and waning
sending out
young branches on
all sides—

hung with cocoons
it thins
till nothing is left of it
but two

eccentric knotted
twigs
bending forward
hornlike at the top

In twenty-four short free-verse lines, the poem describes the tree its title promises. The diction is plain, with none of the allusive density of Canto LXXIV. Nor does intensity come from melodious or figurative language, but from sentence structure: holding in mind the subject "this young tree" in the second line, the reader waits sixteen more lines for the verb "it thins," as the poet observes the trunk ending, the force of the branches stretching up and out.

But objective clarity and the close mirroring of form and content conduct their own historical charge. While "Young Sycamore" may be appreciated on its own, it's illuminating to know the poem responds, as Bram Dijkstra (1969) has shown, to Alfred Stieglitz's 1902 photograph *Spring Shower*. Insider information, perhaps. But I'm convinced there's no better way into Williams's thinking about poetry than his engagement with visual aesthetics. His development as a poet led him into the company of artists, and their example helped him face two crucially entwined questions: what modern abstraction meant to him, and how his art could claim and transform collective energies.

Beginning in the early 1920s, Williams befriended several American artists associated with Stieglitz's gallery at 291 Fifth Avenue in New York. But three painters in the "291" circle came to interest him even more than their gallerist. Marsden Hartley, with whom he edited the magazine *Contact*, fascinated Williams for the vigor of his painting and his almost chthonic faith in his American surroundings—as professed in his early book *Adventures in the Arts* (1921), as well as his advocacy of American Indian painting. Charles Demuth and Williams first met in 1905 over a bowl of prunes in Mrs. Chain's boardinghouse in Philadelphia. Demuth would adapt Williams's poem "The Great Figure" in one of his portrait posters. Williams would dedicate *Spring and All* (1923) to Demuth and write his excellent long poem "The Crimson Cyclamen" in memory of the painter. From their earliest conversations, Demuth and Williams shared an artistic nationalism remarkable for being, unlike other nationalisms of the 1920s and 1930s, free of xenophobia and sentimental nostalgia—suggesting one aspect of "Young Sycamore" that we may not even think to notice: Williams manages, between the world wars, to write a poem in celebration of organic growth and local vigor—the very tone and imagery familiar from the propaganda of National Socialism, which repelled Williams, and the young Soviet Union, which fascinated him, at least until the terrors of the 1930s—and he does so without a touch of ideological cant. This form of artistic nationalism depends upon an ambitious worldliness.

Like his painter friends, Williams never abandoned lessons learned from European Modernism, whose full force he felt, as did

Wallace Stevens, at the Armory Show in 1913. The influence of that event suggests Williams's connection with the third of his closest associates from the 291 group, Charles Sheeler. For Sheeler, precise rendering of American machinery, factories, houses, tools, and furniture celebrated a national past and present, even while achieving an abstraction of sheer fact. Williams and Sheeler also shared an affinity for Marcel Duchamp. As the art historian Wanda Corn has shown, even before Duchamp moved to America he exhibited his own love of *americanisme* (Corn 1999). Sheeler and Williams had no need to import this element. Instead what they found in their French contemporary were lucid, objective forms revealing wonder—whether through abstraction of the part *from* the whole, as in the famous toilet bowl and bicycle wheel, or fabrication of parts *into* a whole, as in *Nude Descending a Staircase*, the painting that so impressed Williams at the Armory Show that, as he tells in his autobiography, he laughed out loud with joy.

This is not to claim a secret meaning to "Young Sycamore." Williams renders the simultaneously real and abstract nature of his perception not by copying the artists of 291 or their French counterparts but engaging their example in the specific energies of speech. Williams's abstraction in "Young Sycamore," a quality one might feel before understanding, proves profoundly sympathetic to Duchamp and Sheeler because it comes neither from general statement nor from subjective impression but from presentation of the tree as object and process, matter and movement, the dynamic relation of parts to whole.

Consider the play of that single sentence over the lines. Williams's definition of the line was a "unit of attention," and by 1927 these are no longer discrete phrasal sets. They not only enjamb but also end in the middle of phrases, seeming at moments to gather their objectivity from near randomness; they include numbers followed by modifiers ("one undulant"), adversatives followed by numbers ("but two"), nouns of action followed by modifiers ("thrust half its height"), and so on. But the verse movement also coheres around lines that are discrete nominal phrases ("this young tree," "pavement and the gutter," "twigs"), participial actions ("dividing and waning," "sending out," "bending forward"), and modifiers followed by nouns ("hornlike at the top"). Given such various and active lineation, these "units of attention" reveal not only quantities and qualities but also velocities, sensations, and states in motion between one another.

Williams's rendering of the tree as interplay of part and whole derives from more than enthusiasm about a new aesthetic approach, more even than wonder at a new conception of reality. The "I must tell you" of the first line imbues the poem with a feeling of need between at least two people. Like the allusion to Count Berchtold in Canto LXXIV, this tone struck by the first line deepens and colors those that follow. Unlike the Berchtold allusion, the urgency of "I must tell you" offers a note of exuberance and generosity. Because we never learn if the "you" in "Young Sycamore" is everyone or one beloved, the address hovers between public and private speech. This ambiguity proves precise in its structure: the intimate spark struck in the first line, but not to return, blends into a tone more objective—and possibly more collective, should the "you" hear what's told, should the readers read the poem. Like Dickinson's "I'm Nobody," "Young Sycamore" ends on the brink between intimate and public experience. The abstract relation of part and whole here matches a social and political vision of "E Pluribus Unum," the surprisingly dialectical motto on the seal of the United States, which Williams quotes in a poem from the early 1920s, "It Is a Living Coral." Each person here becomes part of the many, the totality of social relations.

In many of his best poems Williams follows up on the question implicit in such ambiguity—could modern public life be like love? He does so with full knowledge of the risk. The concept of "E Pluribus Unum" carries more than a little irony here. Dickinson's feeling of being "public like a bog" appears in these poems of the 1920s and 1930s, along with metaphors of pollution, the "unclean," and sewage. Consider the section of *Spring and All* subsequently titled "To Elsie" ("The pure products of America go crazy") or the one later titled "Young Love" ("O 'Kiki' / O Miss Margaret Jarvis") with its intimate address to a woman with whom the poet had an affair, a woman now somewhere in the city "patching up sick school children." These poems bear out Edmund Wilson's description of the climate in which they were written: "Even before the stock market crash of October 1929, a kind of nervous dissatisfaction and apprehension had begun to manifest itself in American life" (2007, 400). This was the same climate that allowed not only the repression of labor and the enforcement of the Volstead Act but also the confiscation by US customs agents in New York of nearly all copies of *Spring and All* on its way from Robert McAlmon's Contact Publishing in Paris. And yet the democratic commitment is real. The "low" or seedy moments do more than provide irony: they speak to a truly inclusive conception of democratic public life.

Williams's most powerful rendering of the "body politic" in which he found himself, at least before the completion of *Paterson*, starts with "The Descent of Winter," his long poem written in series during the fall of 1927 and published by Pound in the fourth volume of *The Exile*. This pursuit continues in full force through the early 1930s, cohering around longer poems such as "The Flower," "Adam," "Eve," "The Crimson Cyclamen," and "Perpetuum Mobile: The City."

"The Descent of Winter" shows Williams at the height of his powers as a maker and thinker. To understand how thought unfolds in the poem, consider a humorous passage on art and economics from one of the prose sections at the center of the series. Here Williams learns that Charles Sheeler has been commissioned to photograph Ford Motor Company's River Rouge Plant in Michigan:

> Henry Ford has asked Chas. Sheeler to go to Detroit and photograph everything. Carte Blanche. Sheeler! That's rich. Shakespeare had the mean ability to fuse himself with everyone which nobodies have, to be anything at any time, fluid, a nameless fellow whom nobody noticed— much, and *that* is what made him the great dramatist. Because he was nobody and was fluid and accessible. He took the print and reversed the film, as it went in so it came out. Certainly he never repeated himself since he did nothing but repeat what he heard and nobody ever hears the same words twice the same. Homekeeping youth had ever homely wit, Sheeler and Shakespeare should be on this Soviet. (1986, 307)

Williams thinks out loud here, arguing that Shakespeare's genius, as well as Sheeler's, lies in ultimate receptivity, the mirroring function of mimetic representation. Taken alone, this claim—one that William Hazlitt made more than a century earlier, in a lecture much admired by Keats—doesn't reveal the poet's thinking; it has the quality, in fact, of premature conclusion, taking into account neither the natural resistance an artist might feel to being a "nameless fellow" nor the underlying nervousness about the ties of capitalism and art.

Williams is not being naive, however. In fact, what's remarkable about this moment is how well it exemplifies another aesthetic notion that had currency among American Modernist artists, one very different from receptive, photographic mimesis—the belief that dialectical movement was inherent in montage. Indeed the movement of "The Descent of Winter" is argument against argument: one strand of assertion receives a turn toward its contrary, oppositions synthesize and then reassert themselves in new forms, tonal as well as rhetorical. Following his bemused endorsement of Sheeler's photographic work at the River Rouge Plant, the poet slips into comedy, casting a marriage plot that manages to wed Sheeler, William Shakespeare, the Bolshevik Revolutionaries, and the über-capitalist, violent union-buster, and racist pamphleteer Henry Ford. "Homekeeping youth had ever homely wit" is the second line from *Two Gentlemen of Verona*, in which Proteus, one of the two young men who will marry by the end of the play, speaks to the other, Valentine, while heading out from his home in Verona to Milan— Williams is wishing Sheeler a successful trip to industrial Michigan. "Homekeeping youth had ever homely wit" contains an affectionate pun too, as Sheeler was at the time painting and photographing interiors, in particular those of his own home in South Salem, New York.

But then, with the completion of the embedded couplet, comes that rhyme with "Soviet." This two-line poem embedded within the prose might work to preempt any claim that Sheeler could be tarred with the brush of an American capitalism in which Williams saw

the unfortunate legacy of Alexander Hamilton. But even for needing to be mentioned, such apprehension stages a moral queasiness
that's more internal and runs throughout "The Descent of Winter."
This same fall and winter of 1927, in the five-year-old Soviet Union,
Stalin would expel Trotsky and Zinoviev from the Central Commit-
tee, offering a strong hint of the terrors to come. Before the Second
World War, Communism in America enjoyed more support and suffered less repression than it would after; the only set of war plans the
US drew up in 1927 were for potential conflict with the naval and
trading power most threatening its dominance, Great Britain. And
yet anti-Bolshevism was already a strong force, too, especially in the
"homekeeping" world of prewar suburbia that both Williams and
Sheeler celebrated as their aesthetic source. Speaking with admiration about the workers' councils in such company, like pretending
to make peace with Henry Ford among the bohemians of 291, Williams reveals serious contradictions in American consciousness as
well as the challenge of making art among them.

Williams responds to this challenge not only with good humor
but also by embracing those same contradictions. His interest in
dialectic, as means of both aesthetic form-finding and political
thinking, appears even more prominently if we turn to the poem
preceding the passage on Sheeler and Ford, "A Morning Imagination in Russia" (1986, 304). The poet here enters the mind of a Russian man after the revolution. He flashes back for a moment on the
czarist years:

> Cities are full of light, fine clothes
> delicacies for the table, variety,
> novelty—fashion: all spent for this.
> Never to be like that again:
> the frame that was. It tickled his
> imagination.

Williams has this man, formerly a bourgeois intellectual, going
through his day in a nearly mystical transport of ordinary life. His
surroundings are a workers' Elysium:

> The very old past was refound
> redirected. It had wandered into himself

the world was himself, these were
his own eyes that were seeing, his own mind
that was straining to comprehend, his own
hands that would be touching other hands.
They were his own!
His own, feeble, uncertain. He would go
out to pick herbs, he graduate of
the old university. He would go out
and ask that old woman, in the little
village by the lake, to show him wild
ginger. He himself would not know the plant.

This experience of immanence shifts, though, as the poem turns toward uneasiness:

We have cut out the cancer but
who knows? Perhaps the patient will die.
The patient is anybody, anything
worthless that I desire, my hands
to have it—instead of the feeling
that there is a piece of glazed paper
between me and the paper—invisible
but rough running through the legal
· processes of possession—a city, that
we could possess—

It's in art, it's in
the French school.

What we lacked was
everything. It is the middle of
everything. Not to have.

The Russian man fears the peril of the communist endeavor, one that would prove fatal. But handling the paper, wanting to know the very experience of handling paper without possession, "a piece of glazed paper / between me and the paper," he becomes indecipherable from the American poet Williams, the "we" now including Russians under the Soviets and Americans under capitalism. Like this, Williams collapses the frame of the monologue. He not only montages the Russian and American speakers but also joins them: true to the dialectical motion of his poem, he has the man begin Russian, then become American, and finally a synthesis. Public and private identities merge here too: the pronoun *we* appears for the first time, and yet this remains the most private section of the poem, spoken in solitary apprehension. *We* now carries the gravity of public address but makes a claim less rhetorical than sympathetic, a claim to the shared experience of a pervasive poverty, the same absence Marx identified in modern man, his lack of feeling without having. The closest the Soviet citizen and American poet come to the opposite, to "having everything by not having," remains through art, sensation, love.

But Williams's clarity differs from photographic mimesis not only because of the dialectic turns in argument and tone: there's also the sympathetic appeal of this figure of the poet himself. He's hopeful, this Rousseauvian who's survived into the age of automized mechanization. Even in his melancholic, isolated, guilty, and sarcastic moods, he appears confident about human potential in "what Plato called 'the cave' of human affairs." In fact he speaks often about public life, doesn't turn from what dismays him, including in himself, but seems most of all to enjoy the embedded messiness.

If sadness lingers even in this figure of the poet, it's the sadness of the love poet, exemplified by the sonneteer who, like his Greek predecessor, claims immortality only through words made deed: "So long as men can breathe and eyes can see / So long lives this, and this gives life to thee." In addition to the magnificent poem beginning "in the dead weeds, a rubbish heap / aflame" and the celebration of the birth of the Polish American girl whom Williams names Dolores Marie Pischak, the fusion of political concern and love poetry reaches its fullest power in "The Descent of Winter" with the lyric beginning "O river of my heart polluted." Here Williams returns to the image of the factory he introduced with his passage on Sheeler at the River Rouge Plant:

> O river of my heart polluted
> and defamed I have compared you
> to that other lying in
> the red November grass
> beginning to be cleaned now
> from factory pollution

Though at night a watchman
must still prowl lest some paid hand
open the waste sluices—

That river will be clean
before ever you will be (1986, 308)

Like "A Morning Imagination in Russia" with its shifting national viewpoint, "O river of my heart" entertains a contradiction it doesn't resolve. The lover sees his heart exceeding factory pollution in corruption and only thereby, like some industrial chemical seeping into the Earth's core, becoming immortal. The final two lines are a curse upon human greed—economic, environmental, erotic—but also a claim to immortality that the same ironic undermining enables.

The marvel of "The Descent to Winter" lies in this contrary. Contingency, disorder, pollution, absurdity, and guilt counterbalance the genuine hopefulness of the poem. The sequence ends with a section of a prose narrative. In the last sentence the poet tells his interlocutor, "You made me think of him." The irony comes from the comic profusion of family stories that's led to this simple statement. The man whom the poet remembers is his uncle—though the storytelling has led, like a colorful and poignant shaggy dog joke, through the nineteenth-century Puerto Rico of the poet's maternal descendants, all before reaching that simple statement "You made me think of him." Structured like this, the conclusion calls to mind a huge mass made to balance on one small corner: entire genealogies of personal experience descend upon six syllables, "You made me think of him." With its more elaborate tone and structure, "The Descent of Winter" ends in the same place as "Young Sycamore," the brink between two people, the new possibility of their connection offered but not yet secured.

In the following years Williams attempts to begin where he ended, between intimate and collective address. While maintaining this position of lover and citizen, and without allowing the dream of local American centrality to become mere cultural nationalism, he now imagines a poem of greater scope.

The eventual answer to his challenge lies in the four books of

Paterson. But "Perpetuum Mobile: The City" from 1936 does just as well to show how Williams, as he remarked of Pound's *Cantos*, "discloses history by the feel of it" in a poem of epic scope but lyrical feeling, addressed to a woman and a city. This poem, with which he ends his 1936 collection *Adam & Eve & the City*, depicts a trip from New Jersey to New York and back. At first the urban destination appears metaphysical, the shared dream of the poet and his beloved. Here's how the poem begins:

> —a dream
> we dreamed
>   each
> separately
>   we two
>
> of love
>   and of
> desire—
>
> that found
>   in the night—
>
> in the distance
>   over
>
> the meadows
>   by day
>
> impossible—
>   The city
> disappeared
>   when
> we arrived—
>
>   A dream
> a little false
> toward which
>   now
> we stand
>   and stare
> transfixed—
>
> All at once
>   in the east
> rising!

All white!
small
as a flower—

a locust cluster
a shad bush
blossoming (1986, 430–31)

After announcing the lovers' separate, mutual desire, the poet describes their reaching a city—literal Manhattan, as well as metaphorical fulfillment—only to find it disappearing around them, and
they're back in New Jersey. New York still shines as promise to the
same desire, unquenched, though they realize their dream's "a little
false ... now."

But then the poet and beloved enter the city *again*, this time as
realists. At first they find a cinematic comedy. The tone of ardor in
the initial lines survives, but like a bright underpainting, showing
through only in the ironic refrain "For love!":

Money! In
armored trucks—
Two men
walking
at two paces from
each other
their right hands
at the hip—
on the butt of
an automatic—

till they themselves
hold up the bank
and themselves
drive off
for themselves
the money
in an armored car—

For love! (1986, 432)

Like the burlesque routine of the workers' council containing
Sheeler, Shakespeare, and the Bolsheviks, this farcical escape of

the armored-truck-drivers-turned-bank-robbers "For love!" makes for effective humor not only because it's rendered with a light but winningly brash touch but also because it tests sympathies. What would any of us do for love? Is our love one of those that need to be hidden? How close is any one person's sex life tied to money?

In the next section of this lurid panorama, Williams presents an image of labor and bodily recalcitrance—a man tying the knotted mane upon the "whorish" head of the running horse he manages, followed by the second ironic refrain, "For love!" But the poem proceeds to its climactic fulfillment in a section that takes realism to its ultimate depths. Here an image of urban consumers leads, like a panning shot, down to a sewer main:

> Guzzling
> the creamy foods
>   while
> out of sight
>   in
> the sub-cellar—
> the waste fat
> the old vegetables
>   chucked down
> a chute
>   the foulest
> sink in the world— (1986, 434)

Out of this flow of waste from the city into the ocean, out of the poet's own admission of disgust, the poem reaches the very different tone of its ending:

> —A dream
> of lights
>   hiding
> the iron reason
>   and stone
> a settled
>   cloud—
>
> City
>
>   Whose stars
> of matchless
>   splendor—

                    and
        in bright edged
                    clouds
        the moon—

                    bring
        silence
                    breathlessly—

        Tearful city
                    on a summer's day
        the hard grey
                    dwindling
        in a wall of
                    rain—

                    farewell! (1986, 435)

The slender, free-verse compression bears a strong undercurrent of
the same nineteenth-century Romanticism with which the poem
opens. "Whose stars ... in bright edged / clouds / the moon bring /
silence / breathlessly" scans as two lines of iambic pentameter that,
while precise in their meaning and their elaborate syntactic placement, have the ring of an ad lib imitation of Keats's "Endymion"
or "Hyperion: A Fragment." Williams has returned to the tone of
the beginning, except, employing a farewell for a coda, he staves
off the feeling of eternal repetition in this cycle of want, fulfillment,
and waste. As with his initial return, when he endeavored to see the
city's underside, so the poet now comes back to love and desire, but
with a difference: they've been tested against mortality.

Likewise, the Romantic mood here becomes the resolution, but
with a difference. Actual material reality, which the poet wanted
to see with disabused eyes all the way down to the level of sewage,
now appears discarded as a possible conclusion and, taken alone,
becomes illusory. The "iron reason" and the "dream of lights" settle
in the final tableau, at this moment of farewell, as dream and fact
fuse and the city becomes indistinguishable from the beloved.

Like this, the poem resolves into its form with both the precision
of a machine and a mysterious, creaturely life. Such synthesis proves
central for Williams. His vision of American society at its best here
resembles his vision of poetic form—unsentimental, even mecha-

nistic. And yet Williams's "machine made out of words" is nothing without the principle of "slack" or "give" required, an element of surprise from within, what Coleridge first identified as "organic form." Consider the passage from the introduction to *The Wedge* (1944) in which Williams offers that definition:

> To make two bold statements: There's nothing sentimental about a machine, and: A poem is a small (or large) machine made out of words. When I say there's nothing sentimental about a poem, I mean that there can be no part that is redundant. Prose may carry a load of ill-defined matter like a ship. But poetry is a machine which drives it, pruned to a perfect economy. As in all machines, its movement is intrinsic, undulant, a physical more than a literary character. (1988, 54)

Williams's identification of the "intrinsic, undulant" movement of the machine, like the messy, human, inevitably dreamed character of the iron city, suggests his power for weaving various strands of argument, affiliation, and sympathy together in one poem. During his last four decades he doesn't submit to the sentimental risk he identifies, but, more important, he continues to open his poetry to those depths of feeling that lie beneath the merely sentimental. He does so by joining his ambitions as a love poet; a poet of observations tuned to the level of unfolding, sensuous experience; a poet whose abstraction of part and whole shows an ironic, sometimes bitter or enraged, but profoundly hopeful conception of the American idea "E Pluribus Unum." In so doing, Williams reveals not only what poetry can be but also where in modern life it will be found.

Lorine Niedecker

Pound's and Williams's influence upon the following generations of American poets appears in movements such as Objectivism, Black Mountain, and the Beats, but the major poets associated with the Modernist direction both understood and exceeded the limitation of those affiliations. Among such writers, Lorine Niedecker and George Oppen remain preeminent.

Born in 1903, Niedecker grew up the daughter of a commercial seine-net fisherman in rural Wisconsin. She dropped out of college to care for her ailing mother; worked as a librarian in Fort Atkinson, Wisconsin; married, and then divorced when both she and her husband lost their jobs in the Depression. In February 1931 she came across the Objectivist issue of *Poetry* magazine, edited by Louis Zukofsky, the young poet who'd given Williams valuable editorial suggestions on "Perpetuum Mobile: The City." Niedecker began a correspondence and then a love affair with Zukofsky and, in the early 1930s, visited New York several times to see him. Zukofsky introduced her to Williams and Oppen, among others. Back in Wisconsin, she worked as a copyeditor for the WPA, a scriptwriter for a Madison radio station, and a custodian at the Fort Atkinson Hospital. In 1963 she married a Milwaukee house painter, Al Millen, with whom she shared the rest of her life.

Biography has a bearing here as Niedecker's poems often portray how given roles, in particular those of gender and class, operate in modern American life. These poems employ candid or confidential speech, and not to depend upon biographical material as any guarantor of value but to reveal social relations and the relations between society and self. For me, this is what makes Niedecker a greater poet than Zukofsky. Neither cared much for the term *objectivist*, an expedient label for one issue of a magazine. But Zukofsky's poems can feel programmatic, cold, didactic—machines made out of words and yet without that "intrinsic, undulant" movement upon which Williams insisted. Niedecker and Oppen, however, reach the height of their powers in the 1960s in poems at once abstract and grounded in a creaturely, living speech register.

Niedecker's development led through surrealism. In 1926, still working as a librarian in Fort Atkinson, the twenty-three-year-old was writing a long poem called "Progression." Here are two characteristic sentences:

> At the Capitol, cheese legislation only sets silk hats
> tipping, rats divine, toward feline waistbands.
> At home, it's blizzard or a curved banana-moon
> on a sash, soap flakes on wash day
> and door knobs wet; hornets' nests in tobacco pipes. (2002, 25)

The subject of "Progression" may seem, as the title suggests, the movement of the poem itself. The pleasure of reading it comes from watching the sharply rendered particulars (those doorknobs wet on wash day) rippling out from the associative rush of the sentences. Niedecker read the first generation of Modernist poets, as well as their Symbolist precursors and Surrealist cousins. She kept a dream journal in hopes of tracing her subconscious. In "Progression" she taught herself to throw quicksands of subconscious implication beneath precise, naturalistic description — "hornets' nests in tobacco pipes."

This is not yet her best work, but even the playfulness ("cheese legislation") reveals a serious preoccupation, the relation of the domestic and the political. As she develops this theme, Niedecker begins the major work she'll continue through her last poems in the late 1960s. Most of all, she becomes more idiomatic: she finds strength in the local midwestern world around her. She renders politics especially through the perspectives of women. Take the poem that begins "In the great snowfall before the bomb":

> In the great snowfall before the bomb
> colored yule tree lights
> windows, the only glow for contemplation
> along this road
>
> I worked the print shop
> right down among em
> the folk from whom all poetry flows
> and dreadfully much else.
> I was Blondie.
> I carried my bundles of hog feeder price lists
> down by Larry the Lug,
> I'd never get anywhere
> because I'd never had suction,
> pull, you know, favor, drag,
> well-oiled protection.
> I heard their rehashed radio barbs —
> more barbarous among hirelings
> as higher-ups grow more corrupt.
> But what vitality! The women hold jobs —
> clean house, cook, raise children, bowl
> and go to church.
>
> What would they say if they knew
> I sit for two months on six lines
> of poetry? (2002, 142)

The poet's changing perspective, her ability both to immerse herself in her subject matter and to remove herself, signals something more mysterious than gritty realism, here and throughout Niedecker— her conception of form. She employs idiomatic American English not as a marker of authenticity; on the contrary, idiom here creates an ironic doubleness. The more Niedecker tunes her language to objective fact, paring her words down to essentials, the more we feel the pull between their meaning within their social context and their meaning as seen from outside. Sometimes they betray their speakers, but often they surprise with lucidity and wit, showing perspicacity and resourcefulness exceeding the situations in which Niedecker's people find themselves. Consider how those double entendres ("suction / pull, you know, favor, drag, / well-oiled protection") point to a particular underside of society most obvious to working women, a whisper chamber where sex and power wheel and deal.

Similarly, in the two short lines containing the play on "rehashed radio barbs" and "barbarous," Niedecker suggests how racism— picked up from broadcasters, such as Father Charles Coughlin, the mid-twentieth-century equivalent of a right-wing shock jock— thrives under a capitalist class that will employ it as a tool to encourage division and competition among its labor force. At the same time Niedecker's formal approach entails more than ironic distancing, and more than mere exposition of her views. In fact she expresses admiration for her subjects, an admiration shaded with irony but not insincere: these really are the people "from whom all poetry flows," people whose language throughout Niedecker's work evinces strength, precision, and emotional range. The rub turns out to be the condition of alienation diagnosed by Marx (whom the young Wisconsin librarian first read in the 1920s), specifically, the growth under capitalism of commodity fetishism, the tendency of social relations to appear as relations to things, and vice versa—what Georg Lukács would elaborate as "reification"—shows even in those innuendos themselves, their confusion of human anatomy and machinery. Niedecker's concern with "reification" lies at the center of her major work. What the laborers and community members of "In the great snowfall before the bomb" wouldn't understand about poetry is *not* its claim to truth and beauty—which they might understand as well as or better than anyone—but the failure of these to translate into objective quantities: two months equal only six lines of poetry.

The poet's not merely a critic of this modern situation; she's caught in it too. She makes her poetry an original response to her society, and yet there are few poets less rhetorical. Niedecker's importance lies in her ability fully to embody her pursuit—of right relation between the self and others, of truth amid uncertainty—in her own new form: the loose yet carefully arranged series-poem she began to favor in the 1940s. In these sequences each poem both holds its own ground and gives to the whole. The constituent poems are discrete: there's no single narrative as in "Mauberley," no consistent reminder of chronology as in "The Descent of Winter." A connective thread appears nevertheless, sometimes as obvious as a common subject, tone, or metaphor, sometimes subtler, and often not there at all. Instead of diffusing meaning and coherence, this arrangement manages both to broaden and intensify.

Consider the three lyrics that open *New Goose*, the first of the major series-poems and the poet's first full-length book, published in 1946:

Don't shoot the rail!
Let your grandfather rest!
Tho he sees your wild eyes
He's falling asleep,
His long-billed pipe
On his red-brown vest.

.

Bombings
You could go to the Underground's platform
For a three half-penny tube fare;
Safe vaults of the bank of England
You couldn't go there.

The sheltered slept
        Under eiderdown,
Lady Diana and the Lord himself
In apartments underground.

.

  Hop press and conveyer
    for a hearse
  Newall Carpenter Senior's
    two patented works (2002, 92)

The first two poems are about hierarchy and violence; both hinge upon a fear of being killed in one's sleep, and both have a lullaby rhythm, appropriate to the opening of a book whose title invokes Mother Goose. The poems also maintain their distance from one another. The first sets a folkloric scene, the second describes London during the Blitz. The first sounds whimsical, the second ominous: after all, there's a big difference between hunting a game bird and bombing a city. The juxtaposition works, in fact, to throw off our sense of scale. That homespun and "homekeeping" lyric on the bird shades over to fright in the line about "wild eyes," just as the second poem wobbles between a sense of terror mixed with class outrage and a lulled calm.

The third poem changes the tone dramatically yet focuses and intensifies the action. Far from the realms of fable or world war, we're among neighbors now in actual rural America—the shift to unrhymed free verse and clipped demotic fragments paralleling the jolt into the present. This poem does pick up on those previous two, however: the premonitions about death have now developed into a real funeral procession. Odd, morbid, and comical, the image of Newall Carpenter Sr. pulled in a hearse made from his inventions, intended for the farming of hops, suggests how Niedecker's preoccupations with ideology, labor, and class (including the displacement of rural Americans by industrial agriculture) will continue throughout the series.

Even as these motifs repeat, the unfolding movement of thought and feeling announces itself in the gap between the constituent parts as the poems change subject, tone, verse form, and speaker. That movement is the motive and means of the poem, the part that convenes with all other parts. What distinguishes Niedecker's management of this force that flows through the gaps or lacunae from the similar practice of her great predecessors and influences, Pound and Williams, turns out to be her balance between confidence and vulnerability. Much more than the hieratic author of *Cantos*, more even than the public-minded love poet of "Perpetuum Mobile: The City," Niedecker renders the intimate voice of the muttered oath, the journal entry, the outburst, the cry. There's no melodrama here, as the paratactic arrangement shows decisive control of such tones. But even as the speakers change, the central voice at the heart of *New Goose* remains that of a young woman striving for her place in the world.

Niedecker abandoned Surrealism after the 1930s, realizing, as Henri Lefebvre once claimed apropos the original surrealism of André Breton, that "the bizarre is a shoddy version of the mysterious from which the mysterious has vanished" (2014, 139). Committing to the mysterious, Niedecker most often inhabits a borderland between collective and individual consciousness. The reader here experiences uncertainty as the poet does, searching for true relation between self and world. This endeavor may never disclose any utopian horizon, may even prove fatalistic, but in such a poem both speaker and reader become something like secular pilgrims on the way toward realization, even when the ending of the poem frustrates their desire.

Following Pound and Williams, Niedecker reintroduces and answers the question of what a modern American poem can be. Here it's worth returning to Georg Lukács. If the Hungarian thinker's theory of reification aligns with Niedecker's portrayal of the twentieth-century American public sphere, his claims about literary genre provide a provocative contrast to Niedecker's form-finding. For Lukács, the novel was the art form in which the self journeys toward its own realization (thus the prominence of the bildungsroman). If nothing else, this was a matter of scale, prose narrative allowing the space for, and necessitating, development toward a goal. In lyric poetry, however, such realization was not the end but the beginning. Lyric poetry was timeless because instantaneous and essentially static. It gave life, Lukács claimed, to "sudden flashes" of an original and emancipated essence: "verse can only weave a garland of freedom round something that has already been liberated from all fetters" (1971, 58). The beguiling and wonderful thing about Niedecker's series poems is that they fulfill both Lukács's definition of lyric and his seemingly exclusive description of prose fiction. *New Goose* could be described as a novel winnowed down to essentials: the protagonist, a young woman in 1940s Wisconsin, tries to find stability just after her father's death. The reader sees her navigating the challenges of work, money, sex, political conviction, and family, as well as the more existential problem of her relation to her surroundings—the "natural" world that's both man-made and not, at times infused with strange sympathies, at other times utterly indifferent. Such a description would be true, but *New Goose* is not a poem imitating a novel. The "essentials" to which Niedecker has winnowed down her lines sometimes turn out to be mundane, even random details, unnecessary to any narrative and yet conductors of energy, objects in a process, moments contributing to an unfolding succession of moments. Entailing more than plot development, this force flows backward as well as forward, suspends as well as reveals.

Niedecker's ability to convey the breadth of prose narrative while achieving the intensity of lyric reaches its height in her 1968 collection *North Central*. In these late poems, the poet's everyday attempts at a truthful relation between self and world appear against the backdrop of the nuclear threat and the war in Vietnam, as well as earlier shocks of modernity still being processed—including the rapid growth and spread of technology, and the advent of Darwinian science.

Consider a section from early in the series poem "Traces of Living Things":

TV
    See it explained—
compound interest
and the compound eye
    of the insect

the wave-line
on shell, sand, wall
and forehead of the one
    who speaks (2002, 239)

These lines deliver a blend of wonder and shock. Their structure itself reveals a canny doubleness: the poet first claims to describe a television program and its seemingly educational content ("See it explained"), then offers her own, far from explanatory programming—a nearly hallucinatory passage, telescoping together the mathematical mechanism of modern capitalism, a timeline of evolutionary biology, and the mass production of televisual technology—all inhering to the anagrammatical play of "compound interest / and the compound eye / of the insect."

This vision of totality slides from wonder into apprehension. Geologic time—going all the way back to the waves of the Paleozoic—appearing on the "forehead of the one / who speaks" may suggest amazement, and the plainness of that phrasing, awe. But this tone also verges on deadpan blankness and the image of our prehistoric past—bad omen. Even the everyday phenomenon of a television broadcast here reveals a relation of utter authority to utter passivity.

That set of doubles correlates with a larger one in "Traces of Living Things" and throughout Niedecker's late poetry: sublime wonder and cataclysmic horror. Consider two consecutive sections from later in the poem—paced as if journal entries, or snippets from a middle American renga:

I walked
on New Year's Day

beside the trees
my father now gone planted

evenly following
the road

Each
    Spoke

        J.F. Kennedy after

        the Bay of Pigs

    To stand up
black marked tulip

not snapped by the storm
"I've been duped by the experts"

—and walk
the South Lawn (2002, 245–46)

Like "TV," these two sections render moments of wonder, catastrophe, and mysterious relation between people and nonhuman life. The poet's quick montage of president and flower, for example, suggests how individual imagination imbues what it sees. Niedecker isn't merely celebrating the subjective powers of the poet, however. A frightening sense of determinism ghosts those six short lines: the president's distance from the life-and-death missions carried out in his name shows an eerie correlation with the metaphor, so striking for its own distance between terms—JFK and a tulip. Such an abrupt splice might even convey the hovering fear of nuclear annihilation. After all, the failed invasion of Cuba will lead a year later to the missile crisis, while "Traces of Living Things" will give way to the final series poem in *North Central*, "Wintergreen Ridge"—in which that nightmare source gets a name: "the grand blow up // the bomb" (2002, 247).

But even here Niedecker's development of her entwining themes, while portraying a deterministic universe in which people may turn out no better than storm-damaged flowers lashing against one another to the death, also intensifies wonder. Considering all experience under the light of modern science, one that now enables humankind to destroy itself and the whole planet, Niedecker in fact releases a fugitive but insistent spiritualism in her poems, leading back past Romanticism—this is not, for example, the lover's lament at the end of Williams's "Perpetuum Mobile: The City"—to a kind of chthonic animism.

The trees the poet passes—while attempting communion with her father, twenty years after the first poems occasioned by his loss—speak. The power of this moment comes from a startling figuration (the word *pun* hardly does it justice): "Each // Spoke" conjures the almost cinematic image of trees radiating evenly as spokes from a hub while the poet walks past, but also introduces the idea that the trees transmit her feelings about her father. The former reading doesn't ironize so much as temper the latter. The objective, even mechanistic image and the mysterious, sympathetic one reveal two poles, two opposed ways of understanding. Niedecker's series poems give form to this same contradiction: their movement lends depth to private, subjective experience even while setting that experience in relation to the objectivity of science and geopolitics. Such movement makes Niedecker more than a realist. Throughout her poems the reader watches as Wisconsin neighbors, seventeenth-century explorers, water flowers, gophers, Red Army soldiers, and scraps of birch bark float up from the page: concrete particularity translated into verbal form. But the concrete in Niedecker is compounded from processes, flows, metabolic rhythms. Her poetry holds a mirror up to the world, and yet this poet knows there's no mirror outside the world. Her greatness lies in her ability to create a unique poetic form from this same situation, one strong with all the lyric pathos of individual longing yet perspicacious enough in its vision of totality to become not only narrative but epic in its imaginative scope.

George Oppen

Like Niedecker, George Oppen endeavored to bring the everyday into startling relief, to return all we take for granted to its original strangeness and importance. Few poets convey the utter shock of being able to talk, breathe, or drive a car as convincingly as Oppen. Even as his poems achieve a nearly scientific clarity, their idiomatic starkness reveals a grounding in collective life. But Oppen's relation to his society remains fraught, and there are few poets whose approach to their own language bristles so often with antagonism. This is not only a matter of rejecting literary conventions, outdated bourgeois values, and so on: plain, colloquial language at times signals immediacy, clarity, and antielitism in these poems, but at other moments the debasing numbness of mass culture. There's a restlessness in Oppen, one that shows in the facts of his biography. The son of a successful San Francisco theater owner, Oppen rebelled against the decadence and emptiness he saw as his father's world.

He left home as soon as he could, visited Pound in Rapallo, fought in the Second World War, and was wounded at the Battle of the Bulge. In the early 1930s, after publishing his first collection, *Discrete Series*—a section of which appeared in that same 1931 issue of *Poetry* that Lorine Niedecker found in the Fort Atkinson library—Oppen gave up poetry for twenty-five years to concentrate his energies on politics, while supporting himself and his family by working as a carpenter. Having joined the American Communist Party in the 1930s, the Oppens organized labor actions in concert with Hollywood communists such as Dalton Trumbo and Ring Lardner Jr., and later in New York with the Workers Alliance. But it wasn't until the election year of 1948 when the Oppens volunteered for Henry Wallace's Progressive Party that they fell under the close scrutiny of the FBI. The couple fled to Mexico in 1951 and lived there for eight years. Returning both to poetry and to the United States in the late 1950s, Oppen published his three strongest collections in quick succession: *The Materials* (1962), *This in Which* (1965), and *Of Being Numerous* (1968). If the poet left poetry for politics, in returning to poetry he never abandoned politics. The central occupation of these books remains social relations, the ways we manage or fail to live together. But the poems are neither agitprop nor sermons delivered to the mirror. They're remarkable for confronting uncertainties they don't pretend to ameliorate. For all their self-consciously epic scope—their Marxian insistence upon seeing discrete phenomenon in relation to totality—they tend toward the interior voice, the individual consciousness speaking its way toward truth.

In addition to reprinting Oppen's 1978 collection *Primitive*, Michael Davidson's edition of the *New Collected Poems* contains a selection of previously unpublished poems. Like Niedecker's "Progression," many of these show the poet thinking not only about aesthetics but about how aesthetics and political thinking meet. Here's one of Oppen's previously uncollected poems—a late one, from the mid-1970s—titled "The Artist":

> he breaks the silence
>
> and yet he hesitates, half unwilling

something comes to his mind
it is something about something

the sea

to ask
where is the sea he asks

where is the shore
he fears as the devil

himself his
cleverness

we move, we move, the mass of the people
moves is he trying to escape? To enter? (2002, 300)

Like Niedecker's, Oppen's colloquial speech has little to do with populism. The lines "something comes to his mind / it is something about something" might even parody plain style—even as they continue to suggest unvarnished sincerity. This poet is caught between states, linguistic as well as existential. He sets out to declare the artist's larger purpose: "He breaks the silence," but a hesitance, the "half unwilling" metaphor that comes to his mind, overwhelms that seemingly communicative task.

That metaphor itself—the relation of land and sea—lies at the heart of Oppen's work. With his nautical imagery he tends to conjure the "ship of state," and yet, a sailor since boyhood on San Francisco Bay, Oppen also conveys the actual sensations of being at sea. In "The Artist" this means simultaneous exhilaration ("we move, we move") and disorientation ("where is the sea he asks // where is the shore / he fears"), the shore standing for the world the artist inhabits with others and also the danger of wreckage, diffusion into the crowd, acquiescence to the limits of the status quo, surrender to the reign of ideology. Refusing to decide whether his desire is "to escape" or "to enter" collective life, Oppen's artist dedicates himself to the threshold itself. In this way he finally does answer the question implied by the poem's title. What does the artist do? He breaks the silence, yes, but he preserves something of silence too: through language he embodies associative, synchronic states of mind and feeling. This preoccupation with organic time, preverbal consciousness, and ineffability crops up often in modern and contemporary American poetry. The "Deep Image" poems of the 1970s, for example, as well as the associative, "elliptical" work of many poets writing today, exhibit the same tendency. The source lies in first-generation Modernists who were Oppen's direct forebears. I have in mind not only Pound's statements concerning Imagism—"the image delivers an emotional and intellectual complex in an instant of time," for all its no-nonsense terseness, suggests a level of mystery—but also Eliot's claim that "the poet is occupied with frontiers of consciousness beyond which words fail, though meanings still exist" (1975, 107). What's unique about Oppen's portrayal of the ineffable, preverbal, or synchronic turns out to be his complete lack of romance. No grail myth, no city of Dioce, no personified river leads from or follows this state in Oppen. Here again he's dedicated to the threshold: conditions of everyday life interest him just as much as their opposite, and are often revealed to be as challenging to linguistic representation as any epiphanic experience. Dismaying, wondrous, or both at the same time, the everyday only rarely meets its match in everyday language, or so Oppen suggests. He responds not with ornate or academic idioms but with a plain American English that he turns against itself, so that his poems often reveal the extreme, fundamental effort of speaking truth.

One of Oppen's best short lyrics, "The Hills" from *The Materials*, shows how such an endeavor works, feels, and provokes:

That this is I,
Not mine, which wakes
To where the present
Sun pours in the present, to the air perhaps
Of love and of
Conviction.
      As to know
Who we shall be. I knew it then.
You getting in
The old car sat down close
So close I turned and saw your eyes a woman's
Eyes. The patent
Latches on the windows
And the long hills whoever else's
Also ours. (2002, 75)

The provocation that the poet directs at himself as well as his reader comes in the first six syllables: "That this is I, / Not mine,..." With a simple distinction between pronouns, one that rules against the possessive, Oppen invokes Marx's argument against private property. One measure of the poet's accomplishment, in fact, might be the simultaneous seriousness and lack of pretension with which he takes up such ideas. Even on the level of style, "The Hills" shows qualities of Oppen's other favorite philosopher, Martin Heidegger, whose elaboration of the fundamental categories of being emphasizes the sensations and intentions related to handling instruments, tools, technology. This engagement with Marx and Heidegger seldom feels doctrinaire in Oppen. The poet maintains rhetorical authority in "The Hills," for example, while admitting an uncertainty so fundamental it applies to his own self-consciousness: "who am I?" is the question he attempts to answer as he wakes, finding himself on the edge between the physical and metaphysical: "Where the present / Sun pours in the present, to the air perhaps / Of love and of / Conviction." In these short lines Oppen portrays a brink between concepts and facts: love and conviction not only feel like facts but often lead to the creation of new material reality, while sun and air may appear immaterial but are physical things. This reversal of expectations informs the remarkable clause "the present / Sun pours in the present," a verbal figure acting as an uncertainty principle: space and time, quality and quantity, motion and place become Möbius strips, and yet a gap remains between them, a quantum loophole eliciting bewilderment and wonder.

"The Hills" tends more toward wonder, as the initial opposition of "I" and "mine" resolves into the "ours" of the ending and the love poet's commitment rhymes with the promise of collective potential. But Oppen's no blithe utopian. In *Of Being Numerous*, his great long poem published in 1968, he seems to submit all he gazes upon to an existential x-ray. Structuring the poem as a statement about the prospects for collective life during the disaster of the Vietnam War, Oppen seldom sounds didactic. Just as the speaker in "The Artist" allows his initial effort at direct public speech to give way to metaphor and subjective impression, so the poet here includes fragments of personal letters, addresses to family members, and moments of inward meditation. The poem feels as much about individual interior existence as collective life.

Consider the thirteenth and fourteenth sections, the former structured around the words *beginning* and *end*, in a spiral-logic resembling the circuit from "Not mine" to "Also ours" in "The Hills":

13.
        unable to begin
At the beginning, the fortunate
Find everything already here. They are shoppers,
Choosers, judges ... And here the brutal
Is without issue, a dead end.
            They develop
Argument in order to speak, they become
Unreal, unreal, life loses
Solidity, loses extent, baseball's their game
Because baseball is not a game
But an argument and difference of opinion
Makes the horse races. They are ghosts that endanger

One's soul. There is change
In an air
That smells stale, they will come to the end
Of an era
First of all peoples
And one may honorably keep
One's distance
If he can.

14.
I cannot even now
Altogether disengage myself
From those men

With whom I stood in emplacements, in mess tents,
In hospitals and sheds and hid in the gullies
Of blasted roads in a ruined country,

Among them many men
More capable than I—

Muykut and a sergeant
Named Healey,

That lieutenant also—

How forget that? How talk
Distantly of 'The People'?

Who are the people? That they are

That force within the walls
Of cities

Wherein the cars
Of mechanics
And executives

Echo like history
Down walled avenues
In which one cannot speak. (2002, 170–71)

In section 13, even before he questions his own stance, the poet's statements about American mass culture sound nothing like mere commentary. The lineation, the active and dramatic grammar (for example, the repetition of "unreal" and "loses"), and the sudden jumps between levels of abstraction render the thinking mind in motion, discovering and living its convictions. This is the dialectical movement evident in Williams and Niedecker, but in Oppen it becomes bare, fierce, explicit. The poet's impassioned, moving, but unsentimental negation of his critical distance at the beginning of section 14, for example, meets its own negation by the end of that section: "Down walled avenues / In which one cannot speak."

Neither optimism nor pessimism, collective nor individual, wins out over the other. Instead they combine to renew a species of wonder, perhaps best expressed by the final word of the poem, occurring in a quote from Walt Whitman's description in his journals of the bronze Genius of Liberty shining atop the Capitol in Washington: "curious."

To my mind, the section that best shows what curiosity means for Oppen—how it is much more than happy, care-free inquiry—is the twenty-fifth:

Strange that the youngest people I know
Live in the oldest buildings

Scattered about the city
In the dark rooms
Of the past—and the immigrants,

The black
Rectangular buildings
Of the immigrants.

They are the children of the middle class.

"The pure products of America—"

Investing
The ancient buildings
Jostle each other

In the half-forgotten, that ponderous business.
This Chinese Wall. (2002, 176–77)

Curiosity in this poem and throughout Oppen leads the individual consciousness toward a vision of totality. Consider the contrast between intense singularity of detail and the ambitious breadth of the subject: the particular fact of young people living in old apartment buildings illustrates the whole power of history.

Oppen's plain style proves itself capable of marvelous complexity. Take the stanza that follows his one-line quote from William Carlos Williams's "The pure products of America go crazy." Oppen slides here into ambiguous syntax. The reader's left to wonder if the participle "investing" applies to the young people who have so recently taken their place in society, one that Ernest Mandel would elaborate under the rubric of "late capitalism" in his 1972 book of that name, one in which the seeming explosion of nineteenth- and early twentieth-century class structure (middle-class kids living in tenements, for example) in fact reveals a situation in which capitalism has saturated society and accelerated its processes, so that everything seems to have become "investment." Or does that word refer simply to the buildings themselves, which in the next line "jostle" for their piece of skyline?

And what of that utterly certain, yet strange, last line, "This Chinese Wall"? The reference continues the architectural motif, hinting that civilization is both more historical and more alien than we imagine. But it also alludes to a passage near the opening of *The Communist Manifesto*: "The bourgeoisie, by the rapid improvement of all instruments of production, by the immensely facilitated means of communication, draws all, even the most barbarian, nations into its civilization. The cheap prices of commodities are the heavy artillery with which it batters down Chinese Walls" (2011, 69). As with the allusion to Williams's "pure products," there's a difference between the phrase's meaning in the original and in its new context. The "pure products of America" who "go crazy" in the section of Williams's *Spring and All* later titled "To Elsie" are distinctly lower class; in Oppen's poem they come to include "children of the middle class" as well. In *The Communist Manifesto*, Marx and Engels's "Chinese Walls" (*chinesischen Mauern*) represent the structures of precapitalist societies that the bourgeois revolution batters down. But in Oppen "This Chinese Wall" becomes the structure of late capitalism itself. Oppen shows as little, or less, contentment with his society in 1968 than Marx and Engels showed with theirs in 1848. There's a graveness here, an admission of the extreme difficulty of meaningful and moral thought and action. There's still a battle ahead, this ending suggests, the big one. And yet the very uncovering of such realities reveals a steely hopefulness.

It's Oppen's unique talent, this gift for embedding such meaning neither in jeweled phrases nor in the display of wit, but in small, seemingly plain interruptions, interjections, momentary blanks, and associative leaps, all deriving from living, idiomatic speech. For all his high seriousness, he entertains an openness, "curiosity" not as preference for the beguiling but as motive for action. And making curiosity his ground note, Oppen doesn't evade his convictions. Nor does he, like some of his postmodern descendants, celebrate the unknown and uncertain for their own sakes. It's simply that his convictions lie in action, change, process, dialectic. These young people he acknowledges in section 25 are part and parcel of the many young subjects of his poems. Portrayal of the young brings Oppen as close as he comes in his austerity to celebration, and (as Donald Davie once pointed out) reveals the poet at his most American, his most Whitmanian.

Oppen's awe regarding human generation is an attitude he shares with Hannah Arendt. A classicist to the core, she identified the ethos of the Greek historians, the public consciousness of polis life, and its long roots in Homeric epic, again returning to the intellectual forefront in modernity, becoming the dominant arena of truth—a progression she allegorizes as History replacing Philosophy, with Marx as the first insurgent historian. If this return to Plato's "cave of the everyday" suggests a loss, it also opens a new possibility: freedom.

But "freedom" has its problems as an ideal. It's worth considering the critique of that word by the same Marxist tradition with which Williams, Niedecker, and Oppen, if not Pound, were well acquainted. Lenin wrote, "'Freedom' is a grand word, but under the banner of freedom for industry the most predatory wars were waged, under the banner of freedom of labor, the working people were robbed" (1987, 3). Echoing Marx's critique of the Proudhonists' misuse of "freedom," Lenin here anticipates an argument Trotsky, after his time in New York, will apply specifically to the United States. Partisan denunciation, no doubt. But are these claims really so outlandish? Turn on a television in America, and you'll hear "freedom" used to sell any and everything from four-wheel drive to foreign wars.

Still, the power of such critique is that it allows the question to remain: what would *true* freedom be like? In Arendt's estimation it remained possible in modern times, but not always, and not as a matter of asserting a sovereign self. True freedom was now an "accessory" to being. Human beings, already thrown into an organic process leading toward nonbeing, now had to confront the modern automatism of functions, pulling in the same direction. This restriction could lead to the daily nightmare of the Stalinist state or to a "freedom" that was itself a new form of domination by the ideological, military, and economic power of capitalism.

Such a philosophy may sound like pessimism, but it made true freedom all the more vital. On the level of individual experience, there was now the possibility for what Arendt called "miracle," a term she reserved not for the works of deities and saints but for the combination of freedom and action in modern human beings:

> History, in contradistinction to nature, is full of events; here the miracle of accident and infinite improbability occurs so frequently that it seems strange to speak of miracles at all. But the reason for this frequency is merely that historical processes are created and constantly interrupted in human initiative, by the *initium* man is insofar as he is an acting being. Hence, it is not in the least superstitious, it is even a counsel of realism, to look for the unforeseeable and unpredictable, to be prepared for and to expect "miracles" in the political realm. (1958, 169)

If we have no claim to immortality beyond what we make of our world and transmit across generations, and if this action itself has the potential to be "miraculous," I'm convinced that the best poems of Pound, Williams, Niedecker, and Oppen are in this sense miracles. In new forms that combined epic and lyric, these poets realigned the frame of what would be possible for their art, and, in turn, their art offered visions of a potential realignment of the relation between self and society. In Pound, a vision of continuity between the self and collective experience glimmers through the admittedly failed, heroic project of creating an alternate modernity out of mnemonic sources both personal and historical. In Williams, the same ambition shows in the less adversarial commitments of a modern love poet refiguring for himself the ideal of "E Pluribus Unum." In Niedecker and Oppen, the relation of self and world occurs on a smaller but no less impressive scale: in Niedecker's montages of the domestic and global; and in Oppen's dramas of the individual mind seeking truth, a clear-eyed sense of potential counterbalances the grave portrayal of social relations. It's this ambition, this critical hopefulness about giving form to aesthetic and social freedom, that undergirds the achievement of all four poets.

John Berryman's Acoustics

In 1989, when Farrar, Straus, and Giroux published the *Collected Poems* of John Berryman, the *New Republic* ran a review by Donald Davie. Against familiar notions of Berryman as poet of the individual tortured psyche—of mental disorder, dipsomaniacal hijinks, erotic banditry, and so on—Davie portrays Berryman not just as a political poet but as one confronting a particular political situation: American imperialism. "He didn't mean to be and yet he was a poet of empire" (2000, 92). It may have been Robert Lowell, Davie argues, who compared twentieth-century America to Augustan Rome with its truculent bloat from republic to empire, but it was Berryman who fully rendered and dramatized the condition. Berryman for Davie remains an artist who "recognizes civic responsibilities; not, as too many commentators would persuade us, a man entranced by his own image in the mirror" (92).

In 2014, a hundred years after Berryman's birth and a quarter century after that *New Republic* review, at least two events made Davie look like a soothsayer. The first was the publication of Philip Coleman's *John Berryman's Public Vision*. Elaborating the whole webbed membrane of political consciousness in Berryman's poems, Coleman offers a reading that feels at the same time definitive and open-ended—a precise and comprehensive portrait promising a robust life to come for Berryman's poetry. The second event was a great example of that robustness, the centenary celebration at the University of Minnesota of John Berryman's birth. Held over one weekend, the celebration brought together scholars from all over the world, students, filmmakers, composers, friends and former students of the poet, and three generations of his close family. The editors of the new centenary editions of Berryman's work, April Bernard, Henri Cole, Daniel Swift, and Michael Hofmann, gave excellent readings from Berryman's poetry and their own.

For my part, the celebration was also just an occasion to listen to Berryman, to hear his poems again, this time in a dialogue containing many voices. In fact, I want to claim that Berryman makes a superlative—if surprising—poet of collective life because of a certain technical gift: his feel for acoustics. I choose the word *acoustics* because it implies not only the management of rhythms, like and unlike syllables, tones, expressive attitudes, and registers of diction, but also the spaces in which such sounds reverberate. These include stanzas (and Berryman was a superlative architect of stanzas) as well as the entire depth and dimension of collective life, the explicit or interpreted distances and proximities between speakers and listeners.

Used to describe how small formal qualities and large historical forces become mutually entailing in poems, *acoustic* contains a revealing contradiction. While the word implies "depth and dimension," it may also suggest its opposite—two-dimensional space. Berryman's contemporary the pop philosopher Marshall McLuhan used the word this way when he related a vision of modern experience as essentially "acoustic." Electronic media, technologies of instantaneous transmission, have returned us, or so McLuhan's excitable prose claims, to a world more tribal than civic in which traditional hierarchies tumble, leaving diverse facets of experience to balance in weird solution as distinctions between background and foreground, cause and effect, society and self, collapse—like so many discrete bodies melting into overlapping information streams. Central to all these transitions for McLuhan remains the shift from a pictorial to an "acoustic" paradigm, characterized by the two-dimensional space of the mosaic in which "components co-exist without direct lineal hook-up or connection, creating a field of simultaneous relations" (2005, 9). Examples include radio and television but also the news-

paper, whose sections and columns not only contain seemingly un-
related information but sometimes perform entirely different social
functions while lying right next to one another.

There's a heavy dose of technological determinism in McLuhan,
and some shambolic vagueness, but his vision of modernity goes a
way toward describing Berryman's own; the dreams of Henry House
are nothing if not "acoustic" environments. In fact, Berryman here
proves the greater thinker about modernity. He sees the paradigm
McLuhan describes as more than technological: he understands it
as the precise stock-in-trade of imperial America — the same power
for whom communications technology has become central in war-
fare as in the glut of postwar cultural production. The power of *The
Dream Songs* in particular comes from the way that amorous, impulsive, short-circuiting Henry makes an American Everyman for his
age. He does so precisely because he includes various and extreme
examples. This occurs even at the level of typography: the proverbial stones that the builder refused here become dialect spellings,
slang words, and accent marks. As for the people in these poems,
Henry not only sympathizes with but sees himself in murderers,
paranoiacs, and sexual deviants, as well as great religious and political figures. He casts himself in the roles of both victims and perpe-
trators. His purview remains mostly national, as he admits to being
a "monoglot of American English" (1969, 52), and yet Berryman
is canny about how this figure appears in an international setting.
Traveling to India in Dream Song #27, Henry makes a grimly comic
parody of a colonialist even while attempting to be a good guest:
"the little people spread, & did friendly things" (1969, 31). These
poems are everywhere polyphonic and everywhere tinged with the
central conflicts of postwar America.

Consider how such political "acoustics" inform Dream Song
#22, which the poet titles "Of 1826," referring to the death of those
famous rivals John Adams and Thomas Jefferson on the same day,
July 4, 1826. Here are the opening two stanzas:

I am the little man who smokes & smokes.
I am the girl who does know better but.

I am the king of the pool.
I am so wise I had my mouth sewn shut.
I am a government official & a goddamned fool.
I am a lady who takes jokes.

I am the enemy of the mind.
I am the auto salesman and love you.
I am a teenage cancer, with a plan.
I am the blackt-out man.
I am the woman powerful as a zoo.
I am two eyes screwed to my set, whose blind— (1969, 24)

The first twelve lines offer a reversal of Whitman's lyric "I" as container of multitudes. In this poem the multitudes show up all right, but they're a nightmarish gaggle. The end-stopped clipping isolates each character, but does anything connect them? Before we can answer, the poem jump-cuts, morphing from a hypnagogic TV set to a nineteenth-century deathbed scene. Can the founding rivals, Adams and Jefferson, Federalist and Republican, reconcile at the end? Can those private selves ever join a redemptive union greater than the sum of its parts? The answer would seem to be no.

But the poem doesn't end before another tone arrives:

It is the Fourth of July.
Collect: while the dying man,
forgone by you creator, who forgives,
is gasping "Thomas Jefferson still lives"
in vain, in vain, in vain.
I am Henry Pussy-cat! My whiskers fly. (24)

Here Henry adopts his feline avatar, echoing those first twelve lines with his own boastful declaration, "I am Henry Pussy-cat! My whiskers fly." The exuberance has a retroactive effect on the preceding lines: despite the obvious grimness of such statements as "I am a teenage cancer, with a plan," these "pure products of America gone crazy" may begin to seem more sympathetic. For one thing, there's the possibility of erotic attraction. Henry Pussy-cat might just enjoy the company of "the woman powerful as a zoo," not to mention "the girl who does know better but." And yet the recuperative potential here goes beyond self-gratification: if only by virtue of its location in the poem, the concluding flare of excitement suggests an adversative turn on that penultimate line at the presidential deathbed, "in vain, in vain, in vain," so that the glimmer of hopefulness extends now to the nation itself.

This may not ensure anything like a "happy ending," and yet the poem concludes with an artist's commitment to his art and to the dissociated people of his society. These isolated flecks from the mosaic of the American populace are for Berryman what the "foul rag and bone shop of the heart" was for Yeats at the end of "The Circus Animal's Desertion." Although Berryman's declaration "I am Henry Pussy-cat! My whiskers fly" remains more ambiguous than that of his great predecessor, nevertheless the imagined public of Dream Song #22 — unctuous car dealers right along with founding fathers — turns out for Berryman to be the source "where all the ladders start" (Yeats 1983, 348).

Berryman's ability to derive lasting poetry from this source depends upon his acoustic sense, in both, seemingly contrary connotations of that phrase. Discontinuous, like nonfigurative shapes on the flattened picture plane of a modern painting, discrete patches of speech in *Dream Songs* turn individual poems as well as the whole sequence into what McLuhan would call "a field of simultaneous relations." Indeed the death of Henry, which occurs in Dream Song #26 but seems to impede neither his carrying on with the events of his life nor his dying again, performs the same function: it confutes linear chronology, exercising the ancient prerogative of lyric to suspend time, to make all time simultaneous.

Still, *The Dream Songs* is more than a mosaic of lexical and narrative discontinuity. Just as the wildly different registers of these poems, their seemingly singular verbal bursts, in fact link up in a grammar of remarkable precision, so the disparate songs become continuous with the storyline of one individual. The feeling that these poems "come off the page," that they take shape right out of the air, startling themselves into the third dimension, depends upon forceful interjections, unexpected idioms, and so on, but also upon the likelihood — though never the inevitability — that such moments will contribute to a narrative, that for all Henry's obvious theatrics and hyperbole, the complaint, the cry, the moan of anguish and desire have their reasons.

Such psychological depths reveal the historical scope of the poem. It's precisely in Henry's isolation, the remove of his subjective states, his dreams themselves, that the social becomes vivid and powerful. The most obvious example is the racial one that Berryman himself mentions in his preface to the complete edition of *Dream Songs* when he describes Henry as "a white American in early middle age, sometimes in blackface." So it's important here to address Berryman's use of blackface in *Dream Songs* — a feature of the work that has understandably given many readers pause. In his introduction to the selection of Berryman's poems he edited for the Library of America, the poet Kevin Young addresses this aspect of *Dream Songs*. "Berryman explores the 'blackness' of whiteness in a way that I have come to admire — even if, from another angle, he might be said to replicate in all too familiar a fashion the constant use of blackness by whites to say the unsayable" (2004, 12). Young makes a crucial distinction: when Berryman employs blackface he doesn't portray black dialect, much less black life, so much as the artificial convention of blackface minstrelsy itself. Strangely, this limitation reveals the strength and honesty of the poetry. For Young, "much of the force of the *Dream Songs*" comes from the way that blackface calls into play the instability of *white* identity. Young quotes Berryman's friend Ralph Ellison's own discussion of blackface: "Here another ironic facet of the old American problem of identity crops up. For out of the counterfeiting of the black American's identity there arises a profound doubt in the white man's mind as to the authenticity of his own image of himself" (12). Social class, marked by race and the history of slavery, informs the very language from which Berryman forms Henry — the private, direct, often offensive and self-destructive thoughts "one" would not normally speak out loud both parallel and create a linguistic underworld. Following Ellison and Young, we can see that the inauthenticity of such language, the way in which it fails to portray black life, makes for an authentic portrayal of the supposedly normative image of the average white male.

The drama created by idioms of different racial provenance rubbing up against one another proves paradigmatic: throughout the poem, private experience gets interrupted when the very language used to translate it can't help but reveal the strain of social and political relations. In a letter to Berryman, Saul Bellow quipped that *The Dream Songs* might as well be titled "The Spiritual History of America Under the Administration of Dwight D. Eisenhower" (2010, 245); he may have had in mind Dream Song #23, "The Lay of Ike," a poem whose choppy, interruptive syntax parodies both broadcast technology and Eisenhower's own less-than-Ciceronian oratory. But the imagery and tone of that poem color others, including many whose occasions remain more obviously personal. The imperial forcefulness and bumptious clumsiness that Berryman sees in Eisenhower, along with the tone of militarism lingering amid the booming prosperity and technological wonder of a postwar economy, appear in Dream Song #69, for instance, when Henry declares a lust so overpowering it could produce "TV spots and skywriting / outlets in Bonn & Tokyo."

One of Berryman's favorite abbreviations, "p.a." for public address, here deserves attention. It shows up in Dream Song #24 when Henry lectures an Indian audience, as well as back in Dream Song #9, a poem remarkable for its engagement with popular culture, electronic media, and state power: Henry's mental anguish finds an image of itself in the final scene of Raoul Walsh's film noir classic *High Sierra* (1941), when Ida Lupino speaks through a California state trooper's microphone, attempting to talk Humphrey Bogart's "Mad Dog" Earl Ray down from a cliff. In all these poems, "public address" suggests a parallel with the poet's own acoustic art. After all, what does the poet do but address others through a conduit connecting collective and personal experience? And yet there's a certain embarrassment: "p.a." may suggest the eminence of the person speaking, but it conjures those institutional authorities—the police as well as academics—to whom people generally aren't overjoyed to listen. Although Berryman himself once confessed to preferring amplification for his readings—explaining to an interviewer that only with a microphone was he able to convey *quiet* moments in his poems—nevertheless in the poems themselves, p.a. systems evoke a Kafkaesque tragicomedy of entrapment within structures of power.

The great wonder of *Dream Songs* lies in Berryman's ability, like Kafka's, to balance his fatalistic tendency with its twin—wonder at the surprise of the inevitable, the beguiling power of becoming. Consider Dream Song #77, the concluding poem in the first volume of *Dream Songs*, as well as the fourth to include that abbreviation "p.a." It's unique not so much for portraying the intersection of private and public consciousness but for exploring how—and why— artworks might strive for such portrayal. Here's the first stanza:

> Seedy Henry rose up shy in de world
> & shaved & swung his barbells, duded Henry up
> and p.a.'d poor thousands of persons on topics of grand
> interest to Henry, ah to those less & none.
> Wif a book of his in either hand
> He is stripped down to move on. (1969, 84)

This is a poem about the life of the writer, and yet Henry's individual travails reveal another subject, more universal and more particular: the sense of time, the sense of being in time, like it or not. The final clause, "he's getting ready to move on," distills the problems inherent to this preoccupation into an effective joke. The imperative of the lyric poet may be *not* to move on, not to "get over" events—sadness as well as love. And to "move on" in a poem may mean to end, to affix the words irrevocably to the page, so that they will always remain still. We can picture Henry himself *moving*, for sure: he can hardly keep still. And what could be a more American ending than moving on—like the hero at the end of a western, his restlessness tinged with equal parts optimism, avoidance, wonder, and wastefulness? But can we really imagine Henry moving on from anything?

After the opening stanza, the meditations on time continue:

> —Come away, Mr. Bones.
>
> —Henry is tired of the winter,
> & haircuts, & a squeamish comfy ruin-prone proud national
> mind & spring (in the city so called).
> Henry likes Fall.

He would be prepared to live in a world of Fall
for ever, impenitent Henry.
But the snows and summers grieve and dream;

These fierce & airy occupations, and love,
raved away so many of Henry's years
it is a wonder that, with in each hand
one of his mad books and all,
ancient fires for eyes, his head full
and his heart full, he's making ready to move on. (84)

Berryman's ambivalent sense of time, of being in time, contains
two sets of contradictions. The first is that of personal and public
life, evident in the contrast between the "grand interest" Henry
himself has in his topics and the disinterest of his audience, as well
as the basic, perceptual disjunction between what Henry experiences internally and what we commonly accept as reality. Henry's
comic complaint, for example, turns "the city" into "the city *so
called*" (my emphasis) so that the alienated poet seems to claim
the prerogative of idealist philosophy to create what he sees. At the
same time such metaphysical, personal preoccupations can appear
illusory, a waste of time, so that the "fierce and airy occupations" of
literature, love, and even consciousness itself turn into mere abstrac-
tions that have "raved away so many of Henry's years." The attempt
to solve this dilemma leads Berryman, Henry, and the reader to an
age-old problem for the lyric poet confronting mortality: the contradiction between organic and inorganic being. "Seedy," the initial
word of the poem, suggests Henry's erotic urges, and sometimes
unsavory style, but also the way any person is bound to biologi-
cal processes and importunate desires to live "for ever." Attempting to solve *this* contradiction becomes part and parcel of that first
one: the poet makes the personal public. Berryman's practice proves
no mere "confessional" act, in the sense of M. L. Rosenthal's persistent but diminishing coinage (1991, 109), because the poet also
makes the public personal. He does so in language that employs
time against time. Casual idioms, dialect spellings such as "Wif"
and "de," and references to his own historical moment, including its
specific technologies, are themselves as contingent or "ruin prone"
as Henry's proud national mind. At the same time they're the nec-

essary material of an artwork striving, if not like Yeats's to ascend "out of nature," at least to render permanent a new fold in reality. The contradiction of the organic and metaphysical develops, then, into a synthesis similar to that of the personal and public: the poem opens a space where each becomes the other.

Throughout his work, such synthesis prevents Berryman's poems from turning into thickets of competing tensions, halls of mirrors in which contradictions face off into infinity. In fact, another word for synthesis might be *direction*. I have in mind the sense of a poem's ending, the impression it leaves of where it has taken the reader and why, and where its affective energies *now* lead. So I want to conclude by examining a late poem that Donald Davie singled out for praise, "Lines to Mr. Frost," a poem that shows Berryman thinking about what poetry as an acoustic art can do, where it can lead, personally and historically—all while addressing the ghost of Robert Frost.

It's significant that Frost should appear at such a moment. If Berryman's immediate predecessors in ventriloquism were Eliot, Crane, and Pound, his forebear in acoustics—this art of getting sound and voice to dramatize historical forces—was none other than the great eclogist writing from north of Boston. It was Frost, after all, who declared in his famous "sound of sense" letter, sent from England to his former student John Bartlett on the Fourth of July 1913, that his metrical art was distinct from that of British predecessors (Frost mentions Tennyson and Swinburne) due to his unique concern with the vocal gestures underlying words, the nonverbal but articulate urge that he calls "the abstract sound of sense" and, in a later letter to Bartlett, "sentence sounds." These "definite entities" are characterized by creaturely rather than semantic intention, by suasion. "The best place to get the abstract sound of sense," Frost writes, "is from voices behind a door that cuts off the words." He illustrates the concept by asking Bartlett to imagine how a few examples would sound:

> You mean to tell me you can't read?
> I said no such thing.
> Well read then.
> You're not my teacher.

He says it's too late.
Oh, say!
Damn an Ingersoll watch anyway.

One-two-three — go!
No good! Come back — come back.
Haslam go down there and make those kids get out of the track.

Those sounds are summoned by the audial imagination and they must be positive, strong, and definitely and unmistakably indicated by the context. The reader must be at no loss to give his voice the posture proper to the sentence. The simple declarative sentence used in making a plain statement is one sound. But Lord love ye it mustn't be worked to death. (1995, 664)

Frost's Fourth of July brag about his originality compared to the likes of Swinburne and Tennyson prefigures Berryman's own "proud" though admittedly "ruin prone" national mind. Likewise Frost's preference for vocal drama ("Lord love ye") over the monotonous repetition of simple declarative sentences anticipates the verbal antics and agonies of Berryman's poems. In fact that imagined pair of walled-off voices, taking on different forms in each of the three examples, might just be the literary parents of Henry House.

Fitting, then, that "Lines to Mr. Frost" contains its own dialogue, this time with Frost's late poem "The Draft Horse," an uncharacteristic, hermetic, and violent dream parable. Here's how Frost's poem begins:

With a lantern that wouldn't burn
In too frail a buggy we drove
Behind too heavy a horse
Through a pitch-dark limitless grove.

And a man came out of the trees
And took our horse by the head
And reaching back to his ribs
Deliberately stabbed him dead. (1995, 665)

Already surprising, this drama becomes even stranger when the speaker responds with peculiar equanimity:

> The ponderous beast went down
> With a crack of a broken shaft.
> And the night drew through the trees
> In one long invidious draft.
>
> The most unquestioning pair
> That ever accepted fate
> And the least disposed to ascribe
> Any more than we had to to hate,
>
> We assumed that the man himself
> Or someone he had to obey
> Wanted us to get down
> And walk the rest of the way. (665)

Now here's Berryman's response in "Lines to Mr. Frost":

> Felled in my tracks by your tremendous horse
> slain in its tracks by the angel of good God,
> I wonder toward your marvelous tall art
> warning away maybe in that same morning
>
> you squandered afternoon of your great age
> on my good gravid wife & me, with tales
> gay of your cunning & colossal fame
> & awful character, and—Christ—I see
>
> I know & can do nothing, and don't mind—
> you're talking about American power and how
> somehow we've got to be got to give it up—
> so help me, in my poverty-stricken way
>
> I said the same goddamn thing yesterday
> to my thirty kids, so I was almost ready
> to hear you from the grave with these passionate grave
> last words, and frankly Sir you fill me with joy. (1969, 249)

Maybe the most remarkable thing about both poems, taken at first blush, remains their startling shifts in the direction not of action so much as tone. Frost imagines a brutal attack, the dramatic culmination of the ominous tone he builds in the first six lines, then has the speaker and his companion respond with neither rage nor terror but acceptance. I'm convinced Berryman's right about the poem: the "invidious draft," for example, hints at universal male conscription, a law in the United States from 1940 to 1973. "Too frail a buggy" pulled by "too heavy a horse" makes a fine figure for the situation Eisenhower himself described in his farewell address when he warned about the "military industrial complex" (1961). But this is not to ignore the obvious: "The Draft Horse" is one strange poem. For all its verbal and dramatic clarity, its relation to its context remains murky.

Responding to "The Draft Horse," Berryman's "Lines to Mr. Frost" reveals its own constitutive tensions. For one thing, there's the disparagement of Frost's "colossal fame / & awful character" that follows and leads back to tribute. More important, the poem balances two seemingly opposite conceptions of history. Deterministic fatalism crops up as the poet states, "I can do nothing." But a sense of history as possibly redemptive shows in the final statement about joy through artwork—a common note in Berryman's last poems, though one that never resolves the ominous undertones. After all, the occasions of speech, the acoustic events Berryman portrays, including Frost's regaling the Berryman family during a visit and Berryman's lecturing his college students, offer some glimmer of hopefulness precisely because they embed their vital messages, including those with international and historical urgency, in the world of everyday mundanity and awkwardness. This is what freedom means to Berryman, a surrendering of the poem to the voices of others. Indeed in his posthumously published collection of essays, *The Freedom of the Poet*, Berryman addresses the condition invoked by that title in an essay on Cervantes, characterizing such aesthetic freedom as "an imaginative collaboration" between the writer and auditor (1976, 151). Giving up ownership of the poem, like Frost's narrator stepping down from his buggy, the poet assumes rather than abandons responsibility. At the same time, freedom now comes from a greater source: the poem gains scope and vivacity from inclusion.

This strengthening surrender is what makes Berryman such a

powerful political poet. Writing about *Uncle Tom's Cabin*, Berryman's contemporary James Baldwin once explained that "the failure of the protest novel lies in its rejection of life, the human being, the denial of his beauty, dread, power, in its insistence that it is his categorization alone which is real and which cannot be transcended" (1955, 23). In "Lines to Mr. Frost" Berryman's rhetorical "message," his direction or directive, couldn't be clearer—he explains Frost's warning regarding an American descent from republic into empire: "you're talking about American power and how / somehow we've got to be got to give it up." But he answers this with "I said the same goddamn thing yesterday," submitting that message to the world of actual speakers. In "The Draft Horse," Frost avoids what Baldwin calls the "categorization" that ruins protest literature, the too-easy matching of schematics to actual human beings by way of an allegory he leaves shadowy, perhaps too much so. Berryman does so through fidelity to the creaturely textures of his subject and his own linguistic material. "Lines to Mr. Frost," and all of Berryman's best work, gathers "beauty, dread, power" because its language carries the historical energy into a vivid present in which excitement and even joy exist right along with outrage and terror.

James Wright's Classicism

There's a description of James Wright's work one often comes across, an account of his breaking through in the early 1960s when he sloughed off the formal constraints of his early style. His poems, or so this narrative tells us, became more authentic in two opposed ways. The recalcitrant facts of the working-class Midwest began to shine through the page with greater fidelity. Here was a poetry of strip mines and foundries, of billboards hanging among dead mulberry trees. By employing the procedures of Spanish and Latin American Surrealist poets, Wright also channeled the subconscious into his poems. Hallways now opened through the stems of elderberry leaves in Ohio, while housewives dreamed of *misterioso* palaces in the air. Wright's readers seem to agree: if this new style could be sentimental and repetitive in places, it nevertheless represented a mature sensibility.

There are reasons for the resilience of this stereotype. For one thing, it conveys some truth. Beginning with *The Branch Will Not Break* (1963), the poems showed an immediate lucidity. With their skeletal verse movement and tonal swerves between demotic homeliness and vatic extravagance, these lyrics sounded like nothing that had come before.

The stereotype also matches our tidy chronologies. We've heard that poets of this generation responded to the upheavals of their age by scrapping rhyme and meter. Wright himself certainly understood the changes in his poetry as something akin to a conversion.

In 1958, the year after the publication of his first book, *The Green Wall* (which Auden selected for the Yale Series of Younger Poets), Wright began correspondences with both James Dickey and Robert Bly. These letters are painful reading. Smoldering with self-hatred and often swirling to over ten pages, they show a mind spun helplessly out of orbit. Wright's teacher Theodore Roethke, who had his own experience with mania and depression, wrote to warn him: "I've been through all this before, through the wringer, bud, so please respect my advice. Once you become too hyper-active and lose too much sleep, you'll cross a threshold where chaos (and terror) ensues. . . . To come to the point: it would set my mind at rest if you would go to see some professional (yes, a psychiatrist) and tell him what's been going on the past two weeks" (Wright 2005b, 26). Neither Dickey nor Bly had this obvious insight. Or else they chose to ignore it: here was a penitent, a fresh recruit to the poetics of the primal each advocated in the journals. Wright was working at the time as a lecturer at the University of Minnesota in Minneapolis, but he began riding the bus on weekends to Bly's farm in the west of the state. It makes me wince, reading the letters, to see the stronger personality dominating the stronger poet. Could this writer whom Auden had praised for his sensitive and discerning intelligence really be swayed by Robert Bly, for whom thought and imagination were forever locked in combat?

But that's where the old conversion narrative founders. Just as Wright's fascination with the irrational surfaced in his earlier poems, especially in the bardic symbolism he learned from Yeats through Roethke, so his love of technique, of measure and proportion, remained in the newer work even when it seeped underground. In one letter, after many sentences of supplication, he complains to Bly himself: "It is my feeling, so far, that your attack on iambics is pretty futile. The selection of a bad line out of one of Shakespeare's sonnets, for example, to show that the English language is unsuited to iambics seems to me a terrible waste of time and energy" (180). The very next day he writes to Donald Hall of "my own personal curse, my equal love of Whitman and Winters" (170). Then there's the case of the poem titled, in the manner of the titles that anthologists often gave to ancient Chinese poems, "Depressed by a Book of Bad Poetry, I Walk toward an Unused Pasture and Invite the Insects to Join Me." With its renunciation of reading in favor of observing ants, who parade past the poet "casting shadows so frail I can see through them," this short lyric might seem to typify the return to the unreflective advocated by Bly. So readers may be surprised to find from the letters whose book actually occasioned the poem. Richard Wilbur's? Howard Nemerov's? No, the poet was Allen Ginsberg and the book was *Howl*. Around this same time, Wright explained in a letter to Donald Hall that Ginsberg "does not move from mastery of formal competence to creation of original art, but rather moves from chaos and sloppiness to their counterparts of commercialism and advertising and back again" (133–34). Wright wanted a departure from traditional forms, and he didn't mind if the result seemed ragged; he even admitted to liking Ginsberg's "Supermarket in California." But he could never give up his own formalism, at least in the deeper sense of measure and proportion, of the vivacious and tensed interplay of parts within a whole. What I mean, in a word, is classicism.

Wright himself often argued for such a view of his poetry. He began a letter to Mark Strand in 1972 with "I have a secret with myself. I love the craft. The nihilists who damn delicacy and balance be damned" (373). In a 1978 interview Wright stated, "As far as I'm concerned I'm a Horatian. I believe in the 'whole' of a poem and the subordination of style to some wholeness of structure and some wholeness of vision about the nature of things" (quoted in Stitt and Graziano 1990, 97). Such hidden sturdiness, such constant belief in the necessity of aesthetic structures, is what makes Wright's work so compelling, though this aspect of his poetry has rarely been appreciated or examined.

Although far from comprehensive, the selection of Wright's letters published in 2005 as *A Wild Perfection* offers some help. The correspondence has none of the slapdash brilliance of Lowell's or the homemade exquisiteness of Bishop's. As Wright approaches middle age, the letters relax to the point of mushiness. Every poet to whom he writes receives praise so lavish that none of it feels believ-

able. The same slackening occurs in his critical prose: casual inter-
views and reminiscences start to replace essays and reviews. But the
early letters are enough to make the book worthwhile. The sincerity
and relentless self-examination show Wright struggling with those
contradictory urges that fuse in his work. Unfortunately, the newest
edition of *Selected Poems* published at the same time as the letters
does little to reveal the true shape of that work. For one thing, the
book's simply too short. The selection offers a mere three poems
from Wright's 1974 volume *Two Citizens*. And it's no wonder: one of
the editors of this selection turns out to be Bly himself, who helped
to convince Wright that the book was a mistake. In fact, it remains
one of the important lost volumes of twentieth-century American
poetry. The editors give equal space, a scanty fifteen pages each, to
Wright's final collections, *To a Blossoming Pear Tree* and *This Journey*,
though the latter remains far superior. Most of the best poems from
that book ("Reading a 1979 Inscription on Belli's Monument," "The
Vestal in the Forum," "Apollo," "Coming Home to Maui") are nowhere to be found. The whole project feels like a missed opportunity.
If there ever was a poet who needed a judicious selection, it's James
Wright. Taken as a whole, his work can seem muddled. He tends to
write the same poem many times over: sometimes he's testing the
limits of an approach, and other times he's simply drubbed by his
own mental current. But to trace his development along the lines of
his best poems is to watch the work establish a shape.

To find what did and didn't change as his methods shifted,
I want to examine two poems, one from before and one from after
his famous breakthrough. Here's the opening octave of "Saint
Judas," the last poem in Wright's second book, which bears the
same title:

> When I went out to kill myself, I caught
> A pack of hoodlums beating up a man.
> Running to spare his suffering, I forgot
> My name, my number, how my day began,
> How soldiers milled around the garden stone
> And sang amusing songs; how all that day
> Their javelins measured crowds; how I alone
> Bargained the proper coins, and slipped away. (1990, 84)

In his introduction to the *Selected Poems*, Bly claims of Wright's leap into free verse that "he no longer fills out the line with reassuring literary language" (2005a, xvi). But there's little that's reassuring or conventional, much less padded, in this sonnet. The starkness of that opening clause, the mordant exactitude of "Their javelins measured crowds," and the cinching effect of the rhymes give the poem its immediacy. These technical accomplishments establish the virtual space of the poem, which every one of the best poems in Wright's first two books attempts to create. I have in mind a place of anguished suspension, a testing ground just outside the bounds of civilization. In "My Grandmother's Ghost" it appears as a blurred limbo where the family property and home have been emptied of all but spectral presences. In "A Note Left in Jimmy Leonard's Shack" it exists as a double bind: the young speaker of the poem stands caught between the incident of near-drowning he has witnessed and the man to whom he should report it, and who he believes will beat him. But in "Saint Judas" Wright has reduced this place, and the drama for which it acts as the stage, to their mythic essentials. Consider the sestet with which the poem concludes:

> Banished from heaven, I found this victim beaten,
> Stripped, kneed, and left to cry. Dropping my rope
> Aside, I ran, ignored the uniforms:
> Then I remembered bread my flesh had eaten,
> The kiss that ate my flesh. Flayed without hope,
> I held the man for nothing in my arms. (84)

Spoken by the ultimate outcast who has nothing to lose or gain, the poem suggests that the foundation of any collective experience lies in basic, selfless, and personal acts of compassion. These poems are simultaneously dedicated to establishing a shared reality and preserving the solitary, inward states they record.

"As I Step over a Puddle at the End of Winter, I Think of an Ancient Chinese Governor," the first poem in Wright's next book, has some remarkable similarities and differences with "Saint Judas." Here's how the poem opens.

> Po Chu-I, balding old politician,
> What's the use?

I think of you,
Uneasily entering the gorges of the Yang-Tze,
When you were being towed up the rapids
Toward some political job or other
In the city of Chungshou.
You made it, I guess,
By dark. (119)

As in "Saint Judas," Wright affects a dramatic turn in the middle of the poem:

But it is 1960, it is almost spring again,
And the tall rocks of Minneapolis
Build me my own black twilight
Of bamboo ropes and waters.
Where is Yuan Chen, the friend you loved?
Where is the sea, that once solved the whole loneliness
Of the Midwest? Where is Minneapolis? I can see nothing
But the great terrible oak tree darkening with winter.
Did you find the city of isolated men beyond the mountains?
Or have you been holding the end of a frayed rope
For a thousand years? (119)

Like "Saint Judas," this poem portrays a tenuous exchange, occurring at one remove from the public world it simultaneously invokes. It creates a similar mood as well, one of querulous melancholy punctured at intervals by an outgoing hopefulness. The obvious difference is prosodic, but there's no significant change in the compactness or efficiency of the writing. Nor has the idiom shifted remarkably. It's tone that Wright now modulates with greater speed and confidence. The new pliancy depends in fact upon the presence of the old metric. The first line's a buckled pentameter (the correct pronunciation of "Po-Chui" demanding three syllables). It's also a good example of deliberately balanced line architecture with its opening and closing nouns, each rooted in an ancient and classical language, framing the two Anglo-Saxon modifiers. From such a base Wright announces his departure: in the second and third lines the truncation in length corresponds with the bathetic undercutting of tone. As in "Saint Judas," these formal procedures work to create a feeling of suspension. The poem stands tensed between the possibility of connection—both Po-Chui's connection with the "city of isolated men beyond the mountains" and Wright's with Po-Chui—and the suspicion that all involved are "isolated men."

Examining this recurring obsession of Wright's, we see how classicism extended beyond technique in his poetry. In that 1978 interview, when Wright invoked his Horatian ideal, he did so while speaking about one of his teachers at Kenyon College, John Crowe Ransom. Wright was immersed in ideas about classical art that Ransom expounded in his essays, foremost the belief that classical art "conducts a sort of experiment in which a purpose is tested to determine whether it is really a practical purpose. It is like the scientific verification of a practical formula" (1984, 90). For Wright, the purpose to pursue is the establishment of a space between private and public life, and he wants his poems to test its viability. Certainly he reveals the old Romantic ambition, the desire to cultivate the illogical network of individual dream life and to protect it against the encroachment of the waking world. But he's also obsessed by a further possibility, the challenge of maintaining some realm in which that subjective experience can be exchanged, in which imagination will not so much overthrow reality as quicken and intensify it. This urge runs beneath every one of his books, so it would be facile to claim that free verse was an improvement in and of itself. Many of the best poems from after his putative breakthrough, poems like "Written in a Copy of Swift's Poems, for Wayne Burns" and "With the Shell of a Hermit Crab," are in traditional measures. Some of his weakest poems depend too entirely upon the starkness of statement that free verse offered him. Yet when he employed them most skillfully, open forms gave him greater range of movement. In the most successful of these poems, the capacity for various tones corresponds with the greater scope of the virtual space he creates.

We're accustomed to following a poet's technical preoccupations toward his or her obsessions. We expect formal tones and structures to direct us toward bedrock convictions and questions. But there's a moment in the development of any of the best poets when the poet has gained enough perspective on the urges behind her or his work that the circuit begins to flow in both directions: the formal specifics often appear now as manifestations of that central vision. Maybe this makes it sound too neat. It's not that the poet has some thesis to demonstrate again and again; such a process would desiccate the poems. The confusion that often attends blind intuition and drive might well remain, but the transaction between the larger convictions and the formal specifics becomes more dynamic, and those specifics become imbued with greater meaning.

Take the so-called surrealistic or irrational content of Wright's middle period. Though often described as a procedure of self-discovery, these feats of association in fact show the poet engaging with his larger ambition: his desire to merge subjective life and fact. Consider a selection of single sentences from the poems in *The Branch Will Not Break*, sentences which display this so-called surrealistic or irrational content:

> Only two boys,
> Trailed by shadows of rooted police,
> Turn aimlessly in the lashing elderberries,
> One cries for his father's death,
> And the other, the silent one,
> Listens into the hallway
> Of a dark leaf. (123)

Or

> Many American women mount long stairs
> In the shafts of houses,
> Fall asleep, and emerge suddenly into tottering palaces. (126)

Or

> After dark
> Near the South Dakota border,
> The moon is out hunting, everywhere,
> Delivering fire,
> And walking down hallways
> Of a diamond. (139)

In each example, some real location opens into a dreamed or mythical space, which we're made to assume represents a deeper reality than the ostensibly real world. But this effect depends upon those factual presences, that drama of boys fleeing the police, those proper nouns America and South Dakota. Whenever Wright attempts to razor out all but the irrational content, he fails. In a poem like "Spring Images," for example, when we're told that "Small antelopes / Fall asleep in the ashes / Of the moon," there's nothing to ground the image (137). It floats around the page like vapor. But in the poems quoted above, such a procedure both enlarges and intensifies the sympathetic force of the speech. The bardic tone gives almost heroic proportion to this landscape of petty criminals, disappointed housewives, moonlight falling on junkyards, working men named Emerson Buchanan and Minnegan Leonard. At the same time, the imagery itself provides an almost microscopic focus, lending full attention to the individual's dreaming and suffering.

By deliberately experimenting with the place of the self in his poems, Wright found another way to fulfill his classical ambition. Perhaps his experiment with the shifting position of the self in the poem comes across most clearly in the lyric "Fear Is What Quickens Me" (123). In this poem Wright creates the composite structure by shifts not so much in tone as in perspective.

1
Many animals that our fathers killed in America
Had quick eyes.
They stared about wildly,
When the moon went dark.
The new moon falls into the freight yards
Of cities in the south,
But the loss of the moon to dark hands of Chicago
Does not matter to the deer
In this northern field.

2
What is that tall woman doing
There, in the trees?
I can hear the rabbits and mourning doves whispering together
In the dark grass, there
Under the trees.

3
I look about wildly.

The modulations are worth tracing from section to section. Wright begins with the blend of bardic authority and creaturely curiosity. Those first two sentences give way to the odd reasoning about the moon, the humans, and the deer. These lines form an argument against the pathetic fallacy, but Wright then moves into the most mysterious section of the poem, in which nature and human emotion seem inseparable. The concluding identification of the poet with the animals suggests that he feels hunted: far from containing multitudes, here he becomes trapped by civilization itself. Feeling these shifts occur in the poem, you understand just how deliberately Wright employs his strategy of pivoting perspective.

In his willingness to push any given poem either toward or away from the suffering self, Wright draws an instructive parallel with his great forebear, Thomas Hardy. Pound once wrote of Hardy that "no man ever had so much Latin and so eschewed the least appearance of being a classicist on the surface" (Pound and Spann 1964, 325). He meant this to refer to Hardy's metrics, his skill for getting quantitative measures to ghost the English meter. But this observation has more than technical applications. Hardy's poems, with their reservoirs of personal grief and their ghostly withdrawals from collective life, seem on the surface as Romantic as those of any other late Victorian. But Hardy's also the savvy architect of novelistic plots, the omniscient narrator of the "Satires of Circumstance," the ventriloquist mastermind of monologues like "The Haunter." His movement between inner and outer vantage points occurs not only from poem to poem but also in the very trajectory of many of his poems. This is what makes both Hardy and Wright secret classicists: classicism in their case shows itself not as poise and urbanity but as the constant desire to embody, and at least in some small measure, ameliorate, the pull between inside and out. Wright's statement about a Horatian "wholeness of vision about the world" never rules out the incompletion, messiness, and disaffection that this dilemma often produces. For sure, in Horace's own poems the Aristotelian ideal of the "golden mean" is itself mediated by the poet's implacable rage against the decadence of Imperial Rome. These countervailing forces of social connection and personal contention are, in turn, given equal presence in the literal and figurative space of the Sabine Farm. Hardy's Essex and Wright's Ohio River Valley stand similarly as achieved feats of poetic architecture in which the fourth wall has been stripped away to reveal a panorama of individual pain and striving.

To call James Wright a classicist, even to call him a secret classicist, might seem to involve some procrustean snipping. What about the raggedness of the poems? What about the extreme emotional neediness? I'm convinced that when these characteristics lent depth and immediacy to the poems, they too derived from the classical vision. When Ransom wrote about the classical artist testing purposes in the manner of a scientist, he made a crucial distinction. He explained that the success of such an endeavor turns out to be the opposite of scientific proof: "Classical art becomes tragic art in the hands of the serious artist. He is the artist who submits the formula to such a searching and sustained experimentation that finally he comes to the place where it breaks down" (1984, 39). I suspect that to anyone familiar with Wright's poetry, that phrase "the place where it breaks down" would immediately suggest his 1973 collection, *Two Citizens*. Bly and others considered the book a breakdown in the worst sense. Wright himself came to disown it.

He was wrong, though you can certainly see why he would be vulnerable to criticism of this collection. The book is personal in the deepest sense: it forms a phantasmagoria, a dream space filled with shape-shifting obsessions. Figures swirl up from the tangle of association, occlude themselves, and then recur pages later in altered forms. Jenny, for instance, the muse and prostitute who appears throughout Wright's books, here becomes a sycamore tree. Her presence glimmers also in the figure of the poet's wife and savior, the constant "you" and "she" of this book, who in turn shows up as the mysterious "little girl who belonged to somebody" in the poem "The Old WPA Swimming Pool in Martins Ferry, Ohio," and then again as the chickadee in the final poem, "The Creature of Creation." Few other collections of contemporary poetry form such motifical integrity out of such seeming diffusion.

The book has found excellent advocates in poet-critics like Alan Williamson and David Wojahn. But the best defense and description of *Two Citizens* comes in Jeanne Foster's "The First Workshop" (2001, 15), a memoir of studying with Wright. As Foster explains, Wright relished "the poem as curse." Arguing that he brought that obsession to bear in *Two Citizens*, she quotes from the final section of the opening poem, "Ars Poetica: Some Recent Criticism" (1990, 224):

> The goat ran down the alley
> And many boys giggled
> While they tried to stone our fellow
> Goat to death.
> And my Aunt Agnes ...
> Threw stones back at the boys
> And gathered the goat,
> Nuts as she was,
> Into her sloppy arms.

"Cursing," Foster writes, "is throwing stones back." That sentence cuts succinctly to the heart of the book: in poem after poem Wright both rages violently against modern America and endeavors to protect the helpless, creaturely life he most values against the threat of violence. This strange dual process, this destructive protectiveness, occurs not only in the dramatic situations of *Two Citizens* but in the language. You sense Wright has set up an echo chamber, a treacherous funhouse of American speech, inside of which he locates and protects the central voice of his poetry. Here for instance is the opening of "Ohio Valley Swains" (233):

> The granddaddy longlegs did twilight
> And light.
> O here comes Johnny Gumball.
> Guido?
> Bernoose got Lilly deVecchis.
> Guido don't give a diddly damn.
> Up on my side of the river
>   The cocksmen ramp loose.
> The bad bastards are fishing.
> They catch condoms.

What are you doing here, boy,
In cherry lane?
Leave her alone. I love her.
They knocked me down.
So I walked on up river,
Outside the Jesus Jumpers' tent,
Oh God our help in ages past,
Our hope in years to come.
Here comes Johnny Gumball.

Comparing such a passage to any from Wright's poems of the early 1960s, you sense his poetry has become less centered on image and more on speech, with all its twisted inflections and sideways bursts. The starkest phrases can take on nightmarish ambiguities. The very name Johnny Gumball, for instance, recurs in the refrain as a menacing threat but also seems patently absurd (his name is Gumball!). Such shifts in tone not only reflect but also determine the action of the poem. Later on we hear the poet shout, "They're hurting a girl down there," and then, soon after, he addresses Guido with "You thought that was funny, didn't you, to mock a girl?" The first sentence suggests a rape, but the second simply some joke, however cruel. Wright brings back the sense of mortal threat at the end of the poem, however, when he declares,

You son of a bitch,
And if I ever see you again, so help me in the sight of God,
I'll kill you. (233)

The true subject of the poem becomes not what Guido has done to Lilly deVechhis but the internal effect of such casual violence, the implosion of the treacherous outside into a self who can only register suffering in an almost schizophrenic swirl of slang and dream patois. The mutual permeation of the collective and personal that Wright worked so deliberately to achieve in his earlier work here becomes a nightmare, national as well as personal. The sarcastic use of the word *swains* in the title, with its suggestion of young men attending upon a knight, carries the same antipastoral effect as the line in "Ars Poetica" in which the poet tells us he does not believe that the boys who stoned the goat "are charming Tom Sawyers."

As the title conveys, *Two Citizens* is both a book about the possibility of making a life in America and a book about the possibility of making a life with one other person: it's a love story. Those two themes intertwine. At the center of the collection lies the poet's love affair with an American woman in Europe. What could have been an escape becomes a reintegration. As in "Saint Judas," the viability of collective life turns out to rest on the most basic connection between two people. And Wright's Europe is no touristic Eden. In a poem called "The Streets Grow Young," about his first summer evening in Paris, the poet alternates between a beery, surrealistic bonhomie and his blank despair at the scenes of suffering that keep edging his gaze. The poem ends with this short section:

> The amused Parisians snickered
> While a retarded fat man on the corner
> Shook a rubber rat in the faces
> Of passing women.
> The poor bastard needs money to die with,
> And he can't even beg. (242)

It's as if the poverty, neglect, and cheap violence of Martins Ferry have followed the poet to Paris. He can't shake them. As the book progresses, he finds he also can't shake his own language. If that language appears as a miasmic swirl in a poem like "Ohio Valley Swains," it also remains his central voice, his instrument of truth. "The one tongue I can write in," he states in the final poem, "is my Ohioan."

The best properties of his Ohioan, both its sincerity and its bent, connotative jazziness, lend their full strength to "Hotel Lenox," the slender erotic lyric that seems to me the best poem in the book. It has never, to my knowledge, been anthologized or much discussed. But consider these lines:

> And she loved loving
> So she woke and bloomed
> And she rose
> And many men had been there
> To drowse awake and go downstairs
> Lonely for coffee and bread.

But she drowsed awake lonely
For coffee and bread.
And went upstairs
With me, and we had
Coffee and bread.
And then we were so happy to see the lovely
Mother who had been her mother a long time.
In this city broken on the wheel
We went back to the warm caterpillar of our hotel.
And the wings took.
Oh lovely place,
Oh tree.
We climbed into the branches
Of the lady's tree.
We birds sang.
And the lemon light flew out over the river. (240)

The way the long "o" sounds create the languorous mood of the opening; the way that mood gives way to the little filmic comedy of people going repeatedly up and down the stairs; the way the clipped syntax balances against the extravagant metaphors; the way those metaphors tease about the actual sex yet do so with neither bashfulness nor vulgarity: such technical skills help to give this poem its gorgeous movement. It's also typical of Wright that the private joyfulness balances against the public realities of the religious art and of historical Paris "broken on the wheel." These inclusions open and deepen the ecstatic moment. The effect depends upon the simplicity and directness of the language, especially in the last five lines. I'm certain that Wright could not have achieved this without the deliberate experiment in speech-based methods that this book allowed him.

Reading the final two collections, you watch Wright following two separate pathways to find seesawing success, until in a group of late poems he discovers a new focus for his classicism. One proof of the vitality of *Two Citizens* lies in the failed poems of his next volume, *To a Blossoming Pear Tree* (1977). As if in response to the criticism of the earlier book, the poet here mutes his speech-based method. The language now sags, in the worst poems, to a kind of barroom storytelling. The poet himself appears less nailed down by anguish than he was, say, at the end of "Fear Is What Quickens Me," and on the whole he fails to make up for this lack of centripetal force with a greater range of attentiveness and sympathy. Wright's best lyrics so often alternate between investment and removal: he balances the suffering "I" against a third-person voice with a wider perspective. But in much of *To a Blossoming Pear Tree* the voice enacts a removal in the worst sense. It advertises its mastery of experience and in so doing enervates the poem. The effect may seem what Bly calls, in the introduction to Wright's *Selected Poems*, "an intelligence like that of Prospero's looking back on a life of many errors but admiring the mysterious wholeness of it all" (2005a, xvii.). But that casual misrepresentation of Shakespeare speaks for itself. Not only is Prospero's wisdom in *The Tempest* the outer layer of his far more outlandish "rough magic," and not only does he enact the farthest thing from a retrospective "admiring the mysterious wholeness of it all" at the very end of the play, when he implores the audience with "Let your indulgence set me free," but he also exists as one element of a larger work of art; he's challenged and quickened at every step by Ariel, Caliban, and Miranda. This new voice of Wright's lacks such tempering and strengthening resistance. The poems center too complacently on anecdotal material.

But if Wright never again created structures as grand as those of *The Branch Will Not Break* and *Two Citizens*, he still found a powerful new mode of classicism in the poems of his last book, *This Journey* (1982). He becomes an observer in these poems. The modulations that he earlier affected through grand modulations of tone and point of view now occur as small shifts of perception. Here's "The Vestal in the Forum":

> This morning I do not despair
> For the impersonal hatred that the cold
> Wind seems to feel
> When it slips fingers into the flaws
> Of lovely things men made,
> The shoulders of a stone girl pitted by winter.

Not a spring passes but the roses
Grow stronger in their support of the wind,
And now they are conquerors,
Not garlands any more,
Of this one face,
Dimming,
Clearer to me than most living faces.
The slow wind and the slow roses
Are ruining an eyebrow here, a mole there.
But in this little while
Before she is gone, her very haggardness
Amazes me. A dissolving
Stone, she seems to change from stone to something
Frail, to someone I can know, someone
I can almost name. (1990, 329)

Reading this poem, I think that the limitations of *To a Blossoming Pear Tree* have been overcome, not by extension but by even greater condensation. That circuit between the individual and the collective that typified the poems of the middle period has been replaced by an exchange between the individual and the work of art. Like the earlier poems, this one works by alteration. The poet insists that the statue's dissolving too: he strikes an anti-Yeatsian note, denying any apotheosis to a state "out of nature." At the same time, so much of the poignancy comes from his attesting to a structure that will outlast him. Between these two senses of the artwork, a space has been created in which the otherness of the human image itself comes into beautiful focus "clearer to me than most living faces."

James Wright's strength remained the short lyric, in which he showed a marvelous ability to focus and conduct intense emotional heat. He lacked the pliancy of mind that many of the best poets of the following generation—Frank Bidart, Anne Winters, Alan Williamson, Robert Pinsky, and C. K. Williams, among others—found in discursive or "antipoetic" registers of speech. But Wright made up for this through his continuing faith in a centering vision. It's there in the earliest poems, those by the GI at Fort Lewis, Washington, writing home to his friends about the cadences of Catullus.

Williams alone of the great American Modernists possessed this generative urge. I mean the desire to build a work founded upon sympathy. Especially with no adequate volume of selected poems, Wright's poetry often seems to pool and tangle together. But wipe away the silt, and the best poems establish a shape, their variety proving the power of their common source.

Palpable Fact:
James Schuyler and Immediacy

Since his death in 1991, James Schuyler's friends have performed the remarkable service of publishing his last poems, diaries, art reviews, his long-out-of-print novel *Alfred and Guinevere*, and a generous selection of letters. What's more, he's earned sensitive and sympathetic readings from critics as distinguished and otherwise divergent as Helen Vendler and Michael Davidson, Wayne Koestenbaum and Christian Wiman, Jed Perl and Maggie Nelson. Even so, Schuyler's achievement sometimes seems at risk of sliding through the cracks. It's not only that he's missing from the *Norton Anthology of Contemporary Poetry* edited by Jahan Ramazani, invisible in R. S. Gwynn's *Contemporary American Poetry* from Longman, and nowhere to be found in Cary Nelson's *Anthology of Contemporary Poetry* from Oxford. No, his elusiveness has more to do with his great virtue, his ability to defy classification. Schuyler's poems elude both traditional and avant-garde notions of how poets find significance in experience and render it in form.

We speak of Schuyler as a member of the "New York School," but that's a slippery term. First applied to painters—abstract expressionists such as Pollock, Hoffman, de Kooning, and Motherwell, artists who seemed the biggest news since the "School of Paris"— "New York School" became a convenient way to refer to those painters of the following generation and their poet friends, a circle centered on the Tibor de Nagy Gallery. Theirs were the anti-credos. "Our program is the absence of a program," John Ashbery wrote in his introduction to the *Collected Poems of Frank O'Hara*: "I guess it amounts to not planning the poem in advance but letting it take its own way" (O'Hara 1971, viii). Even unfettered freedom tends to evolve its own forms, though, and if poems by Ashbery, O'Hara, Schuyler, Kenneth Koch, and Barbara Guest reveal separate sensibilities, there still could be a composite or paradigmatic "New York School" poem. The address in such a poem would feel both intimate and evasive. Tone and register slip and slide, as philosophical speculation gives way to cartoonish banter, emotive declarations branch into private asides. The lines are spontaneous, improvisatory, and urbane, though with a saving vulgarity—suggestive of the influence of French Modernism and Surrealism. (Contemporaries such as James Wright and Philip Levine would, by contrast, find precedents in Spanish and Latin American poetry of the same era.) The speedy syntax for moments suggests the exhilaration of Whitman. But then the accumulation fractures. The poem can't maintain the unity of mind and matter that Whitman and his champion, Emerson, sought in American poetry—nor is it meant to. In fact, this poem suggests that mind and matter don't join but collide, as in Ashbery's lines about what's required of a poet: "The extreme austerity of an almost empty mind / colliding with the lush, Rousseau-like foliage of its desire to communicate" (1986, 235).

Schuyler wrote a similar kind of poem in the 1950s and 1960s. In his 1969 collection, *Freely Espousing*, he keeps a socially alert, discursive tone of voice even as he describes carp flying through forests. As his first full collection, published when he was already in his mid-forties, that book in fact contains several types of poem—Steinian language puzzles, collages, imagist lyrics, campy fantasias, Williams-like street scenes. But as he began his best work, starting with the 1972 collection *The Crystal Lithium* and continuing until his death, he showed an unabashed interest in everyday subjects. He wrote about stays in Vermont and Maine, his depressions, pets, flower gardens, meals, infatuations. The simplicity is not a ruse, but it seduces us into expecting linear development, then eludes that expectation by preserving ambiguities other poets would try to reconcile. These include ambivalent thoughts and feelings, but also different ways of perceiving and making sense of the world. Like the mark-making of those second-generation New York School painters who returned to representation but with the voltage of abstract expressionism still coursing through their brushes, Schuyler's language directly communicates and describes but also achieves complexity and vivacity apart from what it represents.

Schuyler elaborated on such a counterpoint between form and content when he defended his friend Fairfield Porter against critics' claims that Porter's Maine landscapes were mere bourgeois pastoral. Schuyler explains by describing one of the paintings:

> In "Northwest Wind" the paint has its own movement, as brushed, stirred and rippled as the windy grass, trees and water it describes. The paint is not, however, merely a vehicle for description. Nor is it that there is a harmony between matter and manner. It is that there are two distinct things, and if the island and water are, in any sense, an illusion, the paint is itself a palpable fact that holds an imprint of life and infuses life into the image. (1998, 15)

Schuyler's tone suggests he does *not* believe the island and water are illusions: he implies that rejecting subject matter as some middle-brow mirage is just as sentimental as demanding it above all else. On the other hand, he maintains that an artist's given medium must be a vibrant "palpable fact," regardless of what it happens to depict.

This argument seems to me nothing if not an ars poetica. But how does Schuyler translate those painterly concerns in his poetry? Few of his poems illustrate better than the short lyric "Moon," a poem from the early 1980s. By invoking an ancient, and potentially worn, subject of lyric poetry, that title raises an expectation: like a jazz musician playing a well-known standard, the poet renders a familiar motif and reveals his own approach. Here's how Schuyler does so:

> Last night there was
> a lunar eclipse: the
> shadow of the earth
> passed over the moon
> I was too laze-a-bed
> to get up and go out

and watch it. Besides,
a lunar eclipse doesn't
amount to much unless
it's over water or
over an apple orchard,
or perhaps a field,
a field of wheat or
just a field, the kind
where wildflowers
ramp. Still, I'm sorry
now I didn't go out
to see it (the lunar
eclipse) last night,
when I lay abed instead
and watched The
Jeffersons, a very
funny show, I think.
And now the sun shines
down in silent brightness,
on me and my possessions,
which I have named,
New York. (1993, 321)

Enjambment may be Schuyler's most salient means of rendering the counterpoint between abstract and contextual perception: the continuous, explicable thread of his journal-like observations breaks into jagged but constituent parts, thanks to the meticulous dishevel-ment of his lineation. But the very structure of the poem also re-veals such tension. Although Schuyler avoids overt cleverness, he proceeds by a series of eclipses. The title is "Moon," yet he doesn't go out to see the lunar event. He's in New York, yet he imagines being in the country. He praises flowers, yet he enjoys prime-time TV. He alludes to one of his favorite poets, Robert Herrick, yet the confidently casual idiom veils the allusion. Such verbal "eclipsing" might seem like the mere correspondence between "manner and matter" from which Schuyler distinguishes Porter's painting. But this poem depends upon an uneasiness about comparison itself. In the last lines the poet identifies himself and his possessions with the entire city of New York. This claim strikes a comical or "loony" note and, at the same time, suggests how collective life consists of the separate, imaginative lives of individuals, and vice versa.

That off-kilter shift in scale, from the apartment to the metropolis, leaves a peculiar feeling: is the poet's tone exuberant or lonely? I think the answer's both. Schuyler's ability to evoke otherwise exclusive emotions lends "Moon" a quality he admired in Porter's paintings: immediacy. His voice may be talky and explanatory—he "tells" as well as "shows"—but he repeatedly leaves the reader with the given, conflicted emotion, not its abstracted, classifiable residue. Nor does immediacy mean prizing the natural spontaneity of the present tense above all else. There's no romance, as in Ginsberg, with "first thought, best thought." Describing autumn in one of his earlier poems, Schuyler writes, "more litter, less clutter" (33), a line that could be a motto for his poems. Details might appear ordinary or accidental here, but they take on meaning as part of an arrangement winnowed down if not to essentials then to inevitability, to what lasts; such immediacy stretches beyond the immediate moment. And here again Schuyler reveals not only the intellectual framework he drew from his circle of midcentury Manhattan artists but also how he adapted such thinking about painting. Like Porter, who wanted each shape and hue to achieve its full potential apart from, though inside, the composition to which it contributes—a concept not only evident in his paintings but also elaborated in his criticism—Schuyler wanted verbal figures to become palpable facts holding "an imprint of life." He realized, however, that in poems such figures are successive in time. As his work reached its full stride in the 1970s, tonal modulation—that succession of verbal eclipses—became everything for him. Beyond the technical skill they require, these shifts reveal an ambition to bring the structures of his poems as close as possible to the structures of consciousness: ideas, feelings, sights, and sounds quickly change and then unexpectedly return, just as they would in life. But Schuyler's no lover of flux for its own sake. He has an instinct for the shapeliness even the most aleatory poem requires. So many of his poems are occasioned, in fact, by the basic need to give shape to time. Schuyler endeavors to hold together the various facets of daily life, to find form among its freedoms and freedoms among its forms.

The tension between a desire for continuity and the insouciant, disruptive, even iconoclastic force of each new, surprising image or tone becomes prominent in his longer work, in particular the respective title poems of his four final collections — "The Crystal Lithium," "Hymn to Life," "The Morning of the Poem," and "A Few Days." These poems show a remarkable range not only of reference but also of voice: reminiscences of Auden on Ischia exist along with this week's grocery list. Reading these poems, you sense that Schuyler's both breaking out of traditional patterns of association in poetry and attempting to contain every association possible. Here's a swath of "Hymn to Life":

> ... The rain comes back, this spring, like a thirsty dog
> Who goes back and back to his dish. "Fill it up, please," wag, wag.
> Gray depression and purple shadows, the daffodils feigning sunlight
> That came yesterday. One day rain, one day sun, the weather is stuck
> Like a record. Through it all forsythia begins to bloom, brown
> And yellow and warm as lit gas jets, clinging like bees to
> The arching canes where starlings take cover from foraging cats. Not
> To know: what have these years of living and being lived taught us?
> Not to quarrel? Scarcely. You want to shoot pool, I want to go home:
> And just before the snap of temper one had sensed so
> Strongly the pleasure of watching a game well played: the cue ball
> Carom and the struck ball pocketed. Skill. And still the untutored
> Rain comes down. Open the laundry door. Press your face into the
> Wet April chill: a life mask. Attune yourself to what is happening
> Now, the little wet things, like washing up the lunch dishes. Bubbles
> Rise, rinse and it is done. Let the dishes air dry, the way
> You let your hair after a shampoo. All evaporates, water, time, the
> Happy moment and — harder to believe — unhappy. (1993, 219)

Throughout this passage, in subject matter and idiom, the quotidian alternates with the cosmic. We hear about the return of spring, then hear the rain compared to a "thirsty dog." The poet asks a profound and urgent question, "what have these years of living and being lived taught us?," then describes a game of pool. At the end of this passage, the process of shampooing leads to an acknowledgment that all things must pass. Schuyler nuances that acknowledgment: his description of dissolution hardly sounds reassuring, yet the idea that unhappiness may be just as transitory as any other feeling does offer some consolation, as does this poet's ability to complete such transitions in vocal and emotional tone. As with the end of "Moon," his poetry gains force when contradictory feelings are allowed to exist alongside one another, unresolved.

But if Schuyler resists pat conclusions and strives for the "two distinct things" he admires in Porter's paintings, he also renders their synthesis. By separating form and content, he reveals their cat's-cradle of mutual support. Look again at his marvelous sentence in defense of Porter: "It is that there are two distinct things, and if the island and water are, in any sense, an illusion, the paint is itself a palpable fact that holds an imprint of life and infuses life into the image" (1998, 15). Schuyler insists upon the paint's being artifice, a distinct thing, and yet this artifice itself "holds an imprint of life and infuses life into the image."

The same hard-won skill for rendering liveliness distinguishes Schuyler's best poetry. This achievement, as well as its relation to midcentury American visual art, is at risk when Schuyler's left out of anthologies. In his 1959 "statement of poetics" for an anthology that did include him, Donald Allen's *The New American Poetry*, Schuyler wrote that he and his fellow New York poets were "affected most by the floods of paint in whose crashing surf we all scramble" (1998, 1). That metaphor conveys the excitement of the time and place in which he became a poet, but also the feeling Schuyler translates into his rapidly enjambed lines. Even if those lines are about one night in a Manhattan apartment, one lovers' quarrel, one load of laundry, they deliver not only surprise and spontaneity but also a moving and masterful testament to the need to make sense and shape of experience.

Part Two

Biographical Form
Five Poets

Robert Lowell

I want to consider five American poets who make the self their subject and argue for the historical significance of their art, its original openness to personal experience, but also its formal truth. Reading like this means considering the autobiographical nature of these poets' work, but without much concern for the facts of their biographies. To understand that possible contradiction, I take Frank Bidart's introduction to the *Collected Poems* of Robert Lowell as my starting place. "Robert Lowell was above all an audacious maker," writes Bidart. "He became famous as a 'confessional' writer, but he scorned the term. His audacity lies not in his candor but [in] his art" (2003, vii). This argument against M. L. Rosenthal's term "confessional poetry" has the ferocious concision and steeliness of statement familiar from Bidart's poems. Such qualities don't rule out subtlety, either: where another writer might have gone with *mastery*, *genius*, or *greatness*, Bidart chooses a word both more precise and more ambiguous, *audacity*. What difference does this make? *Audacity* describes a daring effort, not its neat completion—fitting for Lowell, who joined autobiographical to historical consciousness in lines marmoreal and spontaneous, well-wrought and risky. Some critics have portrayed him as a foil to avant-garde poets such as Charles Olson, Allen Ginsberg, and John Ashbery, but it's hard to imagine a writer more alert to change than Lowell. Perhaps his fatalism disguises that openness, but Lowell affected vast aesthetic shifts, nearly with each new book. *Audacity* also bears a colorful history: it was the motto of Napoleon Bonaparte—*l'audace, l'audace, toujours l'audace!* Lowell, who not only wrote about Napoleon several times in his poems but, more importantly, revealed in those poems a well-tuned ear for the historicity of individual words, might have appreciated the subtle force with which *audacity* distinguishes Bidart's argument. Even with no such deep background, you can hear it: *audacity* describes boldness that might turn into recklessness, individual defiance of social laws and conventions. I loiter over this one word because Bidart's introduction not only corrects a naive notion of poetry about the self—that it's the natural, unbidden outpouring of a poet's life—but also suggests how Lowell's conception differs from T. S. Eliot's impersonal theory of poetry.

Addressing the difference between the author and the work, Eliot compared the poet's mind, his emotions and experiences, to a catalyst, a thin strip of platinum in a chemical reaction, forming a new acid that "contains no trace of platinum" (1975, 39). As Bidart points out, the seemingly candid or "raw" moments in Lowell's poems are the products of artfulness, not disinhibition. And yet this doesn't contradict the radical shift in American poetry that Lowell leads. I have in mind not just how his poems flout taboos but also how they make personal experience feel much more than *merely* personal. What Eliot calls "platinum" proves vital not just for grounding the existential and political aspects of Lowell's poems but also for revealing them.

Such biographical narratives correlate less with confession—a specific practice that, as an erstwhile Catholic convert, Lowell knew well—than with another religious concept: vision. More social, more "audacious," and more iconoclastic a phenomenon than confession, vision shares its source with poetry: whatever else "visionaries" such as Isaiah and Jeremiah were, they were also poets. For certain, Lowell often seems anything but "visionary" in the conventional sense. He portrays his own embarrassment, mundanity, failure. After his second book, explicit theological coordinates all but disappear. Still, he preserves the *form* of vision, the paradigm in which an individual links the multitude to a totality. Lowell's agnostic turn in the mid-1950s, his reorientation toward personal experience, parallels the same endeavor occurring throughout his society. The literary critic V. S. Pritchett remarks in 1956 upon the "tremendous expansion in autobiographical writing" and attributes it to the "dominant influence of psychoanalytic theory" (quoted in Yagoda 2009, 37). Lowell participates in, but also exceeds, this historical trend. Like Freud himself, and unlike so many memoirists, Lowell sees the development of individual consciousness in relation to history. From his middle period on, he redirects the transformative potential of religious experience into an aesthetics of the encounter, political as well as personal.

But let's consider Lowell's "vision" at the ordinary level first. I mean the way he portrays the very act of seeing. It's remarkable how many of the most intense moments in his poems—how many of the poems themselves—find their occasions in optical disturbances. This motif allows the poet to dramatize questions so basic they could be posed by Socrates, or a child: where does the self end and the other begin? What's the difference between a thing and its image? What makes an image true or false? How trustworthy is personal experience?

Appearing throughout his work, this motif becomes most prevalent in his 1964 volume, *For the Union Dead*. Although *Life Studies* (1959) announces a break from his religious period, a focus on the details of personal life, and a turn toward free verse, *For the Union Dead*, the less declarative, more inward book finds the poet thinking about what poems are and do. If his "visionary" bent was obvious in the earlier work, revealed in vatic lines with biblical and liturgical sources ("On water the Man-fisher walks," "The Lord survives the rainbow of his will," and so on), the poems from his middle period suggest what it means for Lowell to be a visionary if agnostic poet.

Consider the opening of "Myopia: A Night," a poem that traces the passage of one sleepless night during which the poet attempts to see without his glasses on:

Bed, glasses off, and all's
ramshackle, streaky, weird
for the near-sighted, just
a foot away. (2003, 345)

Familiar surroundings have turned strange here, but the strangeness seems to the poet convincingly real; and as the poem slides
from naturalism into allegory, this new reality threatens his life as
a writer—the objects he senses around him are books, but they've
become unreadable: "the books are bluehills / browns, greens,
fields, or color." His home itself has turned into an elemental testing ground, a station on the way to an unknown beyond:

> This
> is the departure strip,
> the dream-road. Whoever built it
> left numbers, words and arrows.
> He had to leave in a hurry. (345)

The suggestion that we inhabit a universe made by a now-
unreachable creator introduces the elevated theological (or *anti*-
theological) tone that burgeons as the poem unfolds. Here are the
final three stanzas:

> Think of him in the Garden,
> that seed of wisdom, Eve's
> seducer, stuffed with man's
> corruption, stuffed with triumph:
> Satan triumphant in
> the Garden! In a moment,
> all that blinding brightness
> changed into a serpent,
> lay groveling on its gut.

> What has disturbed this household?
> Only a foot away,
> the familiar faces blur.
> At fifty we're so fragile,
> a feather ...

> The things of the eye are done.
> On the illuminated black dial,
> green ciphers of a new moon—

one, two, three, four, five, six!
I breathe and cannot sleep.
Then morning comes,
saying, "This was a night." (346)

Like many of his poems from the late 1950s and early 1960s, "Myo-pia: A Night" shows Lowell's conscious and subtle shift in idiom: the writer of ironclad rhyme and meter has become the author of crisp, almost journalistic free verse. But these categories prove unstable. Lowell alternates between the naturalistic scene and a Miltonic vision reminiscent of his earlier poetry. The stanza about Satan in the Garden itself contains plain or "low" diction—for instance, the repeated "stuffed," with its unromantic sexual connotation. And though "Myopia: A Night" ends without having alleviated any of the poet's restlessness, the feeling-tone of that ordinary situation—the insomniac with his bedside clock, worried about aging—now rises to a level of prime significance.

Like many of Lowell's earlier poems, this one portrays a dark night of the soul. Structured as a rite of passage, such narratives—their paradigm being the *noche oscura* of St. John of the Cross—lead most often from bewilderment to renewal. Here the transformative potential of the passage through darkness proves less clear. The laconic concluding sentence, "This was a night," suggests that suffering yields no great wisdom, that no spiritual realm of being exists beyond "the things of the eye." And yet doesn't the strength of "Myopia: A Night" come from Lowell's impatience with his own conclusion, from the feeling that the visionary power of that central stanza has not been quelled? The poem seems almost to swell with the transformative urge it finally disallows.

In another poem from *For the Union Dead*, "Eye and Tooth," Lowell makes such impatience explicit. Once again the poem begins from a problem of vision: the poet's eye has been cut by a contact lens. This time he laces his description with a canny allusion:

My whole eye was sunset red,
the old cut cornea throbbed,
I saw things darkly,
as through an unwashed goldfish globe. (2003, 334)

The last two lines read as a reworking of Paul: "For now we see through a glass, darkly; but then face to face: now I know in part; but then shall I know even as also I am known" (1 Corinthians 13: 12). The allusion has a saving goofiness—"unwashed goldfish globe"! This may not be the fire-breathing Catholic convert of twenty years earlier, but Lowell's urge to break past the screen of mere appearance, to know as also he is known, still sounds as sincere and fierce as Paul's.

In fact, the image of a lens, entrapping the self that strives to break through, appears throughout *For the Union Dead*. In "The Drinker," glass withholds vitality: the alcoholic protagonist looks out his window and "his distracted eye sees only glass sky." In "Fall 1961," glass barely separates the self from the unthinkable Real: describing the dread of nuclear war, while echoing that fishbowl image, the poet declares, "I swim like a minnow / behind my studio window" (329). In the title poem, "For the Union Dead," Lowell remembers the South Boston Aquarium where "once my nose crawled like a snail on the glass" (376). On the other side lies "the dark downward and vegetating kingdom," which the child and adult both desire and fear: beyond our mortal confines may be only this primordial broil, more Darwin's than Paul's.

What all these examples have in common is some realm of being too difficult or painful to face, and such avoidance proves national as well as personal. As Frank Bidart explains, "Like Baudelaire and Eliot (both moralists), Lowell conceives the poet as someone who brings back news of what the world is to a world that has been blind to it" (introduction to Lowell 2006, xiv). Such news in Lowell's middle period has a prominent theme: the spiritual inertia of American private and public life, everything against which "the Sixties" will rebel. This impasse correlates with the challenge Lowell himself faces in writing: what transformative logic will render the poems dynamic if there remains no obvious transformation in the material, and no religious means of breaking past the glass of ordinary life? The solution turns out to be redoubled faith in poems themselves, their ability to portray both the political and personal and, more importantly, to make such fusion a *revelation*, an event in which reality changes, moves. These poems give off a feeling of substance and surprise, of actual living things. Such dynamism prevents Lowell, even at his bleakest, from appearing cynical or lugubrious.

Consider "For the Union Dead" again. While Lowell the Poet proves canny in his arrangement of details and tones, Lowell the Person, the actor who walks through Boston in the present tense, might be mistaken for a passive observer, absorbing all he sees; even as he recounts the story of the all-black Fifty-Fourth Infantry Regiment led by Colonel Robert Gould Shaw and memorialized outside the Massachusetts State House in a bronze relief by Augustus Saint-Gaudens—and even as such images accumulate to a ferocious critique of the American status quo, Lowell nevertheless remains resolutely unrhetorical. Take the following passage:

> There are no statues for the last war here;
> on Boylston Street, a commercial photograph
> shows Hiroshima boiling
>
> over a Mosler Safe, the "Rock of Ages"
> that survived the blast. Space is nearer.
> When I crouch to my television set,
> the drained faces of negro school-children rise like balloons. (377)

That almost unbearable reality, the visionary news of the world that Lowell brings back to the world, here includes not only the dismaying threat of nuclear war but also the everyday brutality of racial segregation. What's more, through his rapid sequence of visual details, he captures the *feeling* of postwar imperial boom-time nearing its end, along with all its exacerbated contraries—luxury and squalor, localism and globalism, high-tech innovation and bestial regression. This vision may prove grim: the image of Hiroshima "boiling" in an advertisement, for example, implies a culture for which mass violence is both omnipresent and blindered from honest consideration: bandying both atrocity and the preservation of private property, the Mosler billboard makes a concise if unwitting indictment of American power, while the children's "drained" faces suggest that they've been sold short, exploited—like those soldiers who were sent with Col. Shaw to certain death at Fort Wagner.

But as with the "blinding light" that metamorphoses Satan to a serpent in "Myopia: A Night," unbearable truths may also reveal desirable potentials. Lowell neither offers nor receives anything like Paul's otherworldly promise to "know even as also I am known," to become both subject and object in permanent realization, yet he continues to pursue what in *Near the Ocean* (1967) he'll call "a loophole for the soul." Even when there's no longer any promise of heaven or assurance from doctrinal belief, a surprising tenderness appears, as in that fugitive moment of curiosity that comes with the simile "rise like balloons." This moment recalls the image with which the poem begins, the poet as a child with his face to the aquarium glass. It also continues the motif of bubbles that Lowell strings across the poem and the book. Like the recurring image of glass enclosures, the bubble stands for isolation, entrapment, the safety of the affluent society, as well as the precarious financial "bubble" of postwar production, the same force that has "gouged" the earth beneath the Boston Commons to create (bubblelike) parking garages, leaving Saint-Gaudens's civil war relief balanced by a splint. But bubbles may also conjure the ordinary, miraculous, fragile suspension of individual lives that must eventually end. They appear first in the opening of the poem when the child at the aquarium longs to burst the bubbles "drifting from the noses of the cowed compliant fish." Then in the quatrain following those above—the second to last of the poem—as if Lowell's detached, urbane intelligence has flared for a moment past rhetoric and into oneiric, prophetic speech, he declares:

> Colonel Shaw
> is riding on his bubble,
> he waits
> for the blessèd break. (378)

The children whose faces "rise like balloons" glimmer, then, not merely as topical images but as part and parcel of a vision. The need to account for them catalyzes the poet's vatic urge, the climactic moment that dynamizes the whole poem, revealing racial segregation not only in the light of history but also in a recurring cycle of suffering that must be broken. And yet, as with the dreamlike image of Col. Shaw riding on a bubble, those children's faces, appearing only for an instant, give off a saving strangeness. "Space is nearer," the poet says as he turns on his television—alluding to how technology has changed everyday life and conjuring the actual *sensation* of the change (377). Likewise the children's faces link up to a thematic presentation of history and at the same time remain inscrutable, mysterious: they have the ambiguity and opacity of actual people.

This Flaubertian or Chekovian side of Lowell nuances and strengthens his countervailing visionary impulse: his truest convictions show not in the stances he takes but in his alertness to actual life, the particularity of lived experience. The poems of his middle period resemble theological scrutiny but with none of the certainties of theology: his agnosticism returns the poet to the people he lives among, returns him to his need to set the self and others in active, living relation. Although fundamental to Lowell's poetry of public conscience, this task proves more specific than writing political poems.

The most moving example from *For the Union Dead* might be a love poem called "The Flaw." It opens with a description of the Maine coast, but the description abruptly breaks off. The very lens through which we're seeing the landscape, the poet's eye, has suffered a hairline scrape—most likely the same cut portrayed in "Eye and Tooth":

> Some mote, some eye-flaw, wobbles in the heat,
> hair-thin, hair-dark, the fragment of a hair—
>
> a noose, a question? All is possible;
> if there's free will, it's something like this hair,
> inside my eye, outside my eye, yet free . . . (373)

The quandary about free will, suggested by the "eye-flaw," turns the reader back to the landscape. How can he and his beloved gain any purchase on their surroundings? What can they leave beyond the gravestones he sees waiting "in couples with the names and half the date"? That dilemma may seem the traditional one for love lyric, which the poet might answer with the Shakespearean promise "that in black ink my love may still shine bright." In fact, Lowell's poem does embody its own promise, launched into the future. But beyond the fact of death, that future remains uncertain. By the end of the poem, husband and wife themselves have become two "motes" or "eye-flaws." Here's the final couplet:

> Dear Figure curving like a question mark,
> how will you hear my answer in the dark? (374)

Except for the tenuous life of images carried through darkness by the optic nerve, as by lines and sentences, there's no reply to the poet's question beyond the act of seeing and the attempt to render faithfully. This is why Lowell makes such a superlative portraitist: the play between the subject as he or she objectively appears in the "real world" and the felt images coursing along the pulse of the artist, this pull between inside and outside, takes on an urgent ethical dimension. I have in mind an "ethics" not characterized by universal or a priori principles but embedded in situations, encounters. Such an approach allows even Lowell's most intimate poems, those entirely free of topical reference, to carry the charge of the best political art.

To understand how this commitment informs the movement of an entire poem, it's worth considering "Epilogue," one of Lowell's last. The poem is both Lowell's statement of dedication to his art and an enactment of that dedication:

> Those blessed structures, plot and rhyme—
> why are they no help to me now
> I want to make
> something imagined, not recalled?
> I hear the noise of my own voice:
> *The painter's vision is not a lens,*
> *it trembles to caress the light.*
> But sometimes everything I write
> with the threadbare art of my eye
> seems a snapshot,
> lurid, rapid, garish, grouped,
> heightened from life,
> yet paralyzed by fact.

All's misalliance.
Yet why not say what happened?
Pray for the grace of accuracy
Vermeer gave to the sun's illumination
stealing like the tide across a map
to his girl solid with yearning.
We are poor passing facts,
warned by that to give
each figure in the photograph
his living name. (838)

Even as he admits that his poems resemble photographs more than paintings, doubling back to correct himself, Lowell adopts the same creaturely responsiveness he admires in the painter's vision. In what sense might he himself be a visionary artist? "Epilogue" offers a microcosmic answer. Bereft of his "blessed structures," this poet faces the withering truth of bare reality. Even when portrayed as a momentary doubt, the narrative structure again suggests a dark night of the soul, a reckoning to occur only after consoling familiar images have been stripped away. Such reckoning takes account of the poet's society, but it must include himself, his failures—right down to that professorial pronouncement against photography that feels specious upon recollection. This bathetic undercutting is not the final gesture of the drama. The concluding phrase of the poem, "living name," suggests the name a person has while living, but also the possibility that he and his name might live *from being named*. It's this trust in the fundamental poetic act of naming—poignantly embodied in the image of recording the names of people in a snapshot—that prevents "Epilogue" from becoming mere decorous valediction on the one hand or mere hangdog regret on the other. Despite its elegiac tone, the poem thrives off a feeling of potential, inherent in the sympathetic circuit between subject and object.

It's significant that "Epilogue" itself contains no names of the poet's contemporaries. Since Lowell's work is replete with names and other proper nouns, their absence in "Epilogue" elucidates a crucial point: though the poet declares, "We are poor passing facts," the final truth of personal experience lies not in facts but in the encounter of mind and feeling with their particularity. Much more than mere representation of facts, Lowell's autobiographical art proves an act, occurring in language with which he wrestles. Had he been a visual artist, his poem-pictures might have been vivid yet ragged, capturing the back-and-forth between artist and subject in high resolution taken almost to the point of brutality—I think of the claim in one of his sonnets that he wants his poems "meat-hooked from the living steer" (590). And yet there's that vulnerable, even delicate aspect again: when he refers to his "threadbare art" some canny dramaturgy may be involved, yet the poignancy proves real. Lowell's sense of what art can be touches always on his feeling for how easily it can *not* be—how the right word or image, almost fleeting, animates its surroundings. Technical mastery alone can't produce but only attend this animation. Far from resulting in journalistic realism, his openness to the chanciness of fact reveals a surprisingly aleatory aspect of Lowell's poems, a faith in the insurgent force of experience. Think of what it *feels like* to read Lowell. What other poems are so well wrought and so jagged, so well plotted and so responsive to generative disruptiveness?

These are not isolated attributes of one poet's style: the blended tones reflect a profound development in the history of the art form, one Lowell doesn't create alone but comes to represent. I mean a new tendency of poetry toward "biographical form." That term was one that Georg Lukács applied to the novel in his *Theory of the Novel* (1915). By "biographical form" Lukács didn't mean the strict tracing of one person's life. He claimed that "the outward form of the novel is essentially biographical," so that even a novel not coextensive with the lifetime of one protagonist takes its essential energy from the desire to understand, and have some say in creating, the shape of one's life (1971, 77). What's so compelling about Lukács's description of biographical form is how it succeeds by failing: "The fluctuation between a conceptual system which can never completely capture life and a life complex which can never attain completeness because completeness is immanently utopian, can be objectivized only in that organic quality which is the aim of biography" (77).

It's worth slowing down to explicate. By "life complex" Lukács implies that any one life includes other people's, along with however many additional external factors. By the "conceptual system" of the novel Lukács means a certain historical situation, one dilemma of the bourgeois revolution that the novel tends to stage—the divide between the conventional, factual world of imposed social structures, which the novel reveals as abstract and arbitrary, and individual subjectivity, which remains interior and also abstract. The "form-giving intention" of the novel doesn't surmount this divide but "renders it sensuous," makes the distance itself palpable and meaningful.

Lukács, who among fellow thinkers of the radical Left was unique for his strong resistance to artistic Modernism and his adherence to nineteenth-century aesthetic ideals, might have been vexed to see his description of "biographical form" applied to poetry. Although he believed all art forms to be historical, he portrayed poetry as less contingent upon the upheavals of history. Nonetheless, his term illuminates the change in American poetry that Lowell represents. In Lukács's history of literary forms, the novel takes the place of epic literature, but the parts of the aesthetic whole now have much greater particularity, making their relation to that whole at times attenuated, as with the difficult split between factual data and subjective experience. Poetry, by troubling the formal autonomy expected from lyric, now stages this same relation to both the epic and the novel. Such poems gather their energetic charge from an extreme tension between particular verbal images and the historical totality those images suggest. We see this throughout those "Modernist epics," in which Odyssean ambition shatters and condenses into imagist fragments, as well as the series poems of second-generation modernists such as Lorine Niedecker and George Oppen. But with Lowell, biographical form becomes the core around which the poems radiate. One result is the still current centrality of the collection of poetry, the expectation that the book itself will reveal a made shape, most often with the figure of the poet at its center, but allowing that figure to refract into others. Think of how in Lowell's collections the biographical material branches into and from historical narratives, translations, portraits of friends and relatives. As Frank Bidart explains, this central image of the self is artifice. What's very real, however, is the process of construction itself, the poet's making this image through observing, asserting, reflecting, constellating, and revising.

Many poets of the generations following Lowell's have found their own ways to maintain the formal integrity of poetry while allowing for the incursion of all that, until the advent of their poems, had seemed mere Eliotic "platinum." None of the four poets whose work I'll next consider shows Lowell's influence at the level of line and sentence. But each faces the same challenge he poses: like Lowell, each makes art from an attempt to understand and shape personal experience, even while admitting the difficulties of doing so when neither a "life complex" nor a "conceptual system" offers completion.

David Antin

Aligning David Antin with Robert Lowell may stretch credulity. In 1972, in an avant-garde magazine called *boundary 2*, Antin published his essay "Modernism and Postmodernism: Approaching the Present in Modern American Poetry." At the center lay an attack on poets he saw as *conservateurs*, writers whose poems led their academic advocates to consider them "the last living generation within the tradition" (2011, 163). These included Delmore Schwartz, Randall Jarrell, and Antin's prime target, Robert Lowell.

Who was this writer laying into Lowell? Having worked at *Art News* with his friend John Ashbery and then as educational director at the Institute of Contemporary Art in Boston, by 1972 David Antin was a forty-year-old professor at the University of California, San Diego, where he also ran the art gallery. Around this same time he was developing his "talk poems," texts he created by transcribing and lineating—with some editing—recordings of talks he gave. While his earliest talk poems are saturated with the meditations on modern aesthetics that you'd expect from someone mulling the work of conceptual artists like Douglas Heubler and Dennis Oppenheim—not to mention collaborating with his wife, the conceptualist Eleanor Antin—these "talk poems" are also shot through with restlessness.

Strangely, such dissatisfaction feels not unlike Lowell's, resulting as it does in such an audacious approach to the formal challenges of writing original poetry and the political challenges of living conscientiously in the present. Antin appears impatient with conventional forms of art and collective life, and yet his attitude's not merely an art school contrarian's—his poems show an intelligence caught in the same situations it addresses. His dilemma is how to break out of closed systems, in art and life. No simple solution presents itself. But like Lowell's interrupting the sound of his own voice in "Epilogue," Antin responds by jarring the balance between the poet and those others who inhabit his poems. Often comical, he gibes at the end of one poem ("what am i doing here?" from *Talking at the Boundaries*) that his definition of poetry could be "uninterruptible discourse" and with the end of the poem everyone might now return to "interruptible discourse" (1976, 3). The joke reveals the extent to which he allows his poems to become permeable to all that would previously have seemed antipoetic, while maintaining the self-contained authority, the "just-thereness" of the artwork.

Consider the first of his talk poems, "Talking at Pomona," in which he offers a funny yet serious take on the predicament of contemporary painting (see facing page).

The entertaining directness of the "talk poem" structure might at first hide the subtlety in this passage. Not only does Antin's caricature of the "little lady from la jolla" show more dimension and sympathy than might be expected, but she comes off no worse than the art school know-it-alls, whose belief in the formal autonomy of their art proves just as contingent as the tastes of this "little lady from la jolla." Most important, the poet himself, nothing if not a "relator," seems caught in the same situation. His regard for the people he portrays remains both critical and Whitmanian: this poet wants to distinguish and discern, yet also include. And his self-referentiality—the creation of this artwork out of the problem of how to create this artwork—neither numbs Antin's talk poems nor prevents moments of surprising emotional force.

the one thing you know from painters who paint is that painting cant possibly be easy they struggle about it because it would be easy if lets say the little lady the proverbial and mythical little lady who down in our area around san diego we think of as the little lady from la jolla the little lady of la jolla has a gold frame painting and that's not what you want to make and she bought it in balboa park and you say "but whats the matter with buying a little painting in balboa park with a frame she hangs it there she looks at it often it gives her pleasure" and that's not what you want to make because what you want to make means something else and i say "but that doesnt mean anything?" no what that means is that that woman has a set of historical tastes that she loves and she is attracted to her taste and she wants to stick to those ideas that she knows very well and she will be satisfied by it the way she will be satisfied by having a particular dish served to her once a week by her cook lets say her spanish speaking cook to whom she doesn't speak because she doesn't speak spanish but this particular dish that she expects regularly her taco dinner and she knows what she wants in art it tastes a particular way now my young artist or old artist doesn't want to make that kind of art because hes not making food hes not making a consumer item youre not making a consumer item youre making a painting and its a big painting and what else is there in the painting that is why are you carrying out this unnatural act say with respect to a large piece of canvas stretched on a support i mean what is this all about I mean there is this thing and its heavy its non-functional it acquires dust and you put colors on it and theres a sigh a tremendous sigh and they point to other paintings that this art that is to say its like with other art and it turns out after a while that this painting relates only to other paintings that is to say it relates to other paintings in the minds of people who relate to other paintings there are a set of people who are painting relators and these painting relators relate your painting to other paintings which is how you know these are paintings (1972, 147)

Antin (1)

Consider how he moves from a discussion of chess to the affecting conclusion of "Talk at Pomona" (186; see facing page).

Insisting upon the social contingency of art work, Antin finally reaches beyond the realm of speculative aesthetics—although he never says "Vietnam," its shadow falls across the lines about war and arbitrary inequity. What's more, the juxtaposition or framing of those lines against the fulsome, concluding phrase, "out of the character of human experience in our world" prevents the latter from sounding orotund and the former from seeming ham-fisted. Even the direct attack on those *retardataire* aesthetics he calls "the arbitrary rules of knot-making" becomes more ambiguous than rhetorical: avoiding any garrulous tangle, Antin's talk poems themselves hold together by constitutive tensions. In fact, the reference to knot-making loops back and gathers a previous discussion of knots earlier in the poems.

Demanding from himself a poetry that would account for the totality of contemporary life, one that sidesteps rhetoric by employing a succession of montages or laminations of various scenes, narratives, and idioms, Antin's practice shows some deep affinities with Lowell's. And yet I think it would be inaccurate to discount Antin's objections to Lowell as the venting of a young radical lambasting an old liberal. So let's rewind here. What of that essay? Beneath the temperamental and stylistic differences, what did Antin so dislike in Lowell, and what might that tell us about his own work?

At first glance the answer would appear to be "not much." Although "Modernism and Postmodernism" shows an emerging writer of capacious intelligence laying out his whole conception of modern American poetry, its central argument seldom exceeds the one expected from that subgenre of literary criticism, the Oedipal screed: "they, the old, are bad, and we, the new, are good." Reading Lowell, Antin objects to a political sonnet from *Lord Weary's Castle* (1946), "Concord," and argues that the poem amounts to a retelling of "The New England Myth," regional lore that "lacks any contemporary reality" (2011, 173). But he avoids the lines of the poem that mount an attack on modern capitalism: even beneath the high, Miltonic tones typical of Lowell's early work, the poet's atti-

. . . shatrandji was the

game of which chess is the trivial example   and it doesnt seem that we have to be especially

impressed with *shatrandji* either   but as *shatrandji* was a game built up out of the human

experiences of its time   arbitrary inequities among people   the facts of unavoidable

war   and the absurd circumstances of luck lying under the feet of ability   it is possible

to construct   make art out of something more meaningful than the arbitrary rules of

knot making   out of the character of human experience in our world

Antin (2)

tude toward "Mammon's unbridled industry" comes across clearly enough as one that, had he fully addressed himself to the lines and sentences, Antin might have found sympathetic, or at least worthy of a more illuminating argument. Antin follows the reading of "Concord" with an indictment of "For the Union Dead," and here his argument hangs by a dubious thread: "Though it is the poet who crouches to his television set," writes Antin of the concluding tableau of that poem, "it is Colonel Shaw who is 'riding on his bubble' waiting 'for the blessed break'" (177). Since what the poet sees on TV are "the drained faces of negro schoolchildren," Antin's implication is that Lowell's aesthetic traditionalism, "The Mind of Europe" as filtered from Pound and Eliot by way of Allen Tate, parallels a political tepidity: the civil rights movement remains an image he watches from afar and merely presents to the reader. But this argument ignores the changes in Lowell's work—changes that led to a cooling of his friendship with the conservative Tate, who disliked *Life Studies* (1959), and a simultaneous warming of his connection with William Carlos Williams—and, more to the point, ignores changes in the poem itself: Antin misses the dramatic shift that occurs with this specific stanza. I mean the jolt into strange, ritual speech, erupting through the already unsettled surface of the poem to identify in the legacy of slavery the foundational crime of American civilization. Ignoring the full depth and scope of Lowell's poems, Antin here seems little more than a self-appointed hatchet man for an avant-garde he conceives as an affiliation of Black Mountain, New York School, and Beat—the poets represented by Donald Allen's anthology *New American Poetry*, as opposed to Robert Pack and Donald Hall's *New Poets of England and America*. Even by 1972 this Manichaean showdown was growing predictable and tired.

And yet despite its "us vs. them," lopsided quality, "Modernism and Postmodernism" reveals two urges that inform Antin's own best work. The first is a desire to represent and enact cultural change. Antin was no identitarian, but spurning academia of the 1950s and 1960s, he wanted a more inclusive American poetry—his gibes about the "parlor conversation" and "poetical Episcopalianism" of poets whose work he dislikes implies it: here was a Jewish kid from

Brooklyn, a City College savant who found in the eruptive art of Whitman and radical Modernism an opening for his own inclusive social vision (175, 180). Attempting to tar Robert Lowell with the brush of Ivy League elitism, he fails; more importantly, though, his essay identifies a cultural fissure much larger than any shift in the personal politics of American poets. The historian Perry Anderson identifies Antin's essay as the "real turning point" in the crystallization of the term *postmodernism* (1998, 15).

In contemporary discussions of poetry, that word often leads to confusion, but Antin's concept of postmodernism proves clear and convincing. How are Antin and other poets of his and subsequent generations "postmodern" writers? Simply by taking the measure of the world around them—a world in which Modernist aesthetic techniques are now used to advertise soft drinks. Near the beginning of his essay, Antin describes his reaction to a recent viewing of Roy Lichtenstein's *Modern Art* series: "It was absurd to see the high art styles of the early twenties and the advanced decorative and architectural styles of the later twenties and thirties through the screen of a comic strip" (2011, 161). The change Antin locates is not limited to aesthetics. Fredric Jameson, the theorist who most convincingly picks up on the analysis of postmodernity where Antin left off, explains that "the postmodern" differs from "postmodernity," the latter term indicating the totality of late-capitalist production, one mode of human history, ours—an era characterized by what Jameson calls the "free play of masks and roles without content or substance" (1996, 19). Aesthetic styles of different historical provenance now seem equally available; as Jameson has it, art in postmodernity tends toward the character of pastiche. But such "free play" is not to be casually accepted and reveled in. Although the conditions of postmodernity remain the air we breathe and can't be denied, the challenge becomes recovery of primary energy, emancipatory potential.

Antin's own talk poems are at their best when he attempts a similar gesture, a reclamation that's more than nostalgia for the past, more than another style of "neo." I find his 2005 collection, *i never knew what time it was* (2005), his strongest. He approaches the motif that title suggests differently here than in "Talking at Pomona." Time appears a source of anxiety for the artist in that earlier poem, since the traditional endeavor of art to preserve experience contradicts the forward-facing commitment of the avant-garde. Seeming to side with the latter, Antin elaborates on two emblems of this uneasiness about art and time—the museum and the shaman (1972, 165–66; see Antin 3).

Antin's ambivalence lies in his inability to reconcile "art youre making now" with a retrospective practice he trusts and respects, though it seems to align with the "arbitrary rules of knot making," or with those American poets he saw as rigid academicians fumbling through the ruins of European culture. In *i never knew what time it was* Antin may never explicitly revise such claims. But in the title poem especially, his meditations on time deepen and change. Not only does he attempt his own "intellectual human shamanism," one that takes into account the challenges facing a postmodern writer, but he also raises his art to a new intensity. And he does so by making it more personal.

Consider the movement between three passages near the end of "i never knew what time it was." Here Antin begins his effort to find the right image for time itself. He describes the carousel at San Diego's Balboa Park (see Antin 4).

Onto this carousel Antin transposes another image of cyclical time, one characterized less by Rilkean wonder and melancholy and more by contemporary ambition and anxiety—the escalator (see Antin 5).

The poet then searches for and finds a replacement for Rilke's elephant—a new way to establish some connection between individual thought and feeling and the seemingly impermeable materiality of everything rolled round not only in "earth's diurnal course" but in the cycles of mechanized modernity. Antin employs a tone that's both parodic and sincere (see Antin 6).

From here the poet segues into the concluding section, an elegy for his father-in-law, a Hungarian poet and painter—Barna Jozef, though he went by the pen name Peter Moor—who was imprisoned by the Hungarian fascists between the two world wars and lived

it is an exercise in humanly
reevoking the world its like an exercise in shamanism   the way a shaman evokes the
presence of the dead person   that is to say someone who is very real and had a very real
effect upon   his wife   and his children   and the tribe   and the shaman draws
upon his reality and brings him there long enough for people to recognize an anterior person
who stood once fully alive   and it may very well be a terrific role that the museum
should play   it often doesn't play at all   and that art history should play
that is to say to play this kind of   intellectual human shamanism and I would say that's a
very respectable role but its not about value nor is it about the art youre making now

Antin (3)

and we remembered going there many years before
when our kid was about the age he seemed in the photograph where we
    were playing football in central park   and I kind of think of the
    seasons as going around like a carousel
        now you may think that's not a good image   because if you watch
    carefully as it all goes around you see that the seasons are not always
    the same   but the carousel is not always the same either   because
    you can't always pay perfect attention to it   and you miss a black horse
        you know its like rilkes poem about the carousel   he seems to
want to pay constant attention   but what he notices is intermittent
    every now and then he spots a white elephant going by   now its
probably the same elephant   but hes not sure about that and he wants
    to let you know that   so he tells you several times   every now and
    then   theres a white elephant   but whos sure it's the same elephant
    (2005, 99–100)
                              Antin (4)

---

        now I have another way of looking for the cycle that would make
    it possible to figure the time   though maybe it's even more bizarre
    suppose you think of yourself on an escalator   youre on an escalator
and   say youre on an escalator going up   youre growing youve got a
    career   youre going up the escalator   and the career is carrying you
almost without effort   you know this is not really true but it feels
    that way   it feels good
        youre doing well you know   youre having shows youre getting
    published youre on an escalator and its going up   but you know at
    some point youre going to be catapulted off the escalator   so how do
    you stay on the escalator (101–2)

                              Antin (5)

---

        all these new people on the escalator are
    making me nervous   I dont recognize them   and since you cant
    recognize the people you keep looking at the escalator to see if the
    escalator has some familiar step   a step with a deformation in it   you
        look for a place where the escalator has something peculiar like gum
    stuck into it   because you know the escalator is a continuing series
    of steps that cycles around and around and around (102–3)

                              Antin (6)

zaha he said *zaha* shaking his head and repeating it over and over
zaha zaha to anything we had to say   it didn't mean anything to me
and of course there was plenty of hungarian I didn't know   so as he lay
there dying I didn't have any idea what he meant later   I tried to look
it up in my hungarian dictionary and I couldn't find anything remotely
like it
     anything but one day im talking to a friend   a marvelous
   virtuoso hungarian violinist named janos negysey   and I tell him
about the word and he thinks a moment   hes a musician and he says
   zaha   its an inversion
     that's *haza*   it means homeland
   so it was as if someone speaking english would say to me
dnalemoh dnalemoh for homeland   so it was homeland he was
trying to say   only I couldn't figure it out   he was somehow trying
   to find the step   his step on the escalator   that particular step that
had lifted him up and had somehow disappeared   and I don't know if
   it was the budapest world that had welcomed him   or the little town
   of keckemet where he had been born
     but he was thinking of his homeland   and of course budapest is
no longer his budapest   and keckemet is no longer the little town
   where his father painted the interiors of churches   but he was
   looking for this one place that he was sure never ever to find again (105–6)

Antin (7)

near the end of his life with the poet and his family in San Diego.
Like those images of High Modernism caught in the postmodern
frame of Lichtenstein's comic strips, and like Antin's own trans-
position of the escalator onto the carousel, this European father-
in-law finding himself in early-1980s Southern California becomes
the occasion of humor and uneasiness. Indeed elegy itself would
seem out of place in an Antin talk poem, too much like the work of
museums or shamans, and yet he concludes the whole talk poem
with his elegy. That ending begins with a description of Peter on his
deathbed (see Antin 7).

The poet mourns here, but he also reclaims more than images
of Peter: he absorbs and renews something of Peter's *volition*, his
effort at reclaiming his past. Given the futility of Peter's desire for
his homeland, there's no victory over death in this ending. But as

with Lukács's conception of biographical form, incompletion preserves possibility, including the possibility that one "life complex" may branch into previously unknown territory—Peter, for example, becomes a central figure in his son-in-law's meditation on time. Instead of depending upon the image of an elephant on a carousel or dried gum on an escalator, the poet now makes his own poem the instrument of reclamation. Even as he elegizes, Antin creates something radical and new: just as discursive and meditative as his previous talk poems, this one also becomes a necessary action, a new shape carved into existence.

It may be the avant-garde who most often demand that art be an autonomous thing or action, and not a representation, but in "i never knew what time it was" Antin the avant-gardist carries his art into reality by seeking greater and greater proximity to personal experience, in a poetry that not only renders that experience but also asks what it is. He's a true radical because of his openness, his wholesome disregard for the kind of reductive argument that would partition narratives of personal experience from avant-garde poetics, and this lends dimension and surprise to all of his best work. Among the generations following Robert Lowell, he remains one of those poets impossible to place on any schema: they pursue the changes in their poetry not as negotiation of allegiances or influences but as obsession. Such poets display something that bridges knowledge and passion, not an attribute—this thing for which English may not have a word—but an ability, an action.

John Koethe

John Koethe is certainly such a poet. In his essay "Contrary Impulses: The Tension between Poetry and Theory," Koethe argues for the old Romantic "impulse of contestation," the resistance of the imagination to the "inexorable encroachment of the real" (2000, 47). He distinguishes the poem embodying this endeavor both from the typical avant-garde poem of today, in which language becomes a tangle of indeterminate signifiers, and from the conventional poem of personal experience, in which autobiography becomes diminished by objectification. So it may come as a surprise, reading much of his best poetry, to see the forms of autobiographical narrative Koethe employs. His work has developed, in fact, on what may seem a steady trajectory toward the biographical approach. Early on, Koethe's voice has the unabashed immediacy of his New York School models. Poems from his first two books, like the love lyric "Your Day," the surrealistic lark "Montana," or the landscape "Mission Bay," wouldn't seem out of place next to the earlier, less discursive poems of James Schuyler. In the 1980s, with the publication of *The Late Wisconsin Spring* (1984), a change occurs—as in fact one did for Schuyler: more introspective now, more Wordsworthian, these poems endeavor to plot the growth of the individual mind. Then in the 1990s, with the collection *Falling Water* (1997), and its title poem in particular, Koethe's poetry reaches its full amplitude.

Koethe has published several collections in the more than twenty years since *Falling Water*, but I want to look in particular at *Sally's Hair* (2006) because it contains the most narrative of any of Koethe's collections and at the same time reveals how thoroughly he's continued his project of contestation. The title poem, portraying a brief college love affair, and "21.1," about a high-school track meet, appear at first to be anecdotal recollections. Koethe's imagery also derives from everyday routines, as in "The dinner, the DVD from Netflix" (2006, 41). His tone often comes across as, to use his own word, "lackadaisical." But Koethe isn't trying to write the kind of autobiographical poem in which crisis and trauma lend the aura of necessity. Significance here comes not from those miniature conversion experiences that punctuate much poetry of personal experience and seem to shape a life into a series of destined stages. Unlike such work—written often under the influence, if not the understanding, of Robert Lowell—these poems dramatize the contradiction between mind and matter as the self attempts to arrange its world, even in the most everyday or seemingly undramatic situations.

It's important here to understand the influence of John Ashbery on Koethe's poems. It shows up in some obvious features of the work: for example, Koethe favors a similar tone of casual colloquiality. But plenty of poets have inherited such traits from Ashbery.

What distinguishes Koethe is that he both understands the obsessions that run beneath that style and brings his own artistic imagination to his response. He reads Ashbery as a poet of personal experience. In his early review of *Three Poems*, Koethe locates a movement in Ashbery's prose poetry between the flights of subjective transcendence and immersion in the everyday. He quotes this passage from Ashbery's prose sequence:

> but our song is leading us on now, farther and farther into that wilderness and away from the shrouded but familiar forms that were its first inspiration. (Koethe 2000, 10)

Koethe then opposes this to the moments in Ashbery that he calls "tunnel vision" (10). He points to the following passage:

> a strange kind of happiness within the limitations. The way is narrow but it is not hard, it almost seems to propel or push one along. One gets the narrowness into one's seeing. (10)

The twenty-six-year-old poet quoting these passages in his review identifies a characteristic opposition in Ashbery. But the poem's also reading him. Over the past few decades, Koethe has made the internal resistance in his own work from the conflicting "shrouded but familiar" forms of the everyday and the "wilderness" of subjective experience. If Ashbery remains the touchstone, Koethe accepts but transmutes the influence. In an Ashbery poem various threads repeatedly approach a synthesis and then fray, suggesting the futility of any union of mind and matter, but in Koethe's poems the structure tends to be more clearly delineated, cohering around biographical form. To put it another way: you could never walk around an Ashbery poem, but despite some weird terrain in places and a few beguiling crevasses where the path of discursive logic plunges away, circumnavigation of a Koethe poem tends to be doable.

In *Sally's Hair* the poet establishes the terms of his pursuit with remarkable variety and lucidity, approaching the process of contestation from various perspectives. The very poet who wrote of the "encroachments of the real" begins his new book with a poem, "The Perfect Life," in which imagination itself becomes the tyrant.

The poem starts with the declaration "I have a perfect life" (3), then things begin to sour. Here's the transition:

> I heed the promptings of my inner voice,
> And what I hear is comforting, full of reassurance
> For my own powers and innate superiority—the fake
> Security of someone in the grip of a delusion,
> In denial, climbing ever taller towers
> Like a tiny tyrant looking on his little kingdom
> With a secret smile. (2006, 3)

The liveliness of this passage comes from the blend of aggressive self-recrimination and measured eloquence. The glide from the iambic pentameter of the first line into the longer lines, the internal rhyme of "powers" and "towers," and the firm placement of individual clauses within the sweep of the long sentence all contribute to immediacy. Koethe's project of contestation feels, therefore, nothing like a rhetorical or systematic approach to writing poems.

And if Koethe presents the imagination as a deluded and deluding megalomaniac in "The Perfect Life," in a poem called "The Middle of Experience" he considers the converse problem: the phenomenon of reality not resisting enough, receding in the face of imagination. Writing about returning to his family home in San Diego after the death of his father, Koethe claims that "nothing was revealed." He states that the house itself, which his parents decorated with the jewel-box aesthetic "of a Fabergé egg," seems "*unbelievable*" (9). Those italics suggest the idiomatic meaning of the word: how oddly impressive the actual objects were. But *unbelievable* also carries is literal meaning: the sense that the objects gave the mind and imagination nowhere to rest. Attempting to locate a sense of home, the poet writes:

> This sense if of an *absence* of a place, a freedom
> From constraint, the freedom of a part of me
> Inhabiting this poem, and a part I left at home.
> I like the image of a lime-green sky
> Above a house two thousand miles away,
> But distance doesn't matter, and the color—well,
> It pleases me, that's all. (10)

Again, formal nuances deliver the larger effect. The rhyme of "poem" and "home," for example, hints at how Koethe's work itself offers, if only provisionally, a space in which objective reality and the imagination, home and freedom, can combine, a space where private life can be preserved but also rendered.

In the attempt to create and maintain such a middle realm, Koethe has developed a unique structure, which many of his poems follow: it begins with the inability to make experience cohere; then comes a Proustian breakthrough, accompanied by a sense of an abiding space where imagination and the everyday commingle; this illusion founders, and finally the poet's left to salvage from the collapse some means of continuance. Not all of the poems unfold like this. Even when they do, Koethe attains great variety. In "The Unlasting," for instance, a poem in the same stanzaic form as Wallace Stevens's "Auroras of Autumn," that method takes the course of meditation. In "21:1," by contrast, it appears in seemingly straightforward narrative. In "Hamlet," the most powerful poem in *Sally's Hair*, Koethe blends those two modes. He recounts his college years and the project of making himself into a poet, which he presents as both wondrous and comically pretentious. The poem leads into a section of reminiscence and mild yet persistent regret, almost risking ponderousness, and then Koethe segues into a final section that dynamizes and delivers on all that's preceded. The poet remembers a performance of *Hamlet* starring Richard Burton, which he and his college friends saw in New York in the mid-1960s, and relates his discovery years later of Burton's performance on DVD. Here are the final lines of the poem:

> I know of course I'm overacting. Burton did it too,
> Yet left a residue of truth, and watching him last Friday
> I began to realize there'd been no real change,
> But just a surface alteration. Sometimes I wonder if this
> Isn't just my high-school vision in disguise, a naïve
> Fantasy of knowledge that survived instead as art—
> Aloof, couched in the language of abstraction, flirting
> Now and then with the unknown, pushing everything aside.
> This place that I've created has the weight and feel of home,
> And yet there's nothing tangible to see. And so I

Bide my time, living in a poem whose backdrop
Is the wilderness of science, an impersonal universe
Where no one's waiting and our aspirations end.
Take up the bodies, for the rest is silence. (82)

The feeling that time has effected no genuine change "but just a surface alteration" seems to leave nowhere for the poet's mind to repose except in the present. The search for home that he pursued in "The Middle of Experience" has here reached an end, with that same rhyme employed again, and yet this attainment offers no satisfaction. The quotation from Fortinbras in the last line brings the melancholic tone to its ultimate depth, with its image of the slain. But even if that note remains the dominant tenor, doesn't "take up the bodies" also carry an almost spiritual connotation? In the play it's Fortinbras's soldiers who "take up the bodies," but those words cross over from script to stage direction: it's the actors and the audience who take up their own bodies at the end of what they've made—together. The words signal that something has transpired, the work of art itself. In this moment, as the fiction itself breaks down, "make-believe" becomes reality.

John Koethe is a vital poet because his deflationary irony and his Romantic ambition combine to form such artful structures. Unlike so many "experimental" poets, he doesn't employ his skepticism as a device to demonstrate again and again the illusory nature of our habits of mind and feeling. Unlike so many poets of personal experience, he doesn't see truth as a set narrative he needs to uncover: it exists instead as an unfolding process. A blend of openness and rigor makes Koethe's poems, for all the "lackadaisical" tones he adopts, crucial embodiments, and not simply reflections, of experience.

James McMichael

On the surface, James McMichael might seem the opposite of John Koethe. Far from contesting objective reality, McMichael remains obsessed with it. But if Koethe strives toward some all-but-illusory synthesis of self and environment, so does McMichael, though he gets there the other way 'round. His poems map the complex circuitries of "the world at large" (the title of his selected poems of 1996) but find their source in the self who suffers, imagines, and strives. And the very structure of a McMichael poem ends up forming a surprising shape, one the poet himself has improvised. *Improvised* might seem a peculiar word, given all the rationality of idiom and scrupulousness of construction in these poems, but McMichael is a poet fascinated by the unexpected yet inevitable paths between one location and another.

McMichael's ability to find unique forms is perhaps most apparent in his best-known, book-length poem *Four Good Things* (1980). How exactly to describe the form of this poem? It moves between an array of subjects: from the real estate development of Pasadena, in which the poet's father was instrumental, to the squalor of England during the Industrial Revolution—in a section that recalls Friedrich Engels's *The Condition of the Working Class in England* (1845); from cartography to hydraulics; from the invention of the cathode ray to the deliberations of an insomniac. But the poet's compulsion to know the world in all its parts turns out to have roots in great personal pain. Here he addresses the effect of his mother's early death:

> With my conception, I was virtually
> coincident with cancer in my mother's body.
> To exist is to be placed outside, where there are
> things to fear. My body. Me. The visible
> pulse at my right ankle, thick blue vein, the skin,
> sunlight on my ankle in a cold house, now. (1996, 100)

At such moments the suffering individual, whose own body often appears exterior and threatening to himself, proves the center of the poem. Despite the civilized, discursive tone, the whole poem turns out to flow from the psychological disruption caused by the mother's death—showing in an extreme desire to understand and order the very world that so threatens the self.

Given the strength with which McMichael conveys this same urge—though now in a different narrative context—and the sheer inventiveness with which he enacts it, the poems in his 2006 collection, *Capacity*, seem to me his strongest work since *Four Good*

Things. Capacity is about nothing less than survival, the attempt of any one self to hold its own in the world. At the heart of the book lies the bare act of reaping sustenance from the planet, which "suffers itself to be turned outside." These poems themselves subsist by a kind of nutritive process. As they range across the various fields of experience and orders of language, they gather into themselves: economics and sex, biology and geography all crop up in this collection. Although McMichael repeatedly returns, as if rediscovering a tonic root, to several images from a book called *The British Countryside in Pictures* (1948), he seems able to import just about anything into the manifold sweep of his poems.

But he's not an Emersonian expansionist such as, say, A. R. Ammons. These poems are more anguished. With extreme concentration on the most minute details, McMichael's voice seems to suffer its progress through the sentences. This prevents his presentation of often scientific material from sounding like the voice-over on a PBS program. The words *I* and *me* never appear in this collection, yet the self remains everywhere present, if only by virtue of its erasure. Often the transitions are driven by what Alan Shapiro, in his introduction to *The World at Large*, identifies as an essentially stoical "penchant for anxiously displacing his attention from people and relationships on to landscapes, houses, objects, plans, or systems" (1996, x). If this tendency often appears in the drama of the poems as evasion or denial, it seldom becomes a weakness of their structures. Instead, as Shapiro explains, the displacements allow this poet to inhabit various vantage points and therefore to connect individual experience with the exterior world.

This process ultimately proves an ethical endeavor, since the compulsion to know the world in all its parts, at its most crucial moments, circles back to what seems to have been displaced: the need to account for others. Indeed encounters between self and the other occur again and again in these poems; even seemingly inanimate objects stage the drama. The book teems with images of one substance entering another: the exact process of chewing and swallowing food, for example; or "huge shield volcanoes" sending up lava through the floor of the North Atlantic; or human birth.

This obsession appears also in the specific turns of the verse movement. Here's a passage from *Capacity*'s opening poem, "The British Countryside in Pictures" (2006, 7–8), in which the poet moves from global economics to the story of one couple in England at the beginning of World War II:

> The desired good was
> useful in the new ideal.
>
> Things become useless in the hoarding of them.
> Needed for a nation's surfeit of goods were buyers
> primed by their wanting. Desire's
>
> deputy was the person in love. An appetite
> need not slacken if what one
> craves is the scarce,
> and there is but the one beloved
>
> only.
>
> No hunger feeds so on itself
> as being able
> never to have one's fill of something prized.
>
> They have become friends.
> It would not have
> occurred to him that she did not love him. Of
> course she did.

These lines may seem to have the deliberate movement of analytical prose, but consider the echoing dactyls of "primed by their," "craves is the," "never to." Like Ezra Pound, from whom he's learned, McMichael tends to weight the beginnings instead of the ends of lines. To my ear, the subtly consistent cadence not only represents but also creates the feeling of rigorous attentiveness that underlies and makes possible the segue from political economy to love story. The music lends substance to the process of the transition itself, the same process that absorbs McMichael throughout this book. I mean the endeavor both to read the self into history and to extract the unclassifiable substance of personal experience from the sheer agglomeration of objective fact that makes up that abstraction "history."

Perhaps this action appears most strikingly in the final poem in the book, "Back." Here the poet imagines the conception, gestation, and birth of a boy who, by the end of the poem, we see gazing into *The British Countryside in Pictures*. Appearing in 1948, at eight years old, the boy happens to be near McMichael's own age. Although this figure remains in the third person, he becomes a surrogate for the author, the closest thing we get in the book to a first person. Here he is, near the middle of the poem, in the infancy of his own consciousness:

> Being is what there is
> when the beings that had come to light are
> no longer there.
>
> Being quenches itself on its
> out-of-this-world pull forward.
> Against the end itself if also
>
> from it,
> craven,
> false,
>
> the imagined turnaround
> backward in time.
> He could
> retrace in reverse each
> percept, act and wish that had
> made up his life,
>
> each one could be discarded, he could
> think it away. (69–70)

As in Koethe's "The Perfect Life," the imagination almost seems like a villain, "craven" and "false" in its attempt to turn back, away from being. Yet that turn is the very action the poem itself pursues as it retraces its way to the womb and then to the postwar boyhood. McMichael may remain an anti-Romantic poet, as Alan Williamson has convincingly claimed. He often seems an antimetaphorical poet too. Yet as he attends to the actual, discrete facts of the physical world, he works toward a result much like metaphor: if not a union of disparate things, then a provisional understanding of their relation. The moments at which this occurs tend to carry intense feeling. Caught between its isolation and the world outside, the self appears at these moments with a creaturely starkness, something like T. S. Eliot's "infinitely suffering thing." Here, for example, is the end of "Back" (74), in which the boy imagines his way into the photographs:

> The span by span erasure of him
> spectral there
> inside the picture's
> outside-of-time
>
> safe spatial harbor,
> he is in repeal,
> exempt,
> the coppice to the left behind the rise
> a boyhood haunt.

The wonder and pathos of this moment glimmers in that curious clause "he is in repeal," which McMichael employs for its original juridical meaning, a temporary stay of banishment or imprisonment. The state from which "he is in repeal" is being itself. Most alive at this moment when he imagines his own erasure, the boy takes part in the fundamental drama of these poems, the individual's attempt to locate a place for himself in the world even as he faces his own isolation.

Better known for the infrastructural sweep of his work, Mc-Michael's also a poet of the kind of centripetal force and barely contained emotional heat more often associated with short lyric. What Lukács called the "form-giving intention" of the novel, which doesn't bridge the split between individual and world but "renders it sensuous," proves central to McMichael's practice. As a poem, *Capacity* comes closer than most fiction to the epic unity toward which the novel strives and from which it fractures into its contingent "organic quality." Confident third-person narration, afforded a wide scope of subjects, conveys that unity. At the same time, in addition to revealing aspects of epic, McMichael's poems court expectations associated with lyric—emotional need; a singular voice; the desiring and suffering first person confronting mortality and necessity. As in such poems as Antin's *i never knew what time it was* and Koethe's "Hamlet," McMichael confronts a "postmodern" situation in which there's no master narrative or monoculture. The poet must piece himself and his world together. It's common these days to hear poets talking about their "projects." But James McMichael's sustained investigation of a small set of obsessions has produced the most integral and surprising structures. What makes him unique in American poetry right now is the strength and subtlety with which he combines conceptual ambition and affective power.

Louise Glück

Both James McMichael and John Koethe are occupied with what Koethe calls "the wilderness of science." For McMichael, it exists as the very field of his inquiry. For Koethe, it forms a backdrop from which the imagination attempts to escape, but which the poet also implicitly trusts. It's hard to think of a poet in whose work "the wilderness of science" has as little presence as in that of Louise Glück. Anyone who's read even a few of her poems will know that her imagination dwells on archetype. No living poet's appeal to myth requires so little willing suspension of disbelief. Glück seems to think and feel in myth. Breaking through silence like fissures through frozen earth, her voice conveys sheerest necessity. But she matches her seriousness with a nearly corrosive skepticism, showing not only in deadpan turns and split-second barbs but also sustained psychoanalytic observation. Such tones work to temper the high romance, but they also intensify: by stripping away all but the essential, Glück ensures that any renewal that follows will be real. Renewal, in fact, has always been her great subject.

I want to look at her 2005 collection, *Averno*, because in this book it's not only the individual psyche for which the poet seeks renewal but also her entire way of understanding the self and the world. Against her characteristic vision of fate, she proposes the possibility of randomness. She still builds her book around a myth, though the myth she chooses proves well suited for those doubts about ordered narratives. In the figure of Persephone, Glück locates a core for several obsessions. This is a book dominated by the aura of late autumn, which the poet entertains both literally and as the classic metaphor of aging. Persephone's the figure who must suffer her hibernal descent to the underworld. Persephone's also the torn daughter, caught between the claims of her mother and those of her lover and captor, Hades. Gluck titles both the third and the final poem in the book "Persephone the Wanderer," and that epithet conveys her odd duality: she's both a figure of cyclical return, of order, and a prisoner of unceasing change who cannot live fully in one place or the other. Such drama correlates with the poet's own urge to examine the difference between her earlier assumptions about the path a life is meant to take (assumptions largely formed by expectations of her mother) and the actual course her life has pursued. In "Prism," the strongest poem in the book, Glück sets the idea of life having "an implied path, like / a map without a crossroads" against the reality of there being "too many roads, too many versions." The poem itself, as its title suggests, works by presenting distinct facets from which the poet endeavors to construct a new whole, even as it continues to break down. Here are the first two sections:

1.
Who can say what the world is? The world
is in flux, therefore
unreadable, the winds shifting,
the great plates invisibly shifting and changing—

2.
Dirt. Fragments
of blistered rock. On which
the exposed heart constructs
a house, memory: the gardens
manageable, small in scale, the beds
damp at the sea's edge— (2012, 505)

This vision of the individual's need to construct her own reality amidst Heraclitean flux carries none of the hopefulness it does, for example, in the tradition of American pragmatism. Chaos is a genuine threat here, fracturing the speech into onciric fragments. The tension between the poet's desire for order and the skepticism that undermines it lends great force to the end of the poem especially. Here are the final two sections:

19.
The room was quiet.
That is, the room was quiet, but the lovers were breathing.

In the same way, the night was dark. It was dark,
but the stars shone.

The man in bed was one of several men
to whom I gave my heart. The gift of self,
that is without limit.
Without limit, though it recurs.

The room was quiet. It was an absolute,
like the black night.

20.
A night in summer. Sounds of a summer storm.
The great plates invisibly shifting and changing—

And in the dark room, the lovers sleeping in each other's arms.

We are, each of us, the one who wakens first,
who stirs first and sees, there in the first dawn,
the stranger. (511–12)

Glück's persistent restlessness quickens the very scene-setting of those first four lines: in each free-verse couplet, a statement is made and then amended, as if the mind of the poet won't allow even the simplest preliminaries to settle. The whole final tableau wobbles on the verge between certainty and irresolution. The lover turns out, disturbingly, to be a stranger. Yet this fright also suggests a return to vitality, a sense that one's immediate surroundings are in fact charged. The crucial line is the fragment "Without limit, though it recurs." In the paradox of such "eternal return," those two opposing ways of seeing the world, the belief in fate and the suspicion that events are actually chaotic, have fused. The self at this moment appears both monumental and tiny. The poet's narration does return us to the grand certitudes of myth: "we are, each of us," delivers the great authority and knowingness particular to the first-person plural, and yet the very idea that this drama happens to each of us leaches distinction from the event. Once again we're back in the frightening unknown. Glück's ability to balance such contradictory feelings and ideas endows her poems with tremendous sharpness and force. In "Prism," as well as "October" and the title poem, she has developed a unique structure for this endeavor, a longer poem in which the constituent sections, each of them conducting the heat of the short lyric for which she has long been known, simultaneously embody and pick apart the desire to give shape to experience.

Of all the poets considered here, Glück may seem the least occupied with politics, the most dedicated to the ancient desire of the lyric poet to transcend history. But *Averno* reveals how her mythical dramas occur not on some transcendent height above collective concerns but *below* them. This becomes clearest in "October," a poem that, without any overt topical reference, proves a meditation upon life immediately after the attacks of September 11. Here's how Glück begins the second section (494):

> Summer after summer has ended,
> balm after violence:
> it does me no good
> to be good to me now;
> violence has changed me.

The poet presumes her task is to connect individual and collective experience ("it does me no good / to be good to me now"). This role feels necessary, though possibly false: if she herself doesn't experience renewal, how can she offer the same? In the fifth section, she claims that the word *hope* itself now appears "false, a device to refute / perception" (498). Scoured down by such skepticism, the poem stands nevertheless as an alternative to despair, a connection between people at the most fundamental level. Here is how Glück concludes the fifth section (499):

> I was young here. Riding
> the subway with my small book
> as though to defend myself against
> the same world:
>
> *You are not alone,*
> the poem said in the dark tunnel.

Delving to the depths of utter loneliness—loneliness that, signifi-
cantly, occurs in public—Glück both recalls Persephone's descent
and alludes to another poetic subway scene, one occurring in T. S.
Eliot's "East Coker." Catching that allusion may not be necessary to
feel and understand the power of "October," but alluding to Eliot,
the poet also reveals her difference from him. In "East Coker," Eliot
conjures that moment when an underground train stops between
stations "And the conversation rises and slowly fades into silence /
And you see behind every face the mental emptiness deepen." Eliot
doesn't give in to despair, but his response to such emptiness is a
dour, meditative act of total renunciation:

> I said to my soul, be still, and wait without hope
> For hope would be hope for the wrong thing; wait without love
> For love would be love of the wrong thing; there is yet faith
> But the faith and the love and the hope are all in the waiting.
> (1962, 126–27)

In contrast, Glück's subway scene proves more creaturely, more
tenacious, and, while not exactly hopeful, dedicated nevertheless to
the idea that art can and will connect disparate individuals.

Poetry critics sometimes like to parade huge concepts in binary
pairs. The avant-garde versus the traditionalists, the raw versus
the cooked, language experiment versus representational narrative, formalism versus historicism. While those pairings identify
crucial concerns, they're often presented in a misleading way. As
their puppeteers face them off in mock combat, they suggest that
poets should have positions, choose sides. But with the best poets
now writing, it's the ability to entertain strong contraries that gives
their work its force. This is not a matter of easy eclecticism. Far from
abandoning critical argument, such poets have internalized argument. Making what Lukács called "biographical form" the armature
of their work, they don't limit themselves with conventional notions
of the authentic self, or the validity of personal experience, but instead open their poetry to uncertainty. In Lowell, the need to give
form to transformative experience when religion itself no longer
seems true leads to an art of the encounter, in which the desire to

account for one's own experience pulls the individual toward others, revealing the basis of a powerful political vision. In Antin, Lowell's putative critic, the urge to make something completely new of the form, instead of guiding the poet away from narrative, brings him into the thick of social and political life. Likewise with Koethe's attempts to follow a Wordsworthian growth of the poet's mind, even while calling into question the reality of such progress; with McMichael's ambition to map the aggregate world of physical fact, even as the isolated self ripples up from the page; and with Glück's tendency to dwell on mythical archetypes even as she undermines such plots. Opposition creates strength. What in lesser poetry would remain mere themes, here become the strongest of formal tensions.

Mah Wallah-Woe

One of the quandaries that all poets encounter, and that in answering they use to define the nature of their work, has to do with perspective. I mean a problem much like the fiction writer's challenge of negotiating the space between her remove as a narrator and her absorption in the lives of her characters. Where is the poet speaking from? Does that speech suggest an open vantage on experience? Does it originate instead in the specific confines of the self, or does it travel between those positions? These are formal questions, but powerful historical currents sluice beneath them. American poetry since the 1950s, with its emphasis on autobiography, has pushed toward constriction. Poets as various as Lowell and Niedecker, Plath and Oppen all write about public life, but compared to their epic-minded predecessors among the High Modernists, they turn much more often to the specific intensities of personal detail, deriving so much of the force of their poems from those very limitations. In fact, from our remove decades later, those autobiographical maneuvers often come across as deliberate attempts to announce newness, to work against Modernist ideas of impersonality.

In the following generation, no poet has defined his work more clearly than Robert Pinsky. You could say that he's done so by going back behind the vantage points of his immediate predecessors, by writing from the widest perspectives. In his first collection of poems, *Sadness and Happiness* (1975), he declared his ambition to understand "the world and all its parts," as the last line of "Tennis" would have it, in downright polemical terms (1996, 220). Even to write a poem called "Tennis," and to follow up on that title with a socially alert and free-ranging discursivity, was to flout conventions of the day, expectations formed by the anguished disclosures of so-called confessional poetry and the inward epiphanies of Deep Image. With his social, reasonable, yet improvisatory voice, Pinsky offered a shift toward inclusiveness.

Reading any of his books since then, you suspect that he can include just about anything. A moment of canniness about this very impulse appears in the poem for which he titles his 1996 collected poems, "The Figured Wheel." Here the image of a vaguely Hindu cycle of being, churning everything in its path, ends with the poet himself:

> ... as it rolls unrelentingly over
>
> A cow plodding through car-traffic in a street in Iasi,
> And over the haunts of Robert Pinsky's mother and father
> And wife and children and his sweet self
> Which he hereby unwillingly and inexpertly gives up, because it is
>
> There, figured and pre-figured in the nothing-transfiguring wheel.
>   (1996, 106)

The effectiveness of that comic moment, the convincing feeling that Pinsky is in fact making a cameo appearance in his own poem that exceeds the scope of his "sweet self," suggests how well he's fulfilled that ambition to write "the world, and all its parts."

And yet. And yet. And yet. If the notion of Pinsky as a poet of global imagination gets to basic truths, it also leaves something crucial to be said about his poems, a contradictory take in the manner of Lionel Trilling's once shocking claim that Robert Frost is "a terrifying poet." For all of Pinsky's public tones and modes of address, he's often a poet of startling intimacy. Despite his monadic vision, it would be hard to find a poet so obsessed with discontinuities. For all of his wholesome reasonableness, there's an abiding melancholy beneath much of his work, a querulous skepticism, a leeriness about consolation. Pinsky's 2007 collection, *Gulf Music*, shows his characteristic skills: a tonal and lexical range that seems as large as the language's, an ability to write in both a pliant metric and a textured free verse, and a deft knack for getting seemingly disparate facets of experience to interlock within the larger mosaics of the poems themselves. But one of the strengths of *Gulf Music* lies in Pinsky's readiness to explore the less evident aspects of his own work.

The very title of the volume, *Gulf Music*, conveys the urge to examine gaps, lacks, and disconnections. This often shows in the forms of individual poems. The first in the volume, "Poem of Disconnected Parts," works by layering a series of strictly end-stopped blank-verse couplets until the disjointed details, often portrayals of political terror and resistance, make a whole. Such a combination of facture and fracture also informs "Poem with Lines in Any Order," which presents spoken pieces of family gossip in fourteen seemingly unconnected lines. Perhaps the most impressive example of Pinsky's work with these jump cuts appears in the title poem, "Gulf Music." Here's an excerpt, a passage that relates the story of a young Jewish immigrant's arrival in the gulf port of Galveston, Texas:

> Morris took the name "Eisenberg" after the rich man from
> His shtetl who in 1908 owned a town in Arkansas.
>
> Most of this is made up, but the immigration papers did
> Require him to renounce all loyalty to Czar Nicholas.
>
> As he signed to that, he must have thought to himself
> The Yiddish equivalent of *No Problem*, Mah la belle.
>
> Hotesy hotesy-ahno. Wella-mallah widda dallah,
> Mah fanna-well. A townful of people named Eisenberg.
>
> The past is not decent or orderly, it is made-up and devious.
> The man was correct when he said it's not even past.
>
> Look up at the waters from the causeway where you stand:
> Lime causeway made of grunts and halfway-forgettings
>
> On a foundation of crushed oyster shells. Roadbed
> Paved with abandonments, shored up by haunts. (2007, 7)

Pinsky's fascination with gaps shows in the formal construction, the overlapping patchiness. An anecdote cuts suddenly into a phrase of nonsense; a rhetorical statement about the past jumps over into a metaphorical description of the Gulf Coast. The poem itself comes to resemble that "causeway made of grunts and halfway-forgettings."

And aren't the improvised, jagged transitions appropriate to the central action of the poem, the narrative of displacement and integration? The figure of the immigrant has always been essential in Pinsky's poetry, as important to it as the farmer to Frost's or the horseman to Yeats's. The immigrant appears in the poems as the hardest worker, the provider, the importer of alien and refreshing customs, the inventor of culture. But he's also the odd man out, the displaced, the individual severed from his own history, the bearer of titanic losses. Even in the very process of becoming a figure for all of our democratic virtues, the immigrant risks losing something of his own human, private self. At the same time that "Gulf Music" celebrates and embodies the ingenuity of the improvising maker, it also relates those subtending sorrows. Language itself here slips repeatedly back into nonsense, a kind of personal creole, as if struggling to capture an imaginative richness that our usual instruments of communication simply can't register. When Pinsky alludes to William Faulkner's statement (from *Requiem for a Nun*) about the presence of the past, Faulkner becomes simply "the man," as if he too might have been forgotten, might have become a haunter.

There's another constitutive absence to this poem. If you read "Gulf Music" without any knowledge of Pinsky's previous work, Morris Eisenberg will seem a perfectly believable, sympathetic character. But he's also the poet's maternal grandfather, a fact that never appears the poem. You would have to know it from Pinsky's "Alphabet of My Dead," a prose poem from his 2000 collection, *Jersey Rain*. The allusion comes off, I think, neither as tricky nor as precious. Instead it gives the poem a dual life: Morris Eisenberg and his family stand isolated by potential forgetting and retrievable by potential acts of memory. In Pinsky's poetry, memory and forgetting entail each other.

Memory's not necessarily a saving grace. At the end of "Gulf Music," in a tone of lament, Pinsky remembers Morris's wife Becky's abandonment of her daughter:

> ... After so much renunciation
>
> And invention, is this the image of the promised end?
> All music haunted by all the music of the dead forever.
>
> Becky haunted forever by Pearl the daughter she abandoned
> For love, O try my tra-la-la, ma la belle, mah wallah-woe. (9)

In the context of this narrative, the syllables "mah" and "woe" are anything but nonsense. Reading this ending, I'm reminded in fact of a devastating sentence from Pinsky's *Democracy, Culture and the Voice of Poetry* (2002): "Dire abandonment, I have read, often makes institutionalized souls, especially children, croon and rock rhythmically: a heartbroken ritual music, a making, a fearsomely minimal created presence" (19). Pinsky's image of the self not only in privacy but also in privation works to counterbalance his global scope. For a supposedly public writer, he has a surprising obsession with the irreconcilable, the neglected.

Pinsky's preoccupation with division and discontinuity extends beyond his examination of the isolated individual: it reaches into an examination of what philosophers might call "quiddity," or "thingness." The central questions these poems raise might be "What are these things that surround us in our lives?" The second section of *Gulf Music* contains a sequence called "First Things to Hand," and Pinsky prefaces the poems with an etymology of the word *thing*, which emphasizes the multiplicity inherent in any single "thing":

> Danish *ting*: a court of justice. Norwegian *ting*: a public assembly; also a creature, a being.
>
> A spoken opinion; an idea; a thought.
>
> A suit; a plaint; a decision; a discourse or a giving voice.
>
> A convocation or parliament of voices.
>
> The *thingstead* is the place of discussion or parley.
>
> From an assembly or law court comes the sense of a matter at hand, an issue for debate. And from that sense comes eventually the nearly opposite sense of a concrete object, a physical or bodily thing. (29)

This concept of an uneasy plurality within the singular suffuses the second section, and indeed the whole book. Consider "Pliers." The poem takes as its occasion the feeling of losing hold, of not being able to cope. Here's how it begins:

> What is the origin of this despair I feel
> When I feel
> I've lost my grip, can't manage a thing?
>
> *Thing*
> That means a clutch of contending voices —
> So my voice:
>
> When my mongrel palate, tongue, teeth, breath
> Breathe
> Out the noise *thing* I become host and guest
>
> Of ghosts:
> Angles, Picts, Romans, Celts, Norsemen,
> Normans,
>
> Pincers of English the conquered embrace. (43)

The second sentence, though it alludes to the history of brutality that trails behind our language, might seem to offer repose and insight by the time it ends; the poet has answered his initial question: the origin of despair, of not being able to "manage a thing," lies in the slipperiness of things themselves. But then the poem takes another turn as it moves toward its ending:

> Embrace
> Of the woman who strangled her sister one night,
>
> All night
> Moaning with the body held in her arms.
> The arms
>
> Of the pliers I squeeze hard squeeze its jaws
> And my jaw
> Clenches unwilled: brain helplessly implicated
>
> In plaited
> Filaments of muscle and nerve. In the enveloping
> Grip of its evolution

Chambered in the skull, it cannot tell the tool
From the toiler
Primate who plies it. Purposeless despair

Spirits
The ape to its grapples, restless to devise.
In the vise-

Grip *Discontent*, the grasper's bent. (43–44)

The anecdote about the murdering sister, like a random slash of
paint across a canvas or a quirked phrase slipped into a jazz solo,
comes out of nowhere. Why does the strange, horrific example
work? I think it does because it conveys ultimate division (murder)
within a relationship that normally suggests ultimate resemblance
and unity. While the murdering sister connects with this theme of
discontinuity, she works as well by not connecting, by remaining
discontinuous. She's the actor who now has become the acted upon,
"helplessly implicated," to steal a phrase from the next tercet. The
poet himself alternates between the position of the actor and the
acted upon, just as he plies his way between the alternating long and
short lines of the tercets. He too becomes, though perhaps in a less
Gothic manner, the grasper wrenched in the grasp of multiplicity.

The image of the poet bent to his task, and bent *by* his task, certainly stands in contrast to the picture of Pinsky as the reasonable
teacher and explainer. That misunderstanding is worth correcting,
since Pinksy's ambassadorial role has a direct bearing on his work—
after all, American social life has long been one of his great subjects.
The usual praise for Pinsky's work as poet laureate, for his renewal of
that slightly silly office, holds that he "brought poetry to the people."
This is not exactly the case. Through the Favorite Poem Project, the
centerpiece of his tenure as laureate, he and his staff gathered poems
from "the people." Watching a Favorite Poem Project video of the
young photographer Seph Rodney reading Sylvia Plath's "Nick and
the Candlestick," or the New York salesman Roger Smith explaining John Ashbery, or the retired teacher Olivia Milward discuss-
ing Goethe, you sense the project has preserved these moments in
which the private and public worlds prove themselves mutually en-

tailing. This is miles away from merely popularizing poetry, much less dumbing it down. If there's a panoramic sweep to the project, an ambition to portray and encourage the nation's mnemonic life, it has its source in the contributions of those separate, private individuals. It's a patchwork.

Throughout *Gulf Music* the poems reveal the same desire, one that has informed Pinsky's work at least since his second collection, *An Explanation of America* (1980). I mean the urge to understand what he calls at the end of that poem "the whole country," a whole that remains "so large, and strangely broken, and unforeseen" (1996, 199). In *Gulf Music* Pinsky recasts that paradox of the broken whole in terms of memory and forgetting, which he sees as inseparable processes within a culture. This cycle informs the very texture of the verse movement. Reading the poems, you sense the extreme singularity, even the forgettability of the examples that Pinsky employs—old baseball players, songs, cartoon characters—even as you watch those details form a whole. In his note to the book, Pinsky relates this process to his ideas about American mass culture:

> Forgetting is never perfect, just as recall is never total: the list or the person's name or the poem or the phone number may be recalled in every detail, but never with the exact feeling it had. And conversely the details may be obliterated, but a feeling lingers on.
>
> That is why the trite notion that Americans lack memory or historical awareness is unsatisfying. *How* might we lack it, severally and collectively? One doesn't need to be a Freudian to understand that memory and forgetting are partial: willful and involuntary, helpless and desperate, in mysterious measures.
>
> Forgetting is not mere absence. The repressed does not simply return, it transforms and abrogates, rising and plunging like a dolphin, or Proteus. (81–82)

In Pinsky's estimation, merely condemning American mass culture turns out to be oddly similar to slavishly consuming it: both stances allow the individual to surrender responsibility to evaluate and cull experience. Pinsky presents mass culture as a phenomenon neither bad nor good in itself. The fact that memory and forgetting entail each other appears likewise as neither wondrous nor lamentable per se; it simply proves the challenge at hand as an individual or a culture attempts creative and moral action. The challenge, as "Pliers" would have it, is to grasp the same force by which we're bent. This endeavor runs beneath so many of the poems in *Gulf Music*. Take the opening of "The Forgetting" (14):

> The forgetting I notice most as I get older is really a form of memory:
> The undergrowth of things unknown to you young, that I have forgotten.
>
> Memory of so much crap, jumbled with so much that seems to matter.
> Lieutenant Calley. Captain Easy. Mayling Soong. Sibby Sisti.

The list of individuals in the fourth line contains both the leading perpetrator of the My Lai massacre and an infielder for the long defunct Boston Braves. Like the mythical Proteus, the cycle of memory and forgetting exists beyond our mortal systems of good and evil. But at the same time as Pinsky presents a monadic whole "beyond good and evil," he dramatizes the necessity of discernment and choice. As the poem snakes its way toward the end, Pinsky addresses Amiri Baraka's anti-Semitic rant at the 2002 Geraldine R. Dodge Poetry Festival in New Jersey:

> Ezra Pound praises the Emperor who appointed a committee of scholars
> To pick the best 450 Noh plays and destroy all the rest, the fascist.
>
> The standup master Stephen Wright says he thinks he suffers from
> Both amnesia and déjà vu: "I feel like I have forgotten this before."
>
> Who remembers the arguments when jurors gave Pound the only prize
> For poetry awarded by the United States Government? Until then.
>
> I was in the big tent when the guy read his poem about how the Jews
> Were warned to get out of the Twin Towers before the planes hit.
>
> The crowd was applauding and screaming, they were happy—it isn't
> That they were anti-Semitic, or anything. They just weren't listening. Or
>
> No, they were listening, but that certain way. In it comes, you hear it, and that
> Selfsame second you swallow it or expel it: an ecstasy of forgetting. (15)

The ending reads not so much as a takedown of Amiri Baraka than as a sudden and disturbing identification. The process of forgetting is nothing new, as the inclusion of Pound in the poem suggests. Nor is it limited to paranoiacs or mindless consumers; it occurs also in the poet's consciousness and in the unfolding skein of his poem. This totalizing view might seem to downplay the moral seriousness of given instances of forgetting, such as that ecstatic nonsense at the Dodge Festival. But by locating such events within a larger cycle, Pinsky not only asks what lasts but also challenges his reader and himself to prove it or make it happen. Earlier in the same poem he throws out this barb:

> You'll see, you little young jerks: your favorite music and your political
> Furors, too, will need to get sorted in dusty electronic corridors. (14)

A funny, cunning tone of reverse psychology quirks these lines. No self-respecting teenager, told her music's ephemeral trash, is going to concede the point; she's going to argue for what she discerns as the best, what she chooses to save from the protean rush of mass culture, just as Pinsky himself does throughout this book. This is why "The Forgetting" reads not as concession but as provocation.

As Pinsky explores the cycle of memory and forgetting in *Gulf Music*, he shows no prejudice in regard to the outcome his poems can pursue or the textures with which he can compose them. If "The Forgetting" reminds us of the acid bath into which time plunges all things, including high art, other poems in the book end up conjuring lasting forces. Take "The Anniversary," which would seem to fit with that given image of Pinsky as the affirmative poet of American public life. The poem, which first appeared in the *Washington Post* a year after the attacks of September 11, reads as a panoramic State of the Union Address in verse. But there's nothing hackneyed, much less jingoistic, about the poem. That's because Pinsky's other tendencies—his melancholic skepticism, his penchant for disconnection and quirkiness—strike a tempering counterpoint with the topical grandeur of the subject. Here are the last twenty lines:

> And if they blow up the Statue of Liberty—
> Then the survivors might likely in grief, terror
>
> And excess build a dozen more, or produce
> A catchy song about it, its meaning as beyond
> Meaning as those old symbols. The *wilds of thought*

Of Katherine Lee Bates: *Till selfish gain*
No longer stain the banner of the free. O
Beautiful for patriot dream that sees

Beyond the years, and Ray Charles singing it,
Alabaster cities, amber waves, purple majesty.
Thy every flaw. Thy liberty in law. O beautiful.

The Rayettes in sequins and high heels for a live
Performance — or in the studio to burn the record
In sneakers and headphones, engineers at soundboards,

Musicians, all concentrating, faces as grave with
What purpose as the harbor Statue herself, *O*
Beautiful for liberating strife: the broken

Shackles visible at her feet, her Elvis lips —
Liberty: not Abundance and not Beatitude —
Her enigmatic scowl, her spikey crown. (21)

You suspect Pinsky might have approached this as if it were a devil-ish homework assignment: "write a poem about America that ends, in full sincerity, with an image of the Statue of Liberty." To achieve that ending he needs to temper the potentially sentimental gesture of describing the monument. We get the idea that the Statue herself might get blown up, and the blithe, skeptical, almost amused tone with which the poet delivers that proposition. There's the workaday detail of the Rayettes in their sneakers. In the final tercet there's the comic moment of comparison to Elvis, as well as the edginess of "scowl" and "spikey." All these tonal nuances, these slight under-cuttings, lend strength to the final image of almost defiant perse-verance.

The wonder of reading Pinsky's poems comes, I think, from his dual perspective, his ability to maintain both sweep and detail. Reading these poems feels like that moment when the airplane as-cends and shapes of highway cloverleafs and baseball diamonds, rivers, industrial yards, and state parks appear with refreshed par-ticularity: jarred from habit, you begin to see the forms they make as they angle against each other, fanning out into a mosaic of plan and accident. But these poems also draw their reader down into the texture of lived experience, like a good walk. There are the bank and the park. There's the street where a turreted Queen Anne stands just around the corner from a row of corrugated trailers. And there are the people who inhabit these structures, the people with their historically created yet resistant inner lives. Theirs turns out to be the most crucial topography of the poems. In *Gulf Music*, more so than in any of his other books, Pinsky has worked to dignify such individuality, giving it the presence and dimension it deserves.

Larry Levis

In Richmond, Virginia, at the corner of Laurel and China, a square of plywood, spray-painted blue, stands bolted to a street sign. A stencil traced from a photo of Larry Levis floats at the center while lines of his poem "Boy in a Video Arcade" race in silver ink around that likeness of their author. I admire the image for its own merits as street art, but there's also some uncanny fit here: Levis's poems themselves read like fugitive infrastructure, stretches of city and countryside poised at the edge of dissolution, yet colored by the imagination that trails through them. To read Levis means to explore how that infrastructure operates, especially as the poems alternate between lyric and narrative, song and story. Maybe to read Levis even more deeply means to ask: what does that movement show us, what does it ask us, about the shapes we live inside and the shapes we make of our lives?

Levis's early poems might not seem to contain his expansive ambitions, but they reveal many of the roots of the later poems. Returning to them after familiarity with the later work often feels like examining a chunk of strata from beneath a family home. In fact, the image of a foundation appears at the very end of Levis's first book, *Wrecking Crew* (1972), in "Unfinished Poem." Here's how that poem concludes:

> I walk the cut road for miles
> where the ground is freezing in the name of the father,
> and the ghost of the cracked snout, and the dull sons

wielding ax handles in the slaughterhouse Day of Our Lord
ruled by bellies. Ruled by the longings of toys
left under houses for years. Left as offerings. Dust.
Puzzles for the woman turned to a doorstep. Over which
you carried all the dead at the moment of your birth. (2003, 20)

The image clusters compressed to the point of detonation, the frag-
mented syntax, the eerie distortion of liturgical idioms, the vague
but insistent anger: these were formal strategies shared by many
poets of the period, poets as righteously indignant at their government as they were totally immersed in Spanish and Latin American
Surrealism. "We were against reason," Levis explained in an interview with Leslie Kelen in 1990, "reason via Dulles and Malaysian
oil rights and other things, against whatever made it possible for our
friends to go off and get killed in Vietnam" (2004, 35). If Levis and
many of his contemporaries soon found their antirational approach
more constrictive than liberating, still, these procedures often allowed them to uncover fundamental images of mind and feeling. In
"Unfinished Poem," for example, the poet unearths two seemingly
opposed urges that will occupy him for the rest of his writing life.
The first is the need to account for others. I have in mind the force
that necessitates not only the shift to the second-person "you" but
also that image of the self carrying "all the dead" at the moment of
its birth. Life in the world of Larry Levis's poems always means life
with other people, even if those others are invisible to us.

And yet the opposite holds true as well. The second urge here
is to render the ultimate singularity of the self, its desires, and the
objects on which those desires fasten. You could say that the whole
framework of the passage works to portray such extreme solitari-
ness: as so often in Levis, the poet appears alone on the road. The
eccentricity of his metaphors and the jumbling movement between
them also lead us to wonder as much about the unique mind that
creates these figures as the world those figures portray.

But the most particular and poignant embodiment of solitari-
ness seems to me the image of abandoned toys. This is a figure to
which Levis returns again and again over the decades. What remains significant every time it appears is the strong feeling of soli-

tude, even isolation. Levis shares this image with Rilke, who himself wrote in 1914 a peculiar essay about children's dolls. To Rilke, dolls are ciphers for our individual yearnings. Abandoned, they become eerie reminders of the failure of any earthbound object of desire. Rilke claims that "the doll was the first to make us aware of that silence larger than life which later breathed on us again and again out of space, whenever we came at any point to the border of our existence" (2018, 56). To arrive at the limits of our existence in the poems of Levis, as in those of Rilke, means to realize our profound singularity, and yet in Levis (the author of *The Dollmaker's Ghost*) the desire to establish some greater connection among others never falls away. Despite his obsession with what he called "the perfection of solitude" (2003, 141), Levis could never be labeled, as Rilke once was by Auden, "the Santa Claus of loneliness" (Auden 1976, 204).

Out of the very tension between his urge to account for and imagine others and his desire to render the profound uniqueness of any one self, Levis wrote much of his best work. He wanted a poem that, while honoring the mysteries of dreams, could traffic among the heat and particularity of the real world—so that, for example, the self at the mercy of oppressive political power, whom we perceive through a jumble of tropes in "Untitled Poem," could become, in "Caravaggio: Swirl & Vortex," the much more moving figure of "my friend Zamora," whose name the poet encounters on the black granite face of Maya Lin's *Vietnam Veterans Memorial* (2003, 148). Beginning in *The Dollmaker's Ghost* (1981), Levis allowed himself more narrative incident in his poems, more abstract meditation, and longer, discursive sentences that unfold through eloquent series of subordinate and coordinate clauses. Here is the opening of one of the poems from that book, "To a Wall of Flame in a Steel Mill, Syracuse, New York, 1969":

> Except under the cool shadows of pines,
> The snow is already thawing
> Along this road . . .
> Such sun, and wind.
> I think my father longed to disappear
> While driving through this place once,

In 1957.
Beside him, my mother slept in a gray dress
While his thoughts moved like the shadow
Of a cloud over houses,
And he was seized, suddenly, by his own shyness,
By his desire to be grass,
And simplified.
Was it brought on
By the road, or the snow, or the sky
With nothing in it?
He kept sweating and wiping his face
Until it passed.
And I never knew. (2003, 52)

"To a Wall of Flame" may seem at first to inhabit the familiar structure of Romantic meditative poems, the ABA arrangement of such old chestnuts as "Tintern Abbey" and "Frost at Midnight," in which the present moment leads to recollection of a past that, in turn, reconfigures the present, to which the poet returns at the end. Levis does inhabit this structure, but with crucial differences. For one thing, he constructs the past out of imagination as much as memory. He writes "I think my father longed . . ." and then he enters that conjectured scene entirely. This moment of transport offers no solving knowledge, as it does in Wordsworth and Coleridge. Instead it burns into the center of the narrative a kind of lyrical brush fire ("his desire to be grass") the meaning of which remains inscrutable even to the father. Levis also complicates the movement between past and present by laminating multiple layers onto each. The poem unfolds, in fact, as a series of time lapses. The 1969 of the title becomes the late 1970s of the opening, which leads to the 1957 of the father's reverie. Then the poet returns to the present, in which he attempts to extrapolate meaning from the imagined scene. And this attempt leads him away in time again, to 1969 and the steel mill of the title:

I remember, once,
In the steel mill where I worked,
Someone opened the door of the furnace
And I glanced in at the simple,
Quick and blank erasures the flames made of iron,

Of everything on earth.
It was reverence I felt then, and did not know why,
I do not know even now why my father
Lived out his one life
Farming two hundred acres of gray Málaga vines
And peach trees twisted
By winter. They lived, I think,
Because his hatred of them was entire,
And wordless. (52–53)

The poem doesn't suggest clear stages for knowledge of the self, the other, and the past. Rather, it depicts a series of overlays, elusive and sometimes illusory slices of time that the individual holds together with both doubt ("I do not know even now") and a faith that ultimately boils down to sheer tenacity ("They lived, I think, / Because his hatred of them was entire"). Formed from glides and segues that both fragment the poem into its constituent moments and incorporate those moments into a sweeping whole, this structure not only reflects but also enacts our deep need to give shape to experience, and while accounting for gaps and discontinuities.

You could say that all poems give shape to experience, but in Levis's work this endeavor often becomes the very subject of the poem, one that he dramatizes by balancing narrative and lyric approaches. These days—long after novels and movies have taken the place of the epic—the poem that combines narrative and lyric has perhaps become something of a default genre. But for Levis, this fusion is never so. He understands its challenges and opportunities, as well as the desires that necessitate it. Foremost, he understands how the lyric/narrative duality so often links with the split between the individual and the culture. That correlation is seldom as simple as it may seem. Song or lyricism can stand for transport, the flight of the subjective self, as in the father's reverie in the car or the son's "reverence" when looking into the flames, while narrative can remain the more social form. But this scheme sometimes reverses itself too. Narrative can figure as personal, as in "telling one's story." Lyric or song can also register as collective by nature: think of ballads or lullabies. After all, what is musical form if not a contract among some community, real or imagined? Even in a free-verse poem with varying line lengths, such as "To a Wall of Flame," the rhythm and lineation themselves are mediating forces, imply-ing that individual expression has been submitted to some outside arbitration. As in a dance, even your most outlandish moves must hold the beat.

Narrative and lyric, self and society—I'm convinced it was the very instability of these categories that, as Levis developed, he learned to employ for intellectual and emotional power. So I want to look finally at "The Spell of the Leaves," from the book *The Widen-ing Spell of the Leaves* (1991). This poem thrives off a shakiness be-tween the self and the other, and between lyric and narrative con-ventions. On its surface, "The Spell of the Leaves" might seem a typical narrative poem. It tells the story of a woman and her son after her husband has left them, then elaborates a series of almost ESP-like connections between the estranged father and son. Here's the opening, in which Levis both sets the scene with all the skill of a superb fiction writer and also cannily subverts his own narration:

> Her husband left her suddenly. Then it was autumn.
> And in those first, crisp days of a new life,
> Each morning she would watch her son, a boy of seven,
> Yawn before mounting the steps, glinting like a sea,
> When the doors of the school bus opened.
> And then she would dress, leaving the back way,
> And hearing or overhearing the screen door close
> Behind her, always, with the same indifferent swish.
> At that hour the frost on the lawn still held
> Whorled fingerprints of cold, as if the cold had slept
> There. Then she would climb in, she told me,
> On the wrong side of the small, open car,
> And sit quite still, an unlit cigarette in her hand,
> And wait for him to come out and drive her
> To work, as always. (2003, 127)

The first thing that strikes me when reading this passage is the beau-tiful precision. Short, sturdy sentences bear great weight gracefully. Levis infuses the moment with pathos but never overinflates his lines. For instance, the simile of the morning sun "glinting like a sea," delayed perfectly by the syntax, before we watch the sparkle from the folding bus doors, makes for a little cinematic marvel. But the real stunner here is the shift in the narration. Because of the pronoun *her* and the declarative sentences in the first lines, the passage has the sound of a story being told by a neutral omniscient narrator. This narrator draws no attention to himself for the first ten lines. So the first-person pronoun in "she told me" arrives as a jolt, introducing a narratorial investment far from neutral. Is the narrator a close friend? A lover? A voyeur? The absent father himself? Some combination of these? We can't be sure. The selves in this poem exist in mysterious and shifting relation to one another. Sometimes these people are painfully distant and sometimes almost permeable. The poem leads us, then, to such questions as, How close can we ever get to one another? How much can we ever know another person? Can we lead our lives together? Or must we finally remain alone?

Such speculations swirl from and return to a central motif in the poem — sleep. The introduction of the narrator as a character intimate with the woman immediately follows the image of a sleeping body ("as if the cold had slept there"). Given that this poem addresses the breakup of a marriage, there's more than a little insinuation rippling beneath that metaphor — who slept where last night, and with whom? But "sleeping together" is one species in a larger order of intersubjectivity — the exchange of what usually remains private, locked in dream life. The poem abounds with images of such exchange. The mother and the son recite a poem by the eighteenth-century visionary poet and madman Christopher Smart. The father attends something that resembles an AA meeting, in which he "steps onto an ark / Of stories, floating" (129). Maybe the most powerful instance occurs near the end of the poem, when the boy, older now, on the way home from school, passes a sleeping homeless man:

> The boy listens & does not listen, both hears
> And does not hear the older students, those
> Already in junior high, lounging outside
> In the corridor, acknowledging each other —
> Their whispers are the high, light rustling of leaves
> Above the vagrant he passes on his way home,

The one intent on sleeping this world away,
A first chill entering the park as he shoves
His chapped hands deeper between his knees—
The boy watches this as if in the sleep of the other (129)

The image of the boy "as if in the sleep of the other" as he crosses the border of selfhood into the consciousness of another, who appears as kind of surrogate for the father, precedes the concluding lines of the poem:

It is as if Time itself
Sticks without knowing it in this wide place
I had mistaken for a moment, sticks
Like the tip of the father's left forefinger
To the unwiped, greasy, kitchen countertop. (129)

The attempt to reconcile, or at least map, the space between people corresponds, and even becomes consubstantial, with the effort to connect isolated moments in a greater expanse of time. And indeed time bends and folds, both in this poem and in the reading of this poem. There are the shifting tenses that have to do with the woman's experience of time, as shaped by her willful forgetting, her disbelief, her grief; there are those that have to do with the conventions of storytelling, moving backward and forward to reflect on narrative incident. And then there's the experience of our needing to reread what we've already read, but with a new perspective on the narrator and on the story being told.

You could say that Levis employs narrative means to reach lyric ends—to break beyond the barriers that channel us through our routine lives, our same old stories. But Levis is too much a realist merely to "employ" narrative. For one thing, the lyric transport in "The Spell of the Leaves" would not be nearly as poignant if we didn't have the story of the family itself, if the poem simply zoomed off into lyric la-la land. Levis trusts the resistance of the real, the palpable life of people and objects that refuse to be aestheticized into vapor. The poem ends with that almost arbitrary, mundane image of the father's finger on a sticky countertop (an image that might seem a parody of Michelangelo's finger of God reaching out to Adam). And for all of his love of curative irrationality and free-flowing subjectivity, Levis tends to portray the dark side of such experience too. If lyric transport, or "the spell," provides a mysterious connection between the mother, the son, and the father, it feels indistinguishable at times from psychic damage, the kind of madness that imprisons the self, like Christopher Smart in his cell in St. Luke's Hospital for Lunatics.

I suspect Levis would sympathize with Whitman in "The Sleepers" when he chants:

> I sleep close with the other sleepers, each in turn;
> I dream in my dream all the dreams of the other dreamers,
> And I become the other dreamers. (1982, 543)

But for Levis, becoming the other dreamers always proves fraught. The father in "To a Wall of Flame," the son in "The Spell of the Leaves," and even the nebulous "you" at the end of "Untitled Poem" remain discrete human beings. At the same time they strive toward a larger, shared vitality, even when it escapes them. Levis writes from this generative place between, where formal tension creates aesthetic power. This may be where narrative selves seek to break out of the structures that bind them and open up to lyric rapture. It may be where lyric selves desire to merge their subjective privacies with story lines that would give shape and meaning to their lives. Levis crafts from his blend of narrative and lyric a gorgeous and surprising poetic infrastructure. But more than that, he manages, with his fused style, to pierce dreams.

Levis achieves this feat not with some kind of Californian woo-woo but through his profound feeling for our lives as citizens. That phrase, "lives as citizens," may sound odd. I don't mean to coronate Levis the laureate of our zoning laws, our divorce rates, our Eisenhower Interstate System. But he realizes something profound about the deep structures of his generation and his era. If his realization could be reduced to a word, it would be one seldom used in discussions of poetry: *mobility*. Levis is the supreme poet of mobility. In his poems we see the American landscape itself as it moves beyond its industrial boom, as it slides from a topography of locale into one of transit. Mobility appears literal, geographic: the poet's life and his poems take place in California and upstate New York, Italy and Utah, Virginia and the Balkans. Mobility proves behavioral too: it includes pharmaceutical and erotic buccaneering, those trips or extracurricular excursions that often appear in the poems. And it includes the permutations of a family that, like so many of his generation, breaks apart and reconfigures—in contrast to the stolidity of the poet's parents on their California ranch.

All of which brings us to a certain presence: the enigmatic father who hovers over all three poems discussed here. He emerges as the poet's actual father, portraits of whom appear repeatedly in Levis's work, including "To a Wall of Flame." But beyond Levis's own father—who comes across as a withholding but ultimately admirable patriarch of the American West—the figure of the father shape-shifts. He appears early on as the autocratic specter against whom a generation rebels, and here he seems to stand for "whatever made it possible for our friends to go off and get killed in Vietnam." In "Unfinished Poem," he is the Grand Guignol who pops up first in the image of the president and then in the distorted Holy Trinity of the slaughterhouse. But less than twenty years later, Levis begins to portray himself as a father in several of his poems—with gorgeous acceptance and generosity in the second half of "Blue Stones," for example, and with unvarnished regret in "The Perfection of Solitude." The figure of the poet as a son and then the figure of the poet as a father—that transition never reads as smooth, never complete. These roles, like all in Levis, exist in a landscape of mobility. Their movement may entail the permeability of selves, "as if in the sleep of the other," and may mean departure away from us into some state of ultimate solitude. One question beneath all of these poems might be, how do we hold together a structure in motion, one not entirely in our power to hold together? I believe that his capacity to render and embody that challenge in the very shape of his poems is what makes Larry Levis not only one of the strongest poets of his generation but also a visionary.

Part Three

Verse Chronicle:
Poems of Force

War and the Iliad

In Marseilles in the late spring of 1942, two writers who would never meet were both struggling to find a berth on a ship to America and both thinking about the same poem. Simone Weil had finished her essay on the *Iliad* two years earlier but still carried the book in her rucksack along with a change of clothes, in case of arrest and imprisonment. Rachel Bespaloff's reading of the poem was likewise colored by the war: her companion that spring, the philosopher Jean Wahl, had been tortured by the Gestapo.

Of the two essayists, Weil remains the better known. "The *Iliad*, or the Poem of Force" follows from the same obsessions found in the letters, meditations, and notebooks Weil wrote while deliberating over her attraction to Catholicism. There's a similar fascination with double binds: suffering and redemption, guilt and expiation descend from abstraction to take on weight in Weil's writing. She has a unique skill for delineating their precise physics. She intuits the ethical center of the poem as if having entered it entirely and felt its properties in action. At the beginning of the essay she writes, "The true hero, the true subject, the center of the *Iliad* is force.... It is that x that turns anybody who is subjected to it into a *thing*. Exercised to the limit, it turns man into a thing in the most literal sense: it makes a corpse out of him" (Weil and Bespaloff 2005, 3). Weil sees force as both the ultimate reality of the poem and the ultimate illusion. Those who believe they've mastered it might be destroyed the next time it seesaws. Homer's poem, Weil believes, reflects force back at the reader; an ethical person must escape the locked cycle of violence and oppression, yet with full knowledge: "Only he who has measured the dominion of force, and knows how not to respect it, is capable of love and justice" (35). Weil's thinking about modernity glimmers through her sentences about Homer. Her conception of the "dominion of force" and her image of inert *things* exerting control over humanity echo the antitechnocratic tones of her essay "The Coming World War," published in 1938. What's more, her sense that men and women can change, can overcome domination, shows the characteristic emphasis upon conversion that fueled not only her religious deliberation but also her earlier political radicalism. Weil's is a twentieth-century Homer.

Bespaloff might have lacked the fire of Weil's prose, and it's probable that before revising her essay for the final time she read and admired "The *Iliad*, or the Poem of Force." But "On the *Iliad*" seems to me the greater of the two essays. Like Weil, Bespaloff comes to that question about art and ethics, but she gives a more surprising, deeper answer. For Bespaloff, art proves the distillation and enlargement of those ecstatic moments when we apprehend ethical truth.

A phrase like "ethical truth" here escapes the neoconservative ring it would gain in the 1980s and 1990s, in critical thought as in politics. It's not that art tells us how to be good. On the contrary: "the step from ethics to morality involves the same betrayal of value as the descent from aesthetic contemplation to hedonism" (90–91). Bespaloff believes that art suspends: it captures and holds ethical truth before it can be polluted by our contingent systems of laws and conventions. Bespaloff's is a modern Homer too: her notion of suspension outside of moral codes rides atop an argument for artistic abstraction, as the novelist Hermann Broch makes clear in his 1947 essay on Bespaloff (included as an afterword to the New York Review Books edition). She finds her paradigm in book XXIV of *Iliad*, when Priam visits the tent of Achilles to plead for the corpse of his son Hector. The grieving king and the killer face each other not with hatred, at least for that moment, but with respect. Priam's act is both horrible to imagine and gorgeous. With his commitment to justice and disregard for established boundaries, "Priam appears in the epic like the poet's delegate," writes Bespaloff. "He typifies the watcher of tragedy, the man who sees it all" (84).

Anyone might disagree with Bespaloff's take on the role of the poet, or Weil's. But even if he or she ends up convinced that art and ethics have nothing to do with one another, the way a poet engages this quandary defines his or her work, whatever the eventual responses may be, and even if they remain implicit or inconclusive. So with Weil's and Bespaloff's examples in mind, I want to consider the results of such reckoning in several recent volumes of American poetry, in particular those that reflect upon the crises of the early twenty-first century—those instances of "force" in Simone Weil's sense that have troubled and deepened individual and public consciousness.

Old War

There's a moment in Elizabeth Bishop's poem "The Moose" when the poet, drifting off during a bus ride, hears the chatter from the seats behind her merging with the voices of grandparents "uninterruptedly / talking, in Eternity" (2008, 160). That border could be the very spot from which Alan Shapiro writes. In his poems, the quotidian realm of family gossip and jokes shades over into the otherworldly. Like those ghosts in the Bishop poem who return to discuss "what he said, what she said ... deaths, deaths and sicknesses," Shapiro believes in the necessity of stories themselves, in their power to offer crucial connection, however tenuous (Bishop 2008, 161).

What makes Shapiro so important right now is not only how he takes over the territory of modern fiction but also taps the reservoir of epic beneath it. The former's impressive enough: while Shapiro's poems maintain the compression and intensity of lyric, they take on story lines we might compare to Philip Roth's or Ann Beattie's, Tobias Wolff's or Ernest Gaines's, as well as the very language of this experience, the twists and bursts, the elegance and saving vulgarity of American speech. His 2008 collection, *Old War*, displays these strengths in poem after poem. At the center of the book lies the desire to maintain love and family in the midst of crisis, including the early deaths of both the poet's siblings, his own divorce, and the international conflict his title suggests. Not only does Shapiro engage multiple subjects, but he makes their multiplicity itself into a poetry remarkable for its integration of subject and form. Even as he avoids overt topicality, these poems show the challenge of holding it all together in the era of "24/7."

Shapiro's portrayal of the present reveals his historical sense. He's as much a modern classicist as Weil and Bespaloff. In the twenty-first century of these poems, force, what Weil calls "that *x* that turns anybody who is subjected to it into a *thing*," appears as a protean shape-shifter. The poet's task, and ours as readers, becomes discovering and salvaging continuity when existence itself seems to channel-surf around us, at turns pleasurable and horrifying. Take the title poem, the first in the book. It begins with a memory of the poet's discovering Thomas Wyatt's poem "They Flee from Me" while visiting "an ancient city / I went to more / Than thirty years ago" (Shapiro 2007, 3). He remembers the poem, and the experience of reading it beside a window, as a place of enchantment, a metaphorical "bower." But then, halfway through, the scene abruptly changes. Here are the last four of the poem's eight stanzas:

> And when the bomb
> Exploded and
> The window shattered
> In a silver shower
> As oddly pretty
> As any in the bower,
>
> A silver shower
> Showering red
> Over the words
> That told how birdsong
> Answered birdsong
> Everywhere overhead,
>
> And everyone
> Who could was running

While the bloody page
Went fluttering out
Into the city
Where the old war raged—

Where was the bower?
And where is it now?
And how do I
Get back to where
The dress is falling
But not yet on the ground? (3)

What's so remarkable about this ending, in addition to the ex-
pert management of sentence, line, and stanza, is the way the form
holds together the seemingly disparate experiences of war and eroticism. For sure, the bombing casts a shadow across the image of the
"bower," and yet irony works not to cancel but to intensify the original desire bound up in the act of reading the poem. In the midst of
the crises that compel Shapiro, the imaginary and real, the horrific
and the sensual, won't remain in their designated categories. He responds neither with postmodern pastiche that would mimic such
scrambling nor with the kind of escapist traditionalism that would
block it out. This poet works not necessarily to overcome predica-
ments but to understand them, experience them more fully, so they
become occasions for genuine response. This is what makes Shapiro
a classicist. His work has that attribute Bespaloff calls "the supreme
detachment of poetry" (Weil and Bespaloff 2005, 48). This has little
to do with emotional "detachment" or lack of sympathy—on the
contrary, she means that the poet, like Priam in the tent of Achilles,
does more than aggressively emote from his assumed stance. Instead he endows his poem with greater emotional power by affecting a suspension, allowing for greater depth of focus. Such a skill
becomes especially effective when it comes to writing within and
about a historical moment.

Take Shapiro's "News Conference," a poem he structures as a
fugal series of questions and answers. Shapiro breaks through those
forms of media transmission that numb not only the daily news but
also a good deal of contemporary poetry. Here's how that poem
begins:

Invisible slow tumbling drift of ash
over the smoking city sifting flake
by flake down out of the Lethe of itself
in a freedom of dispersal beyond belief—

What was the lesson? Steam of whose rage?

particle of particle of dry
continuous blizzard of the long-extinguished
fires of what, in the name of what, now falls
as new flakes falling among the not yet nameless—

What were the numbers saying when they spoke for themselves? (17)

If the italicized questions prove more mysterious, and more insistent and disturbing, than the verbiage of actual news conferences, Shapiro's panoramic description similarly unsettles expectations: as the poem continues, his panning shot joins the war-zone image of the drifting ash with a quotidian American cityscape containing "the hot hoods of jammed traffic." In contrast to the forms of mass media his title invokes, Shapiro's "News Conference" offers a more unsettling, dreamier, and truer link between the wars in the Middle East and us on the other side of them.

This unsentimental engagement with mystery informs the autobiographical sections of this book too. In "Night," in which the poet's deceased brother returns in a dream, the darkness itself becomes a third presence shadowing the brothers, an embodiment of all that was left unsaid between them. At such moments the poems gain power for being unresolved. Shapiro never takes Keats's insistence that the poet remain "capable of being in uncertainties, mysteries, doubts, without any irritable reaching after fact and reason" (1988, 539), as permission to give up on the critical work of the intellect, and yet he pushes himself to the point at which that work can go no further. In this sense Bespaloff's "supreme detachment of poetry" becomes synonymous with supreme engagement. Instead of providing an escape from suffering, these are ways of attending to it.

If the bewildering multiplicity of contemporary life confronts the poet as a challenge, still, much of the power of *Old War* comes from its variety. In the second section Shapiro sets himself up for spontaneity by naming almost all the poems with one word and using that word as the beginning of the first sentence. He titles his third section "From *The Book of Last Thoughts*," and in each of these poems a different character—including a country-western singer, a Catskills comic, and language itself—speaks from the border of life and death. Some of the strongest poems in the book are love poems, written from the early days of a new marriage. Consider "Bower," whose title glances back at that central image from the title poem. Here, in the second of the two long sentence fragments that form the poem, the shadows of husband and wife mingle with those of the branches outside their country retreat:

> Shadow of leaves
> commingling
> with the single
> shadow of our bodies
>
> stirred and lifted
> on the lifting
> scrim between what's
> near and far,
> inside and out,
> all held now
> and slowly moving
>
> toward the sudden rush
> of downpour and
> love cry becoming
> bird call sifting
> in the plush dripping
> of the downpour's
> aftermath. (5–6)

The balance between the short lines and the sinuous sentence structure, held in gorgeous suspension, parallels the subject of the poem, and of Shapiro's whole book—the challenges of holding "near and far, / inside and out" in a way that both maintains the integrity of experience and realizes its multiple facets.

In the early 1990s Shapiro published a collection of essays called *In Praise of the Impure: Poetry and the Ethical Imagination*, a book that celebrated the ways that poetic forms can accommodate the type of narratives we more often associate with prose fiction and essays. He wrote specifically of the power of stories to identify "our provisional position as individuals and cultures in relation to unknown origins and unknown, unknowable ends" (1993, 58). These are the very terms of his own poetry, and the reason I believe thinkers such as Weil and Bespaloff would recognize its power. *Old War* shows Shapiro's prodigious accomplishment, his ability to make lyric art from the stories we tell one another, and to attend to them with a formal classicism that doesn't stiffen but rather enlivens them. He wrests an ethical understanding from the very situations that challenge our too stodgy associations with the word *ethical*—those times when we confront the unknown.

World Tree

What most impressed me about David Wojahn's poems when I first encountered them was their big music, Wojahn's engagement with the actual texture of his medium. I think of a poem from a few years back called "Sawdust" in which the poet conjures the machines in his father's basement workshop with the line "tintinnabulous, their whirr & snarl" (2006, 6). Those four words show Wojahn's range: the movement from arcane Latinate to earthy Anglo-Saxon monosyllables correlates with his grand scope of vision—his ability to render both the bare facts of contemporary life and his sense of human history, as well as his intimations of immortality. Wojahn is obsessed with the entire sweep of human culture and has the tonal and structural gift to paint that whole canvas. His poetry includes allusions to Gnostic devotional poems as well as barroom conversations with Townes Van Zandt. It portrays both Vladimir Lenin and John Lennon. It reinvigorates received forms while allowing the feedback of all sorts of contemporary idioms to leak through the amp.

Back when I first read his poems, Wojahn's ranginess seemed one-half of a dramatic whole—the other being the downward pull of grief. After all, the subject matter of the poems includes the alcoholism and depression of parents, the poet's own melancholy, and the addictions and deaths of loved ones. Wojahn's willingness to take a good look at the worst extends to historical and political

reality too: few poets have written as strongly, for example, about
the degradations of the last few decades of American public life. The
referential largesse of the poems felt, then, like a kind of counterbalance. A collector's wonder at the sheer profusion of culture appeared to lighten the darkness, to prevent the poems from becoming
lugubrious. This still seems the case. But spending more and more
time with Wojahn's 2011 collection, *World Tree*, I've begun to suspect that the imaginative sweep, the inclusiveness, is itself the heart
of his work. This doesn't mean grief and horror have disappeared
from the poems. They haven't. And Wojahn still roots much of his
poetry in the tones and forms of autobiography. But for all its particularity, the self in this book branches well beyond the self: it becomes a representative consciousness. Reading *World Tree*, I think of
a claim Bespaloff makes while considering the figure of Hector: "For
Homer's warrior, glory is not some vain illusion or empty boast; it is
the same thing Christians saw in the Redemption, a promise of immortality outside or beyond history" (2005, 48). Wojahn is a twenty-
first-century poet for sure: *glory* would be an unlikely word in one
of his poems, unless edged with irony. But these poems everywhere
reveal the desire not only to survive but also to remember and be
remembered.

In the second poem in *World Tree*, "August, 1953," for instance,
the speaker imagines the moment of his own birth. Here's the second half of the poem, in which he montages the Gobi Desert in
China with a natal ward in St. Paul, Minnesota:

Mushroom cloud above the Gobi,
.
& slithering toward Stalin's brain, the blood clot
.
takes its time. Ethel Rosenberg has rocketed
.
to the afterlife, her hair shooting flame. The afterbirth
.
is sloshing in a pail, steadied by an orderly who curses
.
when the elevator doors stay shut: I am soul & body & medical waste
.
foaming to the sewers of Saint Paul. I am not yet aware

.

of gratitude or shame.
        I do know that the light is everywhere. (2011, 5)

The poem wends from an elongated free-verse line to the embedded, rhymed pentameter of "I do know that the light is everywhere." The sentences splice from the images of Cold War horror to the mundane detail of the disgruntled orderly, and then to the ecstatic ending. Just as the baby in "August, 1953" exists within the limits of his own body and within history, so too does the poem.

At least since Robert Lowell, poems that balance or counterpose public and private life have become common in American poetry. But Wojahn's originality lies in the ingenious way he employs that form to engage the ancient poetic desire Bespaloff describes: we may never be completely "outside or beyond history" in a poem by David Wojahn, but as he weaves between the world-historical and the personal, this poet renders that desire itself with tremendous feeling, such that supreme ambition and humility seem indistinguishable.

The structures of the book also render the roots and branches of self and world. "August, 1953," for example, follows the opening poem, "Scribal: My Mother in the Voting Booth," which juxtaposes a story of the poet's mother coming down with pneumonia—after waiting in the Minnesota cold to vote for Nixon in 1968—with an account of Sumerian burial rites, then with images of the poet's own son's pneumonia and trip to the emergency room; this latter narrative appears against the backdrop of the 2004 election. If these images of the body politic make a natural transition into "August, 1953," the third poem in the book, "Screen Saver: Pharaoh," picks up on the image of the placenta carried away in a bucket by the hospital orderly. The poem takes place in the late 1970s and centers on a group of hippies who, in their stoned, holistic fashion, have made soup from the placenta of the daughter who's just been born to one of them. The speaker dwells with both irony and genuine nostalgia on that memory, and then as he goes to google his old friends, his screensaver flashes, and the poem ends with a description of that image: a tomb painting of the burial of a pharaoh.

Birth and death, the ancient and the modern, the sacred and the profane, our political life and our individual bodies—such themes weave from poem to poem in *World Tree*. As they recur, do they suggest that meanings run like patterns beneath our everyday experience? Or since these motifs recur in wildly different settings, do they convey how time and circumstance estrange our familiar meanings and confute our attempts at order? Does that concluding appearance of the pharaoh's burial, for example, intimate the greater breadth of a history to which we're connected, or does it simply work as a memento mori? Wojahn doesn't answer these questions. To read these poems means to feel the precariousness and disarray of experience as well as its richness. Weil's conception of force as "that *x* that turns anybody who is subjected to it into a *thing*" courses throughout these poems, and yet in Wojahn's hands that metaphor reveals a flip side, a tentative but insistent spiritualism, most evident in the poet's portrayal of the transmission of images across time.

Two sonnet series at the heart of this book help to elucidate this powerful if subtle portrayal of metempsychosis. The title poem, "World Tree," traces family history through a string of sonnets, each containing references to music and to the (mostly outdated) forms of technology on which it was transmitted. The other series, "Ochre," presents, on facing pages, reproduced images to which the poems respond. The images include photos and drawings of Neolithic cave paintings, early twentieth-century vernacular photography, snapshots from the poet's childhood, an ultrasound printout of his twin sons (taken on September 11, 2001), a digital photo from Abu Ghraib Prison, and a declassified shot of Dick Cheney wearing a gas mask. Here is the first sonnet, "Foot Print & Torch Wipe" (2011, 55), which responds to a cave painting from Chauvet, circa 27,000 BCE:

Something of us to prove our afterlife.
Hurried with charcoal on the cave wall of Chauvet.

The hands drip ochre; they fumble with the Kodak.
What is your mother's maiden name, your wife's

Middle initial? Favorite sport or pet? You have successfully
Changed your password.
            The footprints of the cave's

Last visitor tell us he was ten or twelve.
We know his height—approximately 4′3″.

As his pine pitch torch tapered down, he'd wipe
The ashen top against the cave side, once against an auroch,

Once against a cave bear, the way my father would flick
The wavering orange tip of his Lucky Strike

From his lawn chair to the fireflied grass. Our leavings.
The boy crawled lightward,
      on his feet the pollen of an Aurignacian spring.

Reading this poem again, I'm struck by how the abrupt modulations not only give the verse movement speed and edginess but also render the poem so affecting. Set against the ancient images, those details of the Kodak, the telephone password, and the father's cigarette take on tremendous force: they too seem creaturely imprints, holding their intense singularity within the staggering expanse of time. They're made monumental and minuscule at the same moment—just as our individual lives appear within the larger pattern of history and in their vulnerable particularity; and just as the poem itself gathers authority and historical dimension from the sonnet form while tearing away at that form with the rhythms of free verse, as well as such modern idioms as voice messaging. To attempt to offer "something of us to prove our afterlife" means to feel both enlargement and diminishment.

Giving form to seemingly contrary emotions can often be disorienting, disturbing. In his poems Wojahn faces the terrors of life during wartime, the indignities of a culture that often seems intent on denial, the pain of disease and addiction among family and friends, the private agonies of guilt and self-recrimination, as well as the constant and immediate fact of our mortality. But without skirting such realities, he does something more. Wojahn takes as the epigraph for his title poem, "World Tree," a quotation from Mircea Eliade's *Shamanism*. The quotation describes a ritual meant to enable poetic creation and spiritual freedom: "It is considered best to choose a tree that has been struck by lightning" (Wojahn 2011, 46). Growing from their grounding in the crises, routines, and ecstasies of personal experience and forking out into the entire reach of history, these poems themselves conduct tremendous energy. Contemporary poetry is greater for that voltage.

Emblems of the Passing World: Poems after Photographs by August Sander

In 1929, when August Sander published *Face of Our Time*, his collection of portraits depicting German life, he changed the course of photography. At a time when most art photographers produced what Walker Evans in 1931 described as "misty October lanes, snow scenes, *reflets dans l'eau*, young girls with crystal balls," Sander's documentary approach came as a clarifying, astringent solution. Here were men and women, children and old folks, farmers and bohemians, bricklayers and engineers—all portrayed with startling lucidity (Evans 1980, 185). Evans, who would acknowledge Sander's influence on his own work, hailed *Face of Our Time* as "a case of the camera looking in the right direction among people" (186). More recently Sander has inspired such contemporary photographers as Joel Sternfeld and Alec Soth.

In *Emblems of the Passing World* (2015), Adam Kirsch extends that lineage into poetry. The book includes reproductions of forty-six of Sander's portraits—culled from Sander's *People of the Twentieth Century*, a series that included the photos from *Face of Our Time*—each accompanied by a poem of Kirsch's. The pairings are more than decorous tributes. What makes *Emblems of the Passing World* valuable is the chance to eavesdrop on a conversation between two art forms.

How does a poet respond to Sander's plainness, the almost clinical objectivity with which he renders his human subjects? Kirsch's poems can achieve a similar starkness through "unpoetic" idioms that we would normally expect from essays or editorials. A poet who has published literary criticism as well as studies of Benjamin Disraeli and Lionel Trilling, Kirsch has a talent for abstract statement. Take one of the best poems in this collection, "Farmer Sowing":

> Cities are destroyed by fire
> And rise again;
> Conquering armies melt away,
> Hemorrhaging men;

Leaders proclaim a government
To last forever,
Then walls collapse and refugees
Come pouring over.

Everything passes; he remains
Casting the seed,
Changeless and inescapable
As human need. (2015, 110)

Kirsch keeps the diction plain and leaves the imagery to Sander's photograph. The idea expressed—that while empires fall, farming remains fundamental—may verge on platitude. But through exact management of rhyme and meter, Kirsch reveals the truth in that truism. What's more, such lines suggest that essayistic argument, though hardly fashionable, can be a powerful resource for contemporary poetry.

When the poems don't keep up their side of the conversation, it's because Kirsch allows his argument to stiffen into a position, one that correlates too easily with his "neoformalist" style. He tends to read Sander's images as ironic reminders of the unfairness of life or as memento mori. He concludes too many poems, including otherwise promising ones like "Mother and Child" and "Village Schoolteacher," with a moralizing thud, an effect that belies the openness in Sander's photography. If Kirsch were more alert to surprise, his formalism might transcend to *classicism*, and he might discover more moments like those Bespaloff describes in Homer, when "beneath the marvelous unity of the form, the ambiguity of the real comes to life again" (Weil and Bespaloff 2005, 85).

None of this cancels Kirsch's willingness to learn from a great artist who worked in another medium. And writing about Germany between the two world wars, when many of Sander's photographs were taken, does require at least a dollop of portentousness.

Sander himself hardly escaped history unscathed. His pictures of Jews, blacks, and the disabled didn't square with National Socialist propaganda about the German character. In 1936 the Nazis banned *Face of Our Time* and destroyed Sander's photographic plates. He fled his home in Cologne for the countryside and took his negatives with him. During the war his Cologne house burned down in a bombing raid. One of his sons, a communist, died in a prison camp. Sander himself died in 1964 at the age of eighty seven—appreciated, but without the grand reputation he has now. Kirsch's book testifies to the merit of that reputation, to the specific, unromantic, but wondrous work of a great photographer.

Poets of the Civil War

The Civil War was our defining tragedy. Most of us know that commonplace. But maybe because it's so obvious, the war can also seem a blind spot on our collective consciousness. After the atrocities of September 11, the experts on TV kept referring to the War of 1812 as the last conflict in which an American city had been attacked. Vicksburg and Atlanta could have been cities on the moon to them. You can see how such reasoning works. It's easier to discount the suffering a country inflicts on its own. It's easier, especially since this war ended the abomination of slavery, to gloss over its horror. What makes J. D. McClatchy's collection of Civil War poets so valuable is the power with which it disrupts that trend, corroborating William Faulkner's quip "The past is not dead. It is not even past." It's not necessarily the consistent quality of the work included that gives the anthology its power. Many of the poems, as their editor admits, are second rate; several seem awkward imitations of Milton or Walter Scott. No, it's the immediacy with which poetry itself confronts us. McClatchy explains in his elegant introduction that while there remains no American *Iliad*, he has set out to create a panorama made of the partial glimpses the poems provide.

What does that leave to readers who desire more from poems than historical interest? A good deal. There are six excellent poems by Emily Dickinson, which set explosive interior drama against their uncharacteristic topicality. The strongest poem in the collection is Walt Whitman's devastating "Vigil Strange I Kept on the Field One Night," and the twenty-six pages of Whitman form the center of the book. Fine work by lesser poets also lends power to the anthology. The disillusioned poems of the Connecticut writer John W. De Forest seem to me particularly striking.

But maybe the most impressive selection is that of Herman Mel-

ville. Some of the ornament that Melville could sustain in his mus-
cular prose seems like conventional clunkiness in his poems. But
consider "Inscription," written after the horrific battle of Fredericks-
burg:

> To them who crossed the flood
> And climbed the hill, with eyes
> Upon the heavenly flag intent,
> And through the deathful tumult went
> Even unto death: to them this Stone—
> Erect, where they were overthrown—
> Of more than victory the monument. (2005, 100)

This poem flows from the same impulse that led Melville to give
Billy Budd the subtitle *An Inside Narrative.* It endeavors to remind us
of the ineffable "something more," the incommensurable lost lives
that haunt our official histories. The fact that Melville visited the
front in 1864 carries some interest, but it's not what makes his war
poems superior to much of the political poetry of today. Melville is
a great writer because he registers his convictions in aesthetic form
itself, in the suspenseful surging of the single sentence, in the turn
from the literary adjective "deathful" into the terrible fact of the
noun "death," in the sudden stop that comes with the imperative
in the penultimate line, in the ramifying ending on "monument," a
word he both sincerely means and means to question. It's precisely
this transmutation of movement into action that happens so seldom
in topical poetry. When Rachel Bespaloff writes that poetry "re-
possesses beauty from death and wrests from it the secret of justice
which history cannot fathom" (Weil and Bespaloff 2005, 49), she
may seem to be swelling her organ notes. But she makes a fine distinction in that statement: she implies the power of poetry, even as
it mirrors life, to create a world apart from the one it reflects. This
virtual space of the poem provides not escape but rather an inten-
sification of thought and feeling.

Up to Speed

Rae Armantrout's poems flow from an urge at least as old as Sappho—the desire to peel away "Appearance" and expose "Being." In Armantrout's case, this endeavor reveals the influence of L=A=N=G=U=A=G=E poetry and the poststructural theory that lay behind that movement. Taking the name of a late 1970s literary magazine, this movement insisted upon the "materiality of the signifier." That is, L=A=N=G=U=A=G=E writers wanted to "repossess the word," a task proposed by Charles Bernstein and Bruce Andrews in the introduction to their anthology *The L=A=N=G=U=A=G=E Book* (1984, ix). Repossess the word from what, though? This was less clear. For some, the illusion of transparency, the conception of language as a reliable exchange, loomed as the enemy. For others, "subject positions" of speaking and writing—the asymmetrical power dynamics inherent in the situations from which language issues—were what needed to be exposed. And for a few, the expressive capacities of lyric itself seemed to blame, and a new antipoetry appeared in order. Any of those notions might produce compelling poems. The commitment of such writers to "repossess the word" might even resemble Simone Weil's insistence that the poet be someone "who has measured the dominion of force, and knows how not to respect it" (Weil and Bespaloff 2005, 35).

But how about the actual experience of reading such poetry? Armantrout provides a paradigmatic case. Although her humor works to inoculate her poems against the stiffening effects of doctrine, the original impulse of L=A=N=G=U=A=G=E poetry, to "repossess the word" and thereby expose the fatuity and collusiveness of conventional forms of discourse, remains strong in her work. And since *Up to Speed* (2004) is a book about time, she concerns herself with a parallel claim: that the chronological sequences that make up our commonly accepted narratives are fatuous too.

Armantrout's best instincts are those of the satirist. She has the amusing tone (when she does have tone) of the faux naïf. In her better poems, such as "The Cell Phone at Your Ear May Not Exist," she employs the mashed-up idioms of mass culture, the speech of advertising and tabloids, the banter of clerks at fast-food joints. But imagine if one of the best satirists—say Rochester or Mina Loy—stopped in the middle of a poem to lecture the reader on epistemology. Now imagine that this lecture was always the same. You'd have something like these lines about Christmas that begin the poem "Afterlife":

> Heaven is just this:
>
> Twined strands
> Of winking bulbs
>
> And shiny, fragile ornaments
> Understood to represent grace
>
> Weakly.
>
> It's all this:
>
> The paleness of representation,
> The understanding,
>
> The fond sadness it causes,
>
> The shining circularity. (2004, 9–10)

When you read early Williams, you feel how his verse movement thrives on unpredictability. The mind of the poet might rest on the sheer affirmation of "they taste good to her," the desolate rage of "no one to drive the car," some ad hoc theory about Shakespeare, or any number of other conclusions. Such surprise generates the music of those poems. That's what's missing from Armantrout. You know you're going to arrive in the end at something like those last six didactic lines about the failures of representation. This might seem like challenging avant-garde poetry, but in fact it's too easy to comprehend, too expository.

Recyclopedia: Trimmings, S*PeRM**K*T, *and* Muse and Drudge

Recyclopedia (2006) collects three of Harryette Mullen's book-length sequences, first published by small avant-garde presses in the early

1990s. All three show the poet's characteristic talent for carrying her wordplay beyond whimsy and into crucial thinking about race and gender, sex and violence, economics and aesthetics. Most importantly, Mullen's poems thrive upon the messiness of real life.

Like Armantrout's, her work may suggest affinities with L=A=N=G-U-A=G=E poetry. But for me, the best writing associated with this movement turns out to be the less programmatic. Like Lyn Hejinian's *My Life* (1980), Mullen's early poems show the influence of Gertrude Stein—an understandable model for L=A=N=G=U=A=G=E writers, this modernist intent upon crashing and churning her words into materiality. They're also given to showing up the illusions of seemingly natural speech, exposing the ways our language bites us back. At the same time, and again like Hejinian at her best, Mullen remains bound up in affects, dramatic situations, states over which the individual doesn't have full power.

All three series collected in *Recyclopedia* are mature, moving, and provocative work, but the final one, *Muse and Drudge*, remains the strongest. This sequence of eighty-two untitled, unnumbered poems, each composed of four quatrains, at different times draws on the blues, hip-hop, classical Greek lyric, and contemporary feminist theory. But even given all that cultural framing and the seemingly constrictive force of Steinian condensation, Mullen surprises again and again with the range of real experience she can conjure, enact, parody, praise, mock, and think inside of.

Consider these two quatrains from early in the book:

> black dispatch do do run run
> through graffiti brierpatch
> scratch a goofered grapevine telegraph
> drums the wires they hum
>
> mad dog kiwi antifreezes
> green spittle anguished folks
> downwind skidrowed elbow greasers
> monkey wrench nuts and bolts (2006, 107)

At first glance, since the verse line's so compact and rich, this may seem like Mullen at her most absurd or nonsensical. But these verbal and imagistic clusters resolve into a particular city scene: black kids fleeing the cops, derelicts drinking cheap liquor ("mad dog kiwi antifreezes"), and so on. If that passage shows the careful third-person plotting that Mullen manages, the following quatrains reveal the eroticism near the heart of these poems:

> handful of gimme
> myself when I am real
> how would you know
> if you never tasted
>
> a ramble in brambles
> the blacker more sweeter juicier
> pores sweat into blackberry tangles
> going back native natural country wild briers (101)

The pleasure of reading such lines comes both from the unabashed strength of the voice and the play of a phrase like "handful of gimme" against the elaborate, almost Elizabethan sexual puns. Nuance also informs one of the plainer poems of the series (the one beginning "dark eyed flower / knuckling under") in which the poet bemoans the busyness and tedium of her life and longs for some kind of artist's retreat:

> live in easy virtue
> where days behaving send
> her dance and her body
> forward to a new dress
>
> a pad for writing
> where dreams hit el cielo
> crack the plaster foul mood rising
> it's snowing on the radio (119)

What most impresses me about *Muse and Drudge*, and Mullen's whole achievement, remains the ability of the writer of those first two thick, playful, and emotive examples to be the same writer of softer, subtler moments. The everyday simplicity of the imagined pad of paper, not to mention of the modesty of that desire, contrasts with the grandiose humor of dreams cracking through the plaster into "el cielo." And then the poem ends, delicately, perfectly, on

"it's snowing on the radio," a phrase both idiomatic and ungram-
matical — childishly, wonderfully absurd. This is what I most admire
about Mullen. She's a poet not only of dynamite compactness but
of stunning range.

Tonal variety is more than felicity here, more than a matter of
skill. Mullern's commitment to radical abstraction makes her poems
of race and gender, sexuality and justice, so true to those occasion-
ing forces, so reluctant to paper them over with rhetoric, but to
find and know their forms, and through them the new forms they
inspire in the free imagination of the artist. This is what Rachel
Bespaloff meant when, writing of Homer's talent for hewing figures into existence, she declared, "beneath the marvelous unity of
the form, the ambiguity of the real comes to life again" (Weil and
Bespaloff 2005, 85).

The Epistles of Horace

It's hard for me to resist hearing something American in David
Ferry's translations of Horace's *Epistles*. In his final verse letter, the
one known as "The Art of Poetry," we hear "My aim is to take familiar things and make / Poetry of them" (2001, 169). And isn't this inclusiveness — which takes career advice, war stories, even facetious
mimicry of salesmen, and makes poetry of them — the same blend
of realist pragmatism and libertine imagination that animates, say,
Robert Frost's descriptions of scything, or Frank O'Hara's improvs
on rush-hour New York? Since Horace was the original master of
such counterpoint, we are, true enough, hearing Horatian notes in
these American poets. But returning to David Ferry's rendering
of *Epistles* while thinking about the whole phenomenon of modern
classicism, from Weil and Bespaloff through Harryette Mullen, I
want to stick with that first impression. There's no ulterior motive
hiding in the wings, no claim of cultural nationalism. My interest in
an American Horace has to do instead with describing the achievement of David Ferry. A superlative poet in his own right, Ferry has
published four complete volumes of classical translation in the last
three decades: *The Epic of Gilgamesh*, *The Odes of Horace*, *The Eclogues*

of Virgil, and, in 2017, *The Aeneid*. There are precious few comparable collections of classical translation by first-rate contemporary American poets—Jim Powell's Sappho and Reginald Gibbons's Sophocles are among the few that come to mind. With an ear for the tone of the original and for contemporary "sentence sounds," Ferry has achieved a version of *Epistles* that neither plays fast and loose with the original nor pedantically crabs idiomatic speech. Like a great novelist or movie director dealing with a historical subject, Ferry knows that not only do we read the historical period but, more important, it reads us. Horace offers Ferry a chance to show what his language can do, and the results should encourage anyone interested in an American poetry with historical depth. In such translation, the counterpoint between form and freedom reveals itself in the push and pull between the source and target languages: the original both demands formal fidelity and allows the contemporary poet to explore prosodic and idiomatic resources that might otherwise have lain dormant. This is why translation remains vital to non-translated poetry. Rachel Bespaloff's account of the suspension of conventional moral systems, exemplified by Priam's crossing the battle lines to meet with Achilles, here parallels historical and linguistic border crossing, one that enlarges the target language. Up until now in this consideration of contemporary collections I've examined poets' ethical reckoning as a critical, even grave, endeavor—coming to terms with what Weil called "the dominion of force." But a translation like Ferry's suggests how the same process might also take on a forward-looking, replenishing character, and with a streak of comedy.

In the case of Horace, the balance between traditional verse form and modern idiom reveals more than the translator's technical facility; it shows his understanding of the original. Writing twenty years before the birth of Christ, Horace himself was proud of both bringing the Grecian songs into Italy and portraying everyday Roman life. The play between high and low that appears in specific figures of speech runs in rough parallel with the range of subjects, from Emperor Augustus's chamber to the artisan's hovel—poems that read like an exhilarated, often lurid tour of society itself. So maybe Horace's line on walking shoes will best illustrate how well the Roman verse fits in Ferry's American English. Here's the original: "Si pede maior erit, subvertet, si minor, uret." A "literal" version would be "If it is too big for the foot, it trips him, if too small, it chafes." The line's a short piece of common sense but also a playful ars poetica: Horace's verb is a cognate of *versare*, which means "to turn," and thus of "verse." Before Ferry, the eighteenth-century poet John Gay put this to English in the following embellishment from his poem "Trivia":

> Should the big laste extend the shoes too wide,
> Each stone will wrench th'unwary step aside:
> The sudden turn may stretch the swelling vein,
> Thy cracking joint unhinge, or ankle sprain;
> And when too short the modish shoes are worn,
> You'll judge the seasons by your shooting corn. (1923, 66)

Gay conveys the ars-poetical pleasure by getting his poetic feet to slide into the strictures of the couplet with a periphrastic looseness that not only multiplies Horace's line by six but gives us the image of the undone lace itself, as well as the extravagant pun on "corn." Now here's Ferry's version: "Too big, it makes you stumble; too small, it pinches" (2001, 49). At first it is the no-nonsense brevity that impresses. But then the rhythm asserts itself. The line would almost be unvaried iambic pentameter, except for a syllable thrown in right at the end of "stumble." Hearing the twelve-syllable line is like watching a walker stumbling before regaining his stride. This may sound like cleverness, but the play of traditional form and contemporary idiom gives this rendering of *Epistles* its depth and color. Ferry's version may seem plainer than Gay's, yet the verse line of Gay and his Augustan Age contemporaries, slightly subverted yet still rigorously pentametrical, allows the translator to invoke the tradition of English prosody for his own purposes. If Ferry's line appears simple in instances like this, it's a subtle kind of simplicity—a blend of speech and verse form that has the quiet deftness of Frost's own elongated line "My long scythe whispered and left the hay to make." If such movement intentionally "stumbles" at points, on the whole it shows a fluidity remarkable for correlating with Horace's own movement through varied subject matter. Consider how Ferry's prosody shifts as he translates Horace's address to Aristius Fuscus in the tenth epistle. Writing from his Sabine farm, the poet asks his cosmopolitan friend:

> If we're supposed quote "to live in accordance with
> The nature of things" unquote and therefore have to
> Choose where best to do so, then, I ask you,
> Is any place better for this than the blessed country? (47)

Not only has the translator varied his pentameter with frequent anapestic substitutions—the last line stretches to fourteen syllables— he's inserted the colloquialism "quote ... unquote." The addition serves a practical purpose: it conserves the sound of a familiar maxim spoken with a hint of sarcasm. Yet there's still something impetuously pleasing here: the immediate shiftiness of common speech has challenged what Auden once called "poetry with a capital 'P.'" Since such duplicity in fact serves to delineate precise shades of meaning, the effect feels something like O'Hara's description of stormy weather in Manhattan: "I was trotting along and suddenly / it started raining and snowing / and you said it was hailing / but hailing hits you on the head / hard so it was really snowing / and raining" (1964, 78). Yet Ferry shifts once again, this time back into a more traditional idiom. Here are the lines that follow:

> Is the grass less fragrant or less shining than
> Libyan mosaics? Is the water that does its best
> To burst the leaden pipes in city streets
> Purer than water that makes its murmuring way
> Downhill in mountain streams? In your atria,
> Among your elaborate columns, you've planted trees,
> And houses with views of the fields are always praised.
> Drive nature out with a pitchfork, she'll come right back,
> Victorious over your ignorant confident scorn. (47–49)

Just as nature "comes right back," so Ferry's diction returns to a more Augustan register. If the entire translation were like this, these *Epistles* would be too Olympian; all in the more casual idiom, too showy. Like the atria providing both "elaborate columns" and natural vistas, Ferry's tone gives pleasure through variety. And if the translator continues to vary the meter, he never drags on the rhythm of the pentameter. The second line might have thirteen or fourteen syllables, depending on the pronunciation of "Libyan," yet it maintains accentual-syllabic rigor, and the more traditional ten-syllable pentameter—"To burst the leaden pipes in city streets"—returns in the next line, repressurized.

The larger structure of *Epistles* depends upon these shifts. Throughout the poems Horace organizes—and subverts his organization—by employing sets of doubles: the poems are letters masquerading as poems, and poems disguised as letters; they address Emperor Augustus, and they address errand boys; they retreat from the public arena with scorn for vulgarity, and they circle back with voyeuristic fascination; they offer avuncular wisdom, and they turn on themselves in moments of self-recrimination, calling their own author "a pig from Epicurus's sty, fat, sleek, well cared for" (23). To miss the tonal shifts would be to miss crucial turns on the tour through society that these poems offer. This is why we're fortunate to have Ferry's version. The translator's prosody accommodates both strict iambs and phrases like "couch potato," "hornswoggle," and "snug as a bug in a rug," and the book as a whole benefits from his suppleness.

Ferry's balance of meter and tone should also speak to contemporary poetry's own need to balance tradition and innovation. Horace may stand for the "monumental poet" who writes himself into immortality, yet his monument is a contradiction. He can claim, as he does in one of his most famous odes, that his work is more resilient than the Egyptian pyramids only because the poet's work is made of fleeting human breath. Two thousand years before poststructuralism, Horace was fascinated by the way language shifts beneath us, betrays us even:

> Just as in forests in the changing year
> New leaves come in and the oldest drop away,
> So it is with words: the old ones die away
> And the new ones bloom and prosper in their time. (155)

Reading these lines from the final epistle, the one known as "The Art of Poetry," you hear the artist in his workshop explaining how easily his medium gets corrupted; then you look down to see that all the time that he's talked, he's also fashioned something beautiful and enduring. The problem he states is real: who hasn't heard his or her own dated words crackle off like so many dead leaves? Yet in Horace the challenge of language's transience is playfully expressed in the very speech that forms the work.

For Horace history is not necessarily "the past." He writes in Sappho's or Alcaeus's stanza—or, in the case of *Epistles*, in Homer's hexameter—not to monumentalize the dead but to walk and speak with them. "Words that have fallen may rise again," we hear a few lines after those quoted above, and hear in that "risen" (*renascentur*) the metaphor of seasonal death and rebirth returning, just as Horace tells us old speech may return (155–57).

The Horatian conception of language, in which words turn out as shifty as any other natural process, should quell the notion that only in the last century has philosophy discovered the duplicities of language—or worse, that this is the breaking news all poetry must now address. So-called narrative or scenic poets and their avant-garde counterparts both too often believe this. The former may claim Frost's mantle, but there's very little in them that does not love a wall. Many avant-garde poets, on the other hand, accept that words are duplicitous but take this as permission to give up on subjects. Many would claim O'Hara in their pantheon, but would they deign to depict, believably, a downtown street during lunch hour? This might inconveniently prove that the everyday exists.

It's refreshing, then, to have in living American English the curative clarities of the great comical literary criticism not only of the "Art of Poetry" but of all the *Epistles*, and to consider Horace's conception of history and the present interchanging in language. Such ideas come alive through Ferry's own literal "sense of time"—a crucial skill, this phrase a musician might use to discuss how melodies react to rhythm and harmony. Indeed in Ferry's version of Horace, the literary-historical "sense of time" and the immediate musical "sense of time" are inseparable. Take this passage from the second book of *Epistles*, in which Horace jokes about the suggestion that he compose his lines on the way to visiting friends:

Oh, sure. Tell me about it. First there'll be
A contractor with his gear and all his workmen,
And then a giant crane in the way, first hoisting
A great huge stone and then a great huge log,
And then here comes a funeral procession
Jostling its way along through all the traffic
Of great huge rattling wagons, and all of a sudden
A mad dog runs by one way through the street
And a filthy runaway pig the other way.
"Working on writing sonorous verses enroute?" (137–39)

These lines, chosen almost at random, show Horace to be a master of the kind of comic cinema that could have been filmed by Hawks or Fellini. This passage also sounds like the complaint about the deciduous nature of words: Horace writes poetry, though he says he can't; he's grouchy about his social responsibilities but addresses a friend; he carps about the traffic in Rome, but his *Epistles* everywhere thrive on metropolitan bustle.

This comedy has new life in Ferry's version, in the specific counterpoint between the elaborate parallelisms of Roman syntax and the modern American voice. Like chord changes beneath a melody, the metrical system shows through: eccentric as these lines may be, they're all pentameter, the meter used to attend to Horace since the days of Pope and Gay. But Ferry employs his own instrument, whose range includes the wise-guy interjections "Oh, sure" and "Tell me about it," the rustic contraction "there'll," and the repetition of "great huge"—a phrase teetering between blunt diffidence and childish exuberance in its effort to convey Horace's ironies.

Horace's poetry itself is a form of translation, and not only because of the Greek prosodic form—Horace makes clear the difference between the experience represented and the literary work itself, as if they were themselves the "source" and "target" languages of translation. The difference becomes comic when he convincingly describes walking through Rome even while complaining that his walks distract him from writing. Yet the sincerity—Horace's and Ferry's—is just as real as the cunning. At the very end of "The Art of Poetry," Horace warns his readers away from the character of the poet:

> If he catches a man, he'll read that man to death.
> He's a leech that won't let go till he's full of blood. (185)

Horace is describing another, unnamed poet, but the self-abnegating humor, the deflected candor, is unmistakable. Throughout *Epistles* Horace mediates his didactic tone by admitting his own biases and limits. The variety of Roman life that Horace represents gains profile and dimension when he allows his subjects to break through whatever frame he has placed around them. Reading *Epistles*, you might begin to suspect the bustling life of Rome to be the poet's own creation—and then he stops: he turns on himself in a moment of self-knowledge, whether lighthearted or severe, and leaves his reader stunned, seeing the men and women of Horace's city walking through the streets without him.

"The Wolf, the Snake, the Hog, Not Wanting in Me": Poetry and Resistance

Among contemporary readers, even those passionate about politics, distaste for protest poetry must be endemic. I have in mind the suspicion of didacticism, the feeling that "viewy" poems replace emotion and imagination with tactics. During the Iraq War two American poet-critics, W. S. Di Piero and David Wojahn—who've both written distinguished and original political poetry—published even more forceful articulations. Each pointed to an irony: not only do most protest poems remain mere versified opinion, but they tend to mirror the smugness they rail against. Di Piero described a stand-off in which "absolute pacifism and absolute jingoism each believe that God or Absolute Principle is on its side, which has the irreducible moral value of being right" (2004, 40). Wojahn wrote of these protest poems that "their bad writing connotes a lot of silly, sentimental, and sanctimonious thinking—the very sort of thinking which, allied with greed, helped to bring America into Iraq in the first place" (2015, 32). To read a high-minded anthology such as *Poets against the War* (2003)—as well as recent poems addressing the debacle of the Trump presidency and the bigotry and avarice it represents—is to see what these critics mean. Such poems are predicated upon the assumption of the poet's and reader's being on the same side, and being right; they eliminate what makes any poem feel real and engaging, and so distinct from the language of demagogues: uncertainty.

But does this have to be the case? Maybe what's missing is an account of how uncertainty and conviction might entail each other in political art—and how such art might prove both formally true and politically effective.

A poem of Walt Whitman's provides a good place to start. With its effusion of civic love, "Crossing Brooklyn Ferry" hardly seems a protest poem. It begins to form in a notebook from late 1855. Whitman's still glowing from the letter Emerson sent him in July. He copies over the philosopher's salutation, "I greet you at the beginning of a great career." Then he begins a rough sketch that will burgeon into "Crossing Brooklyn Ferry":

> dazzle in a track from
> the most declined sun,
> the lighters—the sailors
> in their picturesque costumes
> the nimbus of light
> around the shadow of my
> head in the sunset. (Kaplan 1980, 207)

When Whitman finishes the poem the following year, this "nimbus of light" becomes not only a central image but also an entire reimagining of the body politic as a democratic being. Here's how it appears in the third section:

> I too saw the reflection of the summer sky in the water . . .
> Had my eyes dazzled by the shimmering track of beams,
> Look'd at the fine centrifugal spokes of light around the shape of my
>   head in the sun-lit water . . . (1982, 309)

And here's how it reappears in the ninth section:

> Receive the summer sky, you water! and faithfully hold it, till all
>   downcast eyes have time to take it from you;
> Diverge, fine spokes of light, from the shape of my head, or anyone's
>   head, in the sun-lit water . . . (313)

As Whitman repeats it, the image of the nimbus with its "fine, centrifugal spokes of light" melds an ultimate appreciation of selfhood (it comes pretty close to the familiar portrayal of Narcissus) with an ultimate vision of collective exchange. The almost angelic figure of the self—the hub from which stream those lucent spokes of light—can be inhabited by different selves.

The tone feels almost ecstatic, but there's a tension implicit even in the first two syllables Whitman adds to the final poem: "I too." Philip Fisher claims that Whitman's image "eludes what we might call the depression of common experience, the feeling that whatever is there for everyone is unavailable simultaneously to let me experience my own singularity as thrilling" (1999, 68–69). The space between the individual and society proves a potential gulf as well as a connection. And Whitman looks for ways not only to elude this tension, or reveal it as an illusory construct, but also to engage it. If he sees how the democratic project might drift into what Fisher names the "depression of common experience," he recognizes too how independence can shade over into mere selfishness, and worse.

Consider how, in the sixth section of "Crossing Brooklyn Ferry" Whitman takes onto himself the burden of evil:

> It is not you alone who know what it is to be evil;
> I am he who knew what it was to be evil;
> I too knitted the old knot of contrariety,
> Blabb'd, blush'd, resented, lied, stole, grudg'd,
> Had guile, anger, lust, hot wishes I dared not speak,
> Was wayward, vain, greedy, shallow, sly, cowardly, malignant;
> The wolf, the snake, the hog, not wanting in me,
> The cheating look, the frivolous word, the adulterous wish, not wanting,
> Refusals, hates, postponements, meanness, laziness, none of these
>   wanting. (1982, 311)

The sudden plunge into negativity, followed by its absorption into the exultant tone of the whole, may seem one of Whitman's familiar moves. In "There Was a Child Went Forth," it comes with the line about "the blow, the quick loud word, the tight bargain, the crafty lure" (492). In the eighth section of "Song of Myself," it begins with the line "The suicide sprawls on the floor in his bedroom" (195). This modulation is a formal device: by its tempering contrast, it strengthens the celebratory tenor of the whole. But looking at the passage from "Crossing Brooklyn Ferry," you hear how fully experienced such a downward turn can be in Whitman, how far beyond technical maneuvering. It has to do with the very body of the poet: the argument has been circuited through the lyric "I," wired into experience, cut from the surrounding static of public speech.

The poet has reached beyond private grumbling, exceeded the very limits of being an individual. With his rapid series of admissions Whitman sets himself up for the descent to the ultimate depth that comes with those cinching monosyllables, "the wolf, the snake, the hog." There's an undeniable thrill, an exhilaration to this moment. In accepting his degradation, the poet seems to become sheer animal urge and drive, even as he loses his identity.

For sure, the moral system is clear enough—even as he accepts these bad things as his own, we know they're still bad things. But the ambiguity doesn't end there. I mean that Whitman shows evil adopting the various forms of individual withdrawal; his image of corruption here is not, as images of corruption tend to be in Whitman, effete and European. The abject animal reads in fact like the flip side of Whitman's own picture of native self-determination. In his 1855 preface to *Leaves of Grass*, he writes of his ideal citizen: "Obedience does not master him, he masters it" (9). In "The Song of the Broad Axe," his ideal America is a place where "the men and women think lightly of the laws" (335). Admitting in "Crossing Brooklyn Ferry" to the perils that might edge these images, Whitman in fact toughens his convictions about American exceptionalism. His national ideal appears more possible, not to mention less chauvinistic, when we hear him admitting to its real dangers.

Following Whitman's progress, you see this dialectic intensify, even to the point of breakdown. At the beginning of the 1870s he attempts a reply to Thomas Carlyle's "Shooting Niagara" in the prose that becomes *Democratic Vistas*. He finds the Scotsman's antidemocratic essay repugnant, but before identifying in America the "loftiest final meanings, of history and man" (993), he argues with such vehemence against the worst of his own culture that the overall tone of the book becomes deeply melancholic. ("Passage to India," the poem in which he attempts to address the same national malaise, is more balanced but less remarkable than its prose counterpart.) The reasons for his disenchantment lie in the impeachment of Andrew Johnson, the corruption of the Grant administration, and the beginning of the Gilded Age. But Whitman locates such dissipation in the American multitude itself: "The best class we show, is but a mob of fashionably dress'd speculators and vulgarians" (938). His disgust becomes so powerful that it seems at times to apply to the actual existence of his country, the very sweep of its sheer facts, which we normally take to be the material of his poetry. He writes:

> Fearless of scoffing, and of the ostent, let us take our stand, our ground, and never desert it, to confront the growing excess and arrogance of realism. To the cry, now victorious, the cry of sense, science, flesh, incomes, farms, merchandise, logic, intellect, demonstrations, solid perpetuities, buildings of brick and iron, or even the facts of the shows of trees, earth, rocks, etc., fear not, my brethren, my sisters, to sound out with equally determin'd voice, that conviction brooding within the recesses of every envision'd soul—illusions! apparitions! figments all! (985–86)

This is not the Whitman to whom most readers are accustomed. For certain, at the beginning of his 1855 preface to *Leaves of Grass* he did call for a national spirit "untied from strings necessarily blind to particulars and details magnificently moving in vast masses" (5). But even Emerson didn't believe that rocks and trees were illusions! And isn't Whitman supposed to be the poet who finds his muse "install'd among the kitchen ware"? In *Democratic Vistas* itself, Whitman praises such day-to-day realities as "Broadway, the heavy, low, musical roar, hardly ever intermitted, even at night; the jobbers' houses, the rich shops, the wharves, the great Central Park, and the Brooklyn Park of hills" (938). It's not that Whitman has changed his tune but that he sees in his own strongest impulse the temptation toward corruption. He writes of the "arrogance of realism" as if to challenge his own catalogs of facts to maintain the electric spirit he sees flowing through matter. Most crucially, he sees this personal artistic process existing within a larger historical cycle of decay and regeneration.

Such a recognition is precisely what so much current protest poetry lacks. This poetry seems either to accept no responsibility, no complicity, or else to employ such acceptance as a neopuritanical display of election. The motives are understandable. Who genuinely feels, after all, that he or she is responsible for wars begun under the cover of lies? What rational person would see in his or her self the image of Donald J. Trump, not to mention his reptilian cabinet? But if the outrage that boils beneath those questions swells the marches—no mean task—it doesn't, at least on its own, make for good poems. The rendering of consciousness in crisis needs to contain its own countering forces—and this is no mere matter of being "fair and balanced," seeing both sides of a subject, tempering one's rage, etc. A successful political poem might, in fact, prove *more* radical than protest going down on the street: what appears the smaller, even private scale of the poem—because it allows individual consciousness to enter into propositions without certain outcomes— might become the testing site of more powerful challenges to conventions of thought and feeling. If such artwork shows us the totality in which we're caught, those political structures we live inside *and live inside us*, aren't we then impelled to resist more fundamentally?

And isn't this what the most successful protests themselves accomplish? From Seattle in 1999 to the antiwar protests of the early 2000s, from Occupy to Black Lives Matter, the movements of recent memory have varied in terms of their immediate efficacy. The "Battle in Seattle" was, for example, a relative triumph: the WTO talks collapsed as a result of the protests. This happened not only by virtue of persistence—not to mention widespread dismay at images of a militarized police force shooting concussion grenades at unarmed American citizens—but rather because the protesters were able to question themselves, to perform what critical theorists call "immanent critique." Debates within the movement led to the rejection of pressures to stand down. The protest grew more radical, even as it became a collective force open to contradictions and ambiguities—an actual alliance of longshoremen and students, environmentalists and auto workers. Such moments may seem short lived, but even when they effect no obvious change, retreating underground again, they become vital to the future of resistance. Solving contradiction through embracing it, as in Whitman's poems, they offer more than a new moral system with its own repressive features: they furnish a glimpse of genuine freedom, a freedom embedded in responsibility.

There are contemporary poems that respond to our political ex-

perience in this deeper sense, as no mere airing of their "views."
One of these is "Discipline" by Tom Sleigh. The poem is the narrative of a brief encounter. Here's the first half:

> Random meeting at a bar,
>   random association that didn't
> need to happen, was it me
>   feeling and saying what I said,
> shaky after, but at the moment
> loosening to friendship
>   during time of war?—
>
> he had good biceps,
>   straight teeth, fancy sneakers.
> Then he showed a pic of
>   his soldier lover: tall, skinny,
> appealing in a young Abe Lincoln way:
> "When's he come home?"
>   "Six months but he
>
> already got extended ninety days."
> He looked so young—and what? was it
>   heat building in my gaze as we
> stared together, desire crossing
>   boundaries so that me thinking
> I'm straight, my war Vietnam
> began to chafe at strict
>
>   division enforced along lines
> of discipline laid down
> of what naked bodies do
>   and uniformed bodies don't?—
> anyway, shouldn't a patriot want
>   to go to bed to solace a soldier
> as handsome as this one, to feel pressure
>
> of his eyes hard against
>   mine, his body in the line
> of fire conspiring to let me move
>   closer, closer ... (2007, 88–89)

Like Whitman's ideal Americans who "think lightly of the laws," the
poet certainly moves beyond usual boundaries. His transgression
lends the poem both allure and dramatic tension. Narrative allows

Sleigh to dramatize, in isolate moments, the kind of moral ambiguities Whitman disperses throughout his poems. But Sleigh's talent
isn't for narrative alone. Much of the drama here flows from a collision of forms. The poem begins with one convention of storytelling
("I met this guy in a bar . . ."), but the actual story leads us into the
classic triangulation of erotic lyric. And the interior force of desire
not only tempts the poet but also pushes against the exterior plot of
the poem. Neither narrative nor lyric has any set political identity,
and they're fused here anyhow, but the tension between them corresponds roughly with the pull between freedom and constraint, the
transgression as well as the "division enforced along lines" that it
makes apparent. That friction intensifies as the poem moves toward
its ending:

> then the lover took out a letter from his soldier
> that he showed me in a what? subtle gesture
> of flirtation I just as subtly invited,
>
> aware even in my straightness
> I was over the line, voyeur
> to myself, the war, the lover and his soldier
> writing home how hot
> the sun got, he'd shot a rubber bullet
> into a crowd, he was going a little nuts
> like those movies where the soldier always loses it—
>
> the crowd was yelling, running, crossing
> a line, zigging,
> zagging, someone
> stumbled, went down—
> I turned my gaze from the photo's
> smiling eyes, heat building in my looking
> burning off and leaving
>
> us awkward, cooling in
> the once companionable dark:
> "You must miss him."
> "Well, you can see how
> tall he is. His feet hung over
> the edge of the bed. He
> makes an easy target."
> And then we got up to go,

me to come here, losing, then finding another
like him and his soldier
        and the war far away
in these words but still
        going on, each walking his own
shifty line of discipline. (89–90)

The whole poem balances on the fulcrum of that moment when the
poet turns his gaze from the picture. Imagine how much weaker
"Discipline" would be if Sleigh hadn't included those four words,
"building in my looking." It almost seems the erotic attraction has
been heightened by the glimmer of violence. If the poet's interest
had suddenly evaporated after hearing about the shooting in Iraq,
how schematic, how unreal the politics of the poem would have
felt. Desire simply doesn't work that way. As it stands, the poem
complicates our sense of the connection between emotions and beliefs. Sleigh's poem reveals our entanglement in those "shifty lines"
that we often ignore but that still crop up—when a straight person
feels an attraction to someone of the same sex, or a gay soldier has
to hide his identity, or a soldier who doesn't want to fire even rub-
ber bullets is forced ("he already got extended ninety days") into
his frightening role.

But can a poem do more than show us our entanglement? I
think so. At the very end of "Discipline," Sleigh admits that the
people in the poem are virtual, not the actual men in the bar and in
the photo. This might seem to leach power from the artwork. But
Sleigh's turn at the end is no stock, po-mo evasion. As the people
morph into words, they manage two things at once: they confer a
sense of responsibility upon the writer who must render them and,
since they become fictional, allow the kind of creaturely play that
pushes against the lines of our moral systems. After all, the best political poetry collapses the division between play and responsibility.
This happens in Whitman, for example, when we come across such
seemingly contradictory passages as the exalting of those reflected
faces in the water and the grumbling that "the best class we show, is
but a mob of fashionably dress'd speculators and vulgarians." These
passages gain their moral power and endurance from being propo-

sitions rather than rhetorical opinions. As such, they ask us to test the connections between emotions and beliefs, as well as statements and their referents. They compel us to consider a totality that evades our too-easy binaries, to imagine our actions as more mysterious and more vital than simple causes and effects. One result is that we leave the artwork able to praise and protest more fully in the world.

Free within Ourselves

In 1926, when Langston Hughes published "The Negro Artist and the Racial Mountain" in *The Nation*, he appeared to declare the richness and promise of black American literature. After all, the essay concludes with a triumphant call to fellow black artists: "We stand on top of the mountain, free within ourselves" (1994, 58). But this ending can't suppress the tension that troubles the piece and has attended its reception for decades. I have in mind the poet's irritation with those who seemed unwilling to accept their blackness and write from their collective experience. Hughes begins "The Negro Artist and the Racial Mountain" with the following anecdote about his interaction with an unnamed writer—whom biographers and scholars identify as no less a poet than Countee Cullen: "One of the most promising of the young Negro poets said to me once, 'I want to be a poet—not a Negro poet,' meaning, I believe, 'I want to write like a white poet'; meaning subconsciously, 'I would like to be a white poet'; meaning behind that, 'I would like to be white.' And I was sorry the young man said that, for no great poet has ever been afraid of being himself" (55).

What would "being himself" have meant? According to Hughes, black writers need to cultivate roots in common experience:

But then there are the low-down folks, the so-called common element, and they are the majority—may the Lord be praised! The people who

217

have their hip of gin on Saturday nights and are not too important to themselves or the community, or too well fed, or too learned to watch the lazy world go round. They live on Seventh Street in Washington or State Street in Chicago and they do not particularly care whether they are like white folks or anybody else. Their joy runs, bang! into ecstasy. Their religion soars to a shout. Work maybe a little today, rest a little tomorrow. Play awhile. Sing awhile, let's dance! (56)

The objections that a writer like Cullen might have had to these claims only become more obvious in a twenty-first-century context. The poet Gregory Pardlo, for example, in his essay "Revisiting the Racial Mountain," writes of Hughes's portrayal of seemingly authentic "low-down folks" that "it is difficult for the reader to hide a twinge of embarrassment" (2010, 1). All poets work to reconcile intellectual aspiration and instinctual impulse, and for African American poets those tensions prove especially fraught—presenting the risk of communal betrayal on the one hand and racist caricature on the other.

But I'm going to consider two poets whose work suggests not only how poetry benefits from engaging these very tensions but also how such engagement offers a surprising version of Hughes's liberational ideal, his vision of black artists "free within ourselves." Hughes himself, in his best poems, tends to court rather than evade the uncertainties his essay would seem to condemn. I think, for instance, of "Cross," a short lyric whose tightly rhymed form reflects the excruciating situation of a mixed-race speaker whose identity proves far more complex than those caricatures the poet conjures in his praise of "low-down folk." Even in an anthology piece such as "The Weary Blues" there's a significant divide between the narrator who reports about the blues singer and the singer and his song themselves. Perhaps the best example of this same constitutive ambiguity appears, however, in Jean Toomer's *Cane* (1923), a book upon which Hughes lavishes tribute in "The Negro Artist and the Racial Mountain."

Hughes employs that commendation to support his argument about authenticity. Describing Toomer's 1923 collection, he writes, "The colored people did not praise it. The white people did not buy it. Most of the colored people who did read *Cane* hate it. They are afraid of it. Although the critics gave it good reviews the public remained indifferent. Yet (excepting the work of Du Bois) *Cane* contains the finest prose written by a Negro in America" (1994, 56). *Cane* would seem to match Hughes's image of unrefined virtue. For sure the book teems with portrayals of "the common element" Hughes praises, and these include countless instances of impulsive physicality and overt, unabashed eroticism, which may have embarrassed black readers intent upon shedding prejudicial assumptions. But Toomer's rendering of "the common element" in the lyrical prose pieces and interspersed poems that make up *Cane* seems to me remarkable for its nuance.

Consider the motif around which the book revolves, the figure of elusive female beauty. Taking form as the women after whom many of the prose sections are named—"Karintha," "Fern," "Avey," and so on—this figure functions as a shape-shifter whose essence escapes the men who obsess over her, even those who manage to make love to her. Toomer tends to depict her as a native genius of the rural South whose intangible essence appears forever about to vanish. But rather than the resistance of authentic earthiness to linguistic classification, her inscrutability defies the binaries on which Hughes's essay depends. Consider how the narrator of "Fern" describes her:

> At first sight of her I felt as if I heard a Jewish cantor sing. As if his singing rose above the unheard chorus of folk-song. And I felt bound to her. I too had my dreams: something I would do for her. I have knocked about from town to town too much not to know the futility of mere change of place. Besides, picture if you can, this cream-colored solitary girl sitting at a tenement window looking down on the indifferent throngs of Harlem. Better that she listen to the folk-songs at dusk in Georgia, you would say, and so would I. Or, suppose she came up North and married. Even a doctor or a lawyer, say, one who would be sure to get along—that is, make money. You and I know, who have had experience in such things, that love is not a thing like prejudice which can be bettered by change of town. (Toomer 2011, 23–24)

The narrator prefers "folk-songs at dusk in Georgia" to the urban milieu of upwardly mobile blacks. But conjuring Fern's allure, he resorts to a figure of geographic and cultural distance with a phrase Toomer repeats throughout this section—"as if I heard a Jewish cantor sing." And while the narrator declares that "love is not a thing like prejudice that can be bettered by change of town," Fern remains elusive even when she stays in Georgia, where her suitors repeatedly attempt but fail to capture her mysteriously sophisticated nature.

Fern's resistance to geographic binaries corresponds to similar resistances throughout the collection. Toomer's women tend, for example, to wend back and forth across the color line—dangerous enough for them, and worse for those black men who would follow them, as in the section titled "Blood-Burning Moon," which ends with the lynching of a man who provokes his beloved's white admirer. These women also defy easy distinctions between instinct and intellect. In "Esther," for example, the heroine—who's not only more subdued and better educated than most of Toomer's women but so light-skinned that she's described as "white"—surprises her community when she declares her love for King Barlo, a laborer whose attraction for Esther lies in his ability to fuse mind and body in moments of religious vision.

Toomer's skill for making art from the thematic oppositions on which Hughes builds his essay parallels the formal hybridity of *Cane*—its original combination of prose and verse. The best poems in the collection reveal how Toomer's canny negotiation of seeming contraries extends to the specific level of phrase. Consider "Georgia Dusk," a poem describing the ritual character of a feast held in the evening in the cane fields. Here's the second half of the poem:

> Smoke from the pyramidal sawdust pile
>   Curls up, blue ghosts of trees, tarrying low
>   Where only chips and stumps are left to show
> The solid proof of former domicile.
>
> Meanwhile, the men, with vestiges of pomp,
>   Race memories of king and caravan,
>   High-priests, and ostrich, and a juju-man,
> Go singing through the footpaths of the swamp.
>
> Their voices rise ... the pine trees are guitars,
>   Strumming, pine-needles fall like sheets of rain ...

Their voices rise ... the chorus of the cane
Is caroling a vesper to the stars ...

O singers, resinous and soft your songs
    Above the sacred whispers of the pines,
    Give virgin lips to canefield concubines,
Bring dreams of Christ to dusky cane-lipped throngs. (19-20)

This passage forms an extended metaphor: the land and the people who work it become consubstantial, so that by the end of the penultimate stanza the cane itself seems to be "caroling a vesper to the stars." But the fusion depends upon competing registers, tonalities that Toomer doesn't reconcile so much as balance in dynamic, edgy relation.

For one thing, his mastery of the English metrical tradition and his application of "high" diction, such as "tarrying" and "domicile," strike a counterpoint with his "low" subject matter. But the formal contrast mirrors a larger one. Taken at face value, the poet's final invocation to the singers, his request that they "bring dreams of Christ to dusky cane-lipped throngs," would seem to render "Georgia Dusk" a religious poem. I find it impossible, however, to read this passage and conclude that the poet wants the "race memories" of the juju-man and his ilk, or even the "canefield concubines," to be anything other than what they are. Instead the "dreams of Christ," the African American folk traditions, and the bawdy revelry appear suspended, held in solution.

This is Toomer's genius, his ability not to solve contradictions but to build a form in which they're allowed to move, a form that suggests an original and generative conception of freedom. For Hughes—at least the Hughes of "The Negro Artist and the Racial Mountain"—the vision of black artists "free within ourselves" means release from fear of being improper, from the pressure to be white (a motif that recurs in Hughes's autobiography, *The Big Sea*, especially when he writes about his father). But in Toomer, freedom comes from entertaining such antagonisms. Far from simply celebrating the pre-gentrified folk culture of early twentieth-century black Americans, he constructs his characters, and his language itself, from the same contradictions Hughes wishes to erase. For Toomer the *form* of freedom, its action, proves less a breaking-out than a containing, an inclusion of emancipated multiplicities.

This notion of form and freedom suggested by *Cane* receives its most thorough and surprising elaboration in a collection by a contemporary African American poet. I have in mind Thylias Moss's 2004 verse novel, *Slave Moth*. The book delivers great satisfaction even if read simply as a novel. The narrative centers on a slave girl in Tennessee named Varl, taught to read and write because her master, Peter Perry, wants to observe her learning as a kind of experiment. Varl's education, however, leads her to questions that challenge the very foundation of Perry's society. What does freedom mean? How does language relate to the struggle for freedom? Most importantly, how can Varl make the interior liberation she's experiencing manifest in the world? The rigorous curiosity with which Moss attends to these questions makes her collection a vital successor to Toomer's *Cane*.

Moss understands that to examine freedom means also to address form. Slavery, for example, appears as a "deformity," a word that appears throughout *Slave Moth*. "Deformity" also refers in the book to Peter Perry's obsession with oddities of nature: he not only collects animals with deformed features but also owns—and displays for money—an albino and a dwarf. This aspect of the gothic or grotesque reveals Moss's best narrative instincts, as well as the originality of her imagination. For one thing, the malignant weirdness of the society these characters inhabit—one founded on slavery—prevents *them* from seeming the true "freaks." Like this, Moss's characters break past any framing devices. They're never mere stand-ins for some fixed conception of race in American history. Even as she addresses "Big Themes," Moss avoids schematism at every turn; Perry's fascination with deformity turns out to be not only a sign of his brutality but also a means of sustaining some vestige of human curiosity and wonder within the inhumanity of the master-slave arrangement. For Varl, deformity suggests the warped nature of slavery, which she longs to leave behind, but also those complexities she must fathom as she grows into a woman and achieves her freedom. Deformed things, she comes to learn, are not necessarily bad, normal things not always good. As she gains personal resolve, Varl becomes aware of moral ambiguities bound up in her own contradictory feelings. Most importantly, she learns that freedom means more than escape: it takes a form that's more personal, more interior than we might suppose. Moss illustrates the process of self-determination by means of an extraordinary metaphor: she has Varl embroider her thoughts into her clothing, to live inside a literal cocoon of words, the gestating core from which she'll eventually burst into liberation. At the same time, Varl's conception of freedom proves less an achieved state than commonly assumed and more a continuous process, entailing risk, responsibility, and consequence. While Varl certainly wants to escape slavery, she experiences her freedom, and Moss ends the book not when she has been fully emancipated but when she and her lover, Dobb, have fully begun the struggle that will lead to a slave rebellion:

> And I am free now, your freedom doesn't come to you
> because of your location; you have to feel it inside
> or you'd just be a slave in a free place. Lost.
> Inside my cocoon I am already Free.
>
> Inside my cocoon I'm extending Varl's definition to include *Free*. (119)

In these lines from the section of *Slave Moth* titled "Slaughter and the Varl in Me," Varl's emphasis on words themselves suggests not only how freedom and language are bound together but also how Moss's own literary form embodies the pursuit of freedom. I have in mind the way she engages both narrative and lyric expectations. *Slave Moth* rewards the reader on the level of story and character, but there's good reason for the book to be in verse. This novel, after all, is about the acquisition of language in a state of opposition; heavily textured free verse offers Moss a means of establishing Varl's personal echo chamber, that space where her body itself seems at turns to exult and keen. Reading *Slave Moth*, you watch naturalistic scenes morph as lyrical bursts erupt from this interior world where Varl forms compacted charges of phrases. Her quest for freedom runs in parallel not only with the balance between prose and verse but also with the task—Moss's as well as Varl's—of integrating instinct and intellect.

Consider a passage from the first section of *Slave Moth*, in which Varl discusses the figure of the luna moth, whose life cycle she learns about in Perry's *Great Book of Insectean Marvels*:

> —You can fit all my name *Varl* into larva.
> You can fit all my name into something
> that undergoes complete metamorphoses.
>
> Starting tonight
>
> I won't write any more of my thoughts on paper
> though I did like to steal it from my master,
> Ralls Janet especially perturbed by that
> to the amusement of her husband;
> starting tonight
>
> on cloth I stitch my words,
> the larva drawing its silk back and forth
> through squares of cloth
>
> that will be luna wings, dozens
> of specimens stitched together, connected
> into a cocoon I can wear under my dress
> these first squares pinned
> across my chest to change my heart,
> the next ones to be the underside
> of my scarf those days I choose to
> tie up my hair to change my mind
> and then keep it from changing back. (6–7)

If Toomer addresses the seeming contradiction of earthiness and sophistication—the pitted opposites of Hughes's essay—by virtue of his well-rounded character development and carefully tuned linguistic range, Moss does so with metaphor. In fact, this passage offers a metaphor about metaphor-making itself, the attempt to link body and mind, material and idea, in a new form that has been "stitched together, connected." What's so striking is how Varl's deliberation here, her decisiveness, coincides with extreme vulnerability—not only the obvious hazard of an enslaved person's secrecy but also the riskiness of any project so unique, so unlikely.

That is the great virtue of *Slave Moth*: its subject matter, the vexed history of race in America, could easily have led to didacticism, tactics, predictability. Moss's achievement shows in her reckoning with no less a topic than freedom, and yet doing so with an originality so genuine that it verges on the strange, the improbable. Both Toomer and Moss reveal how the strongest poetry comes from courting the very contraries that often frustrate the justifiable desire for stable identities, in art as in cultural life. If there's a lesson in the practice of these two great black poets, it remains relevant to all writers and readers: aesthetic freedom lies not in escape from antagonisms but in the ability to set them in new and generative relations.

Sincerity and Its Discontents

The word *sincerity* has a strange wiggle in discussions of poetry. Some use it as an accolade and others as a criticism, and it's not always that these people disagree about the work at hand. *Sincerity* has simply come to mean various things. Much of its slipperiness derives from being a relatively new word and concept. In *Sincerity and Authenticity* (1972), Lionel Trilling located the origins of sincerity in the Protestant Reformation. Beginning in the sixteenth century, there appeared new images of the writer as the individual believer speaking from faith alone, and later, the citizen acting within democratic structures. And in fact, if you look up the definition of *sincerity* in the *OED*, you'll find the following definitions, substantiated with quotations from sixteenth-century English ecclesiastical texts:

> the character, quality, or state of being sincere. 1 : a. freedom from falsification, adulteration, or alloy; purity, correctness. *Obs.* b. genuineness (*of* a passage). *Obs.* 2 : a. freedom from dissimulation or duplicity; honesty, straightforwardness. b. of feelings: genuineness. c. *pl.* sincere feelings or actions. (2018)

Such definitions, translated into social ideals, found natural fruition in America, itself the result of those historical currents. But even here "sincerity" arrived with its undercurrents of discontent. D. H. Lawrence suspected as much when, in *Studies in Classic American*

Literature, he claimed that American aspiration rose not from ideals of freedom but from refusal and alienation. Behind the advertised values of public-spirited straight talking lies "something grimmer, by no means free-and-easy," Lawrence pronounced, adding that "you have got to pull the democratic and idealistic clothes off American utterance" if you want to understand the life of this new republic and the art made from its speech (1968, 5).

You don't have to buy his sociological conclusions to see the literary value of Lawrence's identifications. So much of the best American poetry gains its strength from pitting the public communicative urge against the naked discontent that those "democratic and idealistic clothes" attempt to cover. Think of Whitman, who even as he offers "every atom" of himself in the unfolding of his poem admits that in the eye of an ox there seems to be "more than all the print I have read in my life." Think of how even as Whitman celebrates civic life, he repeatedly throws out images from which his citizens might recoil, right down to "the sick-gray faces of onanists." Or consider how Dickinson, although she directly addresses her reader and invites her into genuine exchange, exclaims "how public, like a frog" it is to speak one's self to the civic world, that mucked tangle of the marketplace that feels like "an admiring bog." This tension between the urge toward sincerity and the underlying dissatisfaction that torques it remains a generative force in our poetry. To evaluate the poems of our own moment, we need to understand it.

Maybe the first step would be to cut sharper contours around our idea of "sincerity." In so many of the formative arguments of modern and contemporary poetry, it receives only the roughest definition. Take Louis Untermeyer's *Modern American Poetry,* his anthology of 1919. This was a dramatic act of taste-making, and a successful one commercially: Harcourt put the book through seven printings. Opening his introduction with a declaration of America's "poetic renascence," Untermeyer bases his polemic on a celebration of sincerity. He claims that the poets in his anthology have sloughed the constraints of lyric convention: "The result of this has been a great gain both in sincerity and intensity; it has enabled the poet of today to put greater emphasis on his emotion rather than on the shell that covers it — he can dwell with richer detail on the matter instead of the manner" (ix).

From a contemporary vantage the book seems daft, and not only because Untermeyer gives himself more space than he gives Emily Dickinson. His whole argument turns out to be a rehash of Wordsworth's famous call for a "selection of language really used by men," except without the "coloring of imagination," upon which Wordsworth also insisted. To Untermeyer, "sincerity" means merely one idiom that he values above all others. He prizes "the use of a simpler and less stilted language" at all costs, and the results are often poems like Richard Hovey's "A Stein Song" ("With a stein on the table and a good song ringing clear").

A reaction against the febrile parlor poetry of the turn of the century, Untermeyer's anthology remains a period piece. But we can still see its arguments burbling up now and again, as if during the whole last century American poetry and its criticism have been locked in a rinse-and-spin cycle between sincerity and its discontents. *Modern American Poetry* itself, for example, although it contained minimal selections from Pound and Eliot, flowed in clear opposition to the claims of those classic Modernists. The call for "sincerity" streamed up against Eliot's famous arguments for "impersonality," which appeared the same year in the pages of the periodical *The Egoist*. Open to any chapter in the history of American poetry and you'll see the debate swirling away in some new permutation. A more recent instance appears in Louise Glück's essay "Against Sincerity" from the early 1990s. Glück argues that poetic truth stands apart from mere fact, and she takes "sincerity" to stand for the ingenuous desire for a one-to-one relation between what happened and what's written. The only problem is, who can imagine an intelligent person disagreeing? Are there really serious readers who want writers merely to be trusty reporters? To be fair, we should see Glück's essay in context. In several places in her book of criticism *Proofs and Theories* (1995), she seems compelled to make an antiliteralist argument, one that carried more force twenty five years ago during the glut of "trauma narratives" and the poetry that drew support from it. This was work that in its bareness showed a surface resemblance to Glück's own poetry of personal crisis but little of its strengthening skepticism. Her distinction in "Against Sincerity" was a refreshing backward swipe against the Richard Hoveys of the day. But set apart from its context, her argument teeters. It comes to resemble the claims of a movement that has no relation to her own superlative practice. I mean those poets who are truly "against sincerity," period. For these writers, the very idea of the poem as the speech of a subjective self endeavoring to find some truth, however provisional, seems hopelessly Romantic. As the poet and critic Danielle Chapman explained in her essay "Bad Habits," these poems have become "so familiar by now that they could appear in a Girl Scout handbook of the *avant-garde*" (2005, 324). Chapman points out the irony: by preserving the author's thoughts and emotions behind an embroidered curtain of free association, these poems exhibit the most encrusted Romanticism imaginable. Oddly, the effect turns out to be the same as that of naive, deadly earnest "sincere" poetry: experience and language remain in fixed relation, and the poems go static.

At this point it may seem that the word *sincerity* would best be avoided in discussion of poetry. And yet I'm convinced that because of its very instability the concept of sincerity remains crucial to an understanding of American poetry: it locates fundamental tensions from which poems arise.

In order to explain those tensions, I want to introduce two additional terms that may seem just as troublesome as *sincerity*. The first of these is *rhetoric*. One way that poets have declared both their sincerity and their newness for at least two hundred years now has been by attacking rhetoric. When Wordsworth argued for a "selection of the real language of men in a state of vivid sensation" (2011, 597), he wasn't only advocating new registers of speech: he was also condemning what he called "personifications of abstract ideas" (600). He wanted his representations of people to deliver the imprint of real people and not to exist merely as stand-ins for arguments. That Romantic belief in the power of the image as an actual thing carried over into Modernism and was best summed up by Pound, who famously wrote that the genuine poetic image was "that which presents an emotional and intellectual complex in an instant of time" (1968, 4). He thought of this presentation as profoundly antirhetorical, declaring with characteristic crustiness that "the 'image' is the furthest possible remove from rhetoric. Rhetoric is the art of dressing up some unimportant matter so as to fool the audience for the time being" (1974, 95). Such convictions continue to inform contemporary poetry. You can hear Pound echoing, for example, in Robert Creeley's influential and downright utilitarian claim that "form is never more than an extension of content" (Olson 1997, 241).

Of course all these statements are themselves rhetoric, and even the poems written in their spirit never scrap rhetoric entirely. Wordsworth's leech gatherer and Pound's apparitional faces in a crowd both seem to me like "personifications of abstract ideas." Maybe it's impossible to erase the sound of persuasion or argument from any speech meant to move a reader or listener. Certainly in American poetry of recent decades, the emphasis on the image that began to filter into classrooms long ago as "show, don't tell" seems to have shifted: many of our most prominent poets often work in discursive or essayistic registers. And this shift bears directly upon concepts of sincerity. On the one hand, rhetorical argumentation figures as a turn away from sincerity—encouraging skepticism about naive or self-justifying claims of authenticity; on the other hand, by emphasizing the pursuit of truth, such methods sometimes align with sincerity.

One of the many compelling things about Tony Hoagland's poems is that he takes rhetoric itself as one of his central subjects. Big pronouncements, sudden adversative turns in thinking, long elaborations of examples employed to adduce a point—these are not only recurring features of Hoagland's poems but also their very substance. There's a counterforce to all the arguments as well. Hoagland is obsessed both by the maneuvers of thought that we employ to make sense of fact and experience and by the tension that occurs when fact and experience resist those maneuvers. Take the first five lines of his 2010 book, from the poem "Description":

A bird with a cry like a cell phone says something
to a bird which sounds like a manual typewriter.

Out of sight in the woods, the creek trickles
its ongoing sentence; from treble to baritone,

from dependent clause to interrogative. (3)

The humor of these oddball similes and metaphors comes not only
from the juxtaposition of pastoral detail to human systems of technology and grammar but also from the underlying sense that the
comparisons are a bluff, the natural world will slip free from the
poet's extravagant attempts to catalog it. Similar resistance to his
own efforts at classification occurs in all the strongest of Hoagland's poems, including "Hostess," "Complicit with Everything,"
and "The Story of the Father." Hoagland appears in these poems
as a nearly compulsive describer, and yet he allows the refreshing
strangeness of the world to push back. His ability to engage such
tension seems to me his great talent and a sign of his sincerity. His
irony may be highly developed, but it seldom acts as armor. This
poet gravitates toward moments when the individual finds himself
embarrassed, caught out, and therefore forced to confront uncom-
fortable truths.

The tension between eloquence and fact that informs "Description" corresponds in *Unincorporated Persons in the Late Honda Dynasty* (2010) with another internal resistance, the weird contradiction about contemporary American life that you pick up even from
that title, the idea that we're conditioned, determined by the imperial forces of mass culture, and at the same time oddly and alarm-
ingly free because of it as we float around in our indeterminate postmodern wash.

Hoagland's ability to match formal challenges with serious social
concerns should make for strength and subtlety in the poetry. But
this sociopolitical territory is also where the exhilaration of his rhetorical approach runs into pitfalls. Consider the opening of "Hinge":

Last night on the TV the light-brown African-American professor
looked at the printout analysis of his own DNA
and learned that he was mostly Irish.

I can't go back to Africa now, he thought,
controlling the expression on his face,
his big moment onscreen already turning out
different than he had imagined.

Nor would he ever be able to say the sentence,
"I be at the crib"
with the same brotherly ease as before. (2010, 43)

The first three lines work as a fine lead-in. But then the poem takes a wrong turn. The idea that a light-brown African American man, and a professor to boot (readers will recognize Henry Louis Gates Jr.), might be surprised by having European ancestry, and might consider a DNA readout as the ultimate verdict on racial and cultural heritage, feels dubious enough for starters. But the sudden move into the omniscient third person, conveying the presumption that the poet knows exactly what the man was thinking, is the real trouble here. The professor's thoughts turn out to be cartoonish at best. These thoughts read less like interior monologue and more like gags at the expense of the professor, whom Hoagland makes not only gullible but affected: "his big moment onscreen already turning out / different than he had imagined."

The problem is not simply that Hoagland has made some political blunder. He's been criticized often for his poems about race—in particular, a poem called "The Change" from his previous volume *What Narcissism Means to Me* (2003). But the riskiness of addressing race in America, and inhabiting seemingly "incorrect" tones or attitudes, might have been refreshing. The real snag has to do with the management of rhetoric. The narration operates at a supreme distance from the material, so that the true subject turns out to be the poet's performance of a joke at the expense of a famous intellectual, who becomes little more than a "personification of an abstract idea." To be sure, "Hinge" contains a turn at the end in which the reality of America's racial history becomes suddenly much more real to the speaker; "The Change" offered a similar ending: the narrator, who spends most of the poem entertaining derogatory thoughts about an African American tennis player, comes to admit that the times are changing. In both cases the turn feels insufficient, not because some proper ideology has been flouted but because the shift seems too consciously schematic.

Such reduction occurs elsewhere in the book. When Hoagland writes in another poem that Britney Spears "looks a little chubby in a spangled bikini" as she dances before "fanged, spiteful fans and enemies" (2010, 20), he resorts to types, images that may have particularity so far as the poet's phrase-making is inventive and amusing but that exert little pull of their own against the plotting of the poem.

And that plotting shows through too often. For example, Hoagland tends to tie off his poems with summations that often sound, despite their hard-won and tough-love tones, like tidy morals. Here's a nearly random sample of endings:

—But that is how you build your castle.
That is how one earns a name
like Jason the Real.
                    —"Jason the Real" (51)

All that talk about love, and *This*
is what that word was pointing at.
                    —"Love" (18)

That was part of the composition.
That was the only kind of freedom
we were ever going to know.
                    —"Jazz" (72)

That was the plot.
That was our marvelous punishment.
                    —"Voyage" (87)

Hoagland may often advertise his spontaneity with goofy imagery and phrasing, but in these passages he points you to the meanings of his own poems with all the rigid authority of a traffic cop. He may often play the naïf or the anti-intellectual, and yet he's much more comfortable in the world of categorical signs and markers than in the thick of actual experience. As his commentary piles up and his tactics of argument repeat themselves, you begin to suspect that this poet has never had an experience for seven seconds without beginning to structure it into some clever speech.

Oddly, this is the very narratorial distance that Hoagland isolates and questions in his excellent essay "Fear of Narrative and the Skittery Poem of Our Moment," when he discusses a type of contemporary poem dominated by irony. The trouble with such a poem, he explains, is that it remains "safely told by a narrator who operates at an altitude above plot, narrating from a supervisory position.... It is distinctly externalized. *Distance* is as much the distinctive feature of the poems as play; distance, which might be seen as antithetical to that other enterprise of poetry—strong feeling" (2006, 176). Reading *Unincorporated Persons in the Late Honda Dynasty*, I find myself wondering: Is the flaw here that Hoagland writes the same poetry that he complains about in his essay? Is the problem with Hoagland's rhetoric simply the distance it cleaves between the poet and his subjects? I don't think so. From Horace through Pope to Auden, great poets have long depended upon rhetorical distance. At times their imagery even seems clearly subordinate to their argument, as the people in their poems appear like those "personifications of abstract ideas" that Wordsworth railed against. And these are still great poets.

No, what makes Hoagland's rhetoric feel so "rhetorical" in the pejorative sense has to do with the second in my pair of admittedly troublesome terms: I have in mind this poet's peculiar lack of "music." The absence contributes to the ease with which many of his weaker poems can be summed up by pat phrases. It's not just that his tactics of argument become monotonous. When you turn, for example, from "Hinge" to the next poem in the book, "Foghorn," you encounter this opening:

> When that man my age
> came towards me in the fast-food restaurant
> with his blue plastic cafeteria tray
>
> and stood next to the table where I sat alone
> (there was no place else to sit),
> I looked up at him in welcome. (45)

The lineation has little tension, the nouns and verbs exert no sway because they have so little particularity, and the voice itself remains anecdotal. It's unfortunate that Hoagland allows this mode to dominate because the best poems in *Unincorporated Persons in the Late Honda Dynasty* deserve to be read and admired—and studied by aspiring poets.

A poet's musical skillfulness means more than the ability to establish a measure or set vowels and consonants ringing against each other. Sometimes music comes from such patterning of sounds. Sometimes it comes from starkness. It can derive, too, from the shifting of tones, the pacing of associative leaps, the timing of statements. Whatever its source, music affects the semantic meanings of a poem. For one thing, sound intensifies the words and phrases and therefore underlines their denotative content. But though we're used to connecting form and content, they can also proceed in counterpoint. Music maintains a distance from logical sense—if it didn't, all poems would be entirely onomatopoetic.

Because of this distance, music may resemble rhetoric: it unfolds as an abstract ordering pattern and yet remains at one remove from semantic meaning. But if music proves the more fugitive or ineffable of the two terms, it also has something rhetoric doesn't— bodily force, sway. The sounds of poems produce their own images and have their own animal alertness. In this way music can become a mark of sincerity in the best sense: genuine music allows the reader not only to witness but also to feel the twists and turns of consciousness in action. Music can thereby make a vital counterpart for rhetoric—preventing the strategies of argument in a poem from coming across as strategies. Reading, say, Robert Hass or C. K. Williams at his most discursive, I seldom sense any contrivance—because the music offers an almost creaturely element of unreason, amplitude, and surprise.

Williams provides an excellent example. After his death in 2015 I found myself returning to his poems of the prior fifteen or twenty years: during this late period, because he was so prolific, critics had a hard time catching up with Williams. There was also an earlier "breakthrough narrative," leading many readers, or so it seemed, to focus on and favor his poetry of the late 1970s and early 1980s. The publication in 1977 of his third book of poems, *With Ignorance*, marked an exhilarating moment in American poetry. Williams had moved on from his earlier style, a kind of Spanish surrealism that he quickened with his own, Nixon-era political rage. The newer poems maintained that anger but now registered the social world with greater fidelity. Williams had a nearly faultless ear for how his contemporaries actually spoke. With his characteristic long lines, he could begin a poem like this:

> If you put in enough hours in bars, sooner or later you get to hear every
> imaginable kind of bullshit. (2006, 129)

Social life didn't dampen but captured and conducted the heat of Williams's concerns. And his work wasn't mere gritty realism. The colloquial directness could accommodate a more philosophical, discursive tone of speculative yearning. If this opened whole regions of experience, it also incurred a risk—rhetoric. The challenge for Williams became to balance corporeal rawness and metaphysical fluency, and this stands out boldly in two successive book titles from the late 1980s and 1990s, *Flesh and Blood* and *A Dream of Mind*.

Although his late work remains voluminous and contains some poems that are transitional or repetitive, the many superb poems share an ambition to weave together abstraction and embeddedness, argument and expression. Take the title poem from his 2005 volume, *The Singing*. It begins with the poet encountering a young black man rapping to himself as he walks down the street:

> I was walking home down a hill near our house on a balmy afternoon
> under the blossoms
> Of the pear trees that go flamboyantly mad here every spring with their
> burgeoning forth
>
> When a young man turned from a corner singing no it was more of a
> cadenced shouting
> Most of which I couldn't catch because the young man was black
> speaking black

It didn't matter I could tell he was making his song up which pleased me
    he was nice-looking
Husky dressed in some style of big pants obviously full of himself hence
    his lyrical flowing over (552)

The young man then begins to sing the word "Big," referring to
the poet's height. But when the poet smiles in response, the rapper
begins to chant "I'm not a nice person." "The Singing" concludes
with these lines:

No one saw no one heard all the unasked and unanswered questions were
    left where they were
It occurred to me to sing back "I'm not a nice person either" but I
    couldn't come up with a tune

Besides I wouldn't have meant it nor he have believed it both us knew
    just where we were
In the duet we composed the equation we made the conventions to
    which we were condemned

Sometimes it feels even when no one is there that someone something is
    watching and listening
Someone to rectify redo remake this time again though no one saw nor
    heard one was there. (552–53)

If the encounter Williams portrays in "The Singing" brims
with tension, so does the poem itself. Its very form establishes this
counterpoint: the long, unpunctuated lines at times correspond with
flowing, long sentences, and at times contrast with abrupt, staccato
statements. Likewise the tone shifts between an almost rhapsodic
register, as in the opening ("a balmy afternoon under the blossoms,"
"the pear trees that go flamboyantly mad," "burgeoning forth") and
one of painstaking, reflective analysis. Williams's poem proceeds
by a series of alternations in which "musical" and "rhetorical" approaches temper one another. The result is a remarkable example
of sincerity in the best sense: the poet remains open to instability
and uncertainty as he searches for some form of right relation between himself and his subject. That relation never fully material-
izes in the actual narrative. Not only does the young man remain
inscrutable to the poet; any promise of redeeming presence, any

hope of connection with others, seems to fall away with this final statement. But the statement wouldn't have the power it does if Williams hadn't sustained connection, both with his subject and with his reader, if he weren't both inclusive and discerning, expressive and argumentative, responsive simultaneously to ideas and sensations. This embodied engagement is the element of music, the singing after which the poem's titled. The conventions that the poet and the young man share turn out to be "the conventions to which we were condemned," and yet the ending doesn't feel like a deadlock because the poem allows those conventions, if only for a moment, also to be what they are earlier on that same line — "the duet we composed the equation we made." Like the rapper singing "Big," the ending allows exchange between the self and others to remain precarious, even as the very "singing" of the poem, the process of its becoming, establishes a shared reality.

If Hoagland's collection exhibits the opportunities and risks of rhetoric, and if Williams's "The Singing" reveals how music can lend depth and subtlety to those same methods, Atsuro Riley's astonishing and original debut collection, *Romey's Order* (2010), suggests the potential of a poetry based almost entirely on music. Thriving off their sonic richness, these poems are about the attempt to make sense of the world, to account for all the strange and disparate details that enthrall consciousness, and to hold them in some kind of meaningful relation. The book is one long series, the protagonist a boy nicknamed Romey, the son of a Vietnam veteran and the Japanese woman he brought back with him to the South Carolina low country. As the father works the rivers as an odd-job man, the son himself plies the shallows and the woods, the fairground and the campground. As he wanders, he concocts an entire vocabulary, one that mixes southern dialect and smatterings of Japanese with his own inventions. Riley often takes the prosepoem as his form, yet the improvised vocabulary always provides musical force. Take, for example, the beginning of the opening poem, "Flint Chant":

Once upon a time a ditchpipe got left behind behind Azalea Industrial, back in the woods backing on to the Ashley, where old pitch-pines and loblollies grow wild. A mild pesticide-mist was falling and mingling with paper-mill smell and creosote oil the morning he found it. The boy shook and sheltered in its mouth awhile— *hoo-hoo! hey-O!* —and bent and went on in. It was like a cave but clean. He C curved his spine against one wall to fit, and humming something, sucked his shirttail. He tuned his eyes to what low light there was and knuckle-drummed a line along his legs. (2010, 3)

There's a lot to marvel at here. Riley seems to weave effortlessly between his narration and the interior thoughts of the boy. I also admire how the rhymes and half-rhymes not only help to prevent the prose from becoming prosaic but also manage to convey the palpability of the world the boy encounters—those textures as beguiling and various as "pesticide-mist" and sucked shirttails. What moves me most about this passage, though, is how Riley crafts from seemingly modest material a profound evocation of the work of poetry: in the abandoned "ditchpipe" Romey brings himself, and the readers of the poem, into a space where the world, the self, and language all become simultaneously rich and strange. This poem's about the very music of poetry. Or, to be more precise, it's about searching for and finding that music. Like the father in the book, Romey (and it's hard not to hear both the verb *roam* and the name Riley in Romey) turns out to be a kind of modern hunter-gatherer. He tries to make some kind of sense—his "order"—from everything that surrounds him. He must piece himself and the world together.

This is what makes Riley such an American poet. The world that he and his protagonist encounter is always the New World, one in which few ready traditions offer consolation or furnish tools for understanding. The social interactions in the book tend to be odd and even frightening, not least of all because Romey is an Asian American boy in the rural South. The poem "Diorama," for example, portrays a summer fair where the attractions include a game called "Shoot the Gook Down," and where Romey overhears gossip about himself:

I wonder does her boy talk Chinese?
  You ever seen that kind of black-headed?
Blue shine all in it like a crow. (28)

In "Strand," Riley provides this two-line portrait of the father:

Jim Beam *&* Jim Crow drive him through, like Jesus does some others.
Sure I'm evergreen for Wallace but I'm not no kkk. (12)

Such passages are presented without any commentary. Riley never *explains*, for example, how ironic it is that a father of a mixed-race boy would support the notorious segregationist George Wallace. But if this poet seems wise to reserve judgment of the details he presents, avoiding any overtly rhetorical claims about them, nevertheless his analytic mind is always alert. As much as Hoagland, Riley is fascinated by the friction between the individual's desire to shape experience and American culture's ready-made, often unsatisfying categories for experience. The father may seem foolish when he uses two available markers ("Wallace" and "kkk") to explain his politics. But he's engaged here in something like Riley's own project of using the available and often impoverished nouns around him to construct a self-determined and original life from what he's been given.

What makes Riley a master of these constructions is his ability to order details such that his speaker not only perceives but also questions and evaluates. Often this appears as a kind of dance between the child's perception and the adult's narration. Consider this passage from "Scroll," in which Romey pores over a book of Hokusai's prints of Mount Fuji:

The boy took to night-gnawing and nursing this old (folding-out) book of mountains, his mother's. He nosed, naturally, and licked at the milkish-mushroomy cover-threads. He finger-hankered, unfolding, for something, something, something. He "read."

Look! Mama's cradle-place. Pines. Lakes. Reeds. Cranes. Plum-blooms (pink-tendered leastways: cherry, could be) and willows. A blue-carved C of wave.

The boy (bellied-down, and trawling) traced and craved. (36)

Riley's inventiveness with interior dialogue, his forging of chewy neologisms and unexpected compounds like "milkish-mushroomy" and "pink-tendered," both conveys the thoughts and feelings of the child grappling to understand and shows the poet himself scavenging in the unknown where he searches for "something, something, something." At times the voice of the poet and the voice of the child seem inseparable, and at times their difference becomes obvious — for instance, in the comic remove from the child's point of view affected by the quotation marks around the word "read," with its subtle half-rhyme against "threads." Romey's attempt to hold all the facets of the mixed-up realms of family and culture in some kind of order becomes Riley's own effort to give these memories a shape that feels beautiful and true. The challenge of recovering childhood experience, creating for it an entire vocabulary, and then crafting from this argot an original music, may seem as daunting a task as moving Mount Fuji to South Carolina. But the success of *Romey's Order* is not that it pulls off some staggering feat. Riley doesn't so much recover the past as join memories and the very process of memory itself into a new, vivacious action.

Anyone who's had occasion to read a stack of new poetry books will know how widespread concept books have become: I have in mind those collections in which thematic structures order the energies of individual poems, in the manner of rhetorical claims, if not always with overt rhetoric. Riley's work, though it hardly follows any trend, suggests how fruitful such a method might be, how sincere. He deploys high-resolution images, both visual and aural, and sets them in paratactic relation, without any commentary between. But the success of his poems doesn't depend upon the absence of abstraction any more than the problems with some of Hoagland's poems derive from his rhetorical approach. As Riley arranges his details, especially as he negotiates the distance between his child protagonist and adult narrator, he fuses feeling with thought. There's a genuine metaphysical core to these poems: Riley asks not only how an individual can give shape to his or her own life through memory, imagination, and artfulness but how he or she can do so in a specifically American situation. His answers are sincere because we feel both the attempt of the imagination to transcend its contingent circumstances and the obdurate reality of those circumstances. The ditchpipe abandoned behind Azalea Industrial is both Pan's instrument of magic and a ditchpipe. The tension between the world of fact into which each of us is born and the desire to forge our own new worlds results here in beguiling music, bringing these poems to life with all their sinew and subtlety.

Having considered sincerity through the filters of "rhetoric" and "music" and in the work of three contemporary American poets, I find a couple of beliefs implicit in my conception. The first is that true sincerity must be open to change—must be dynamic. This means considering sincerity not as an attribute but as an act. I'm imagining a process that changes as the correspondences between the speaking self and the world change too. Such a sincerity might even contain its own discontents, counterforces that flow against what the *OED* calls "purity, correctness," "honesty, straightforwardness," and "freedom from falsification, adulteration, or alloy." The second belief is that sincerity entails some understanding of the relation between the speaking self and history—not only how the self inhabits history but, more importantly, how history inhabits the self.

With these beliefs in mind, I want to conclude by looking at two contemporary poems that take the measure of our moment. Both balance upon a metaphor connecting speech—the actual minute phenomenon of it—to historical totality. In so doing they test sincerity in the most active sense. They both attempt to establish communication even as they strip away the covering of conventional exchange, much as Lawrence recommended. In each the subjective imagination speaks to public realities while remaining true to itself. Although one of them seems more successful, these are both poems I admire. To me they suggest that some of the most exciting work in American poetry right now occurs when skepticism and emotional seriousness flow together, their collision driving the movement of the poem.

Here's how Maurice Manning begins "Where Sadness Comes From":

Don't go back to say it came from way
back when. It did, it did, but now.

When you said did just now did you feel
a little dip, a curtsey in

the middle of the word, almost
another syllable but

not quite? We like to say a word,
a single word can make us feel.

There, there it is again, this time
a falling down at the end of feel.

You feel it, how that little sound
goes dropping down and hangs alone. (2010, 89)

Up to here, the poem might resemble some of those in the "Girl Scout handbook of the *avant-garde*." The voice works to atomize itself even as it unfolds, keeping the focus on the "materiality of language." But Manning's skepticism is more than mere show. As the tetrameter halts and proceeds and the voice weaves between the inward, almost oneiric address with which the poem begins and the outward questioning, the lines take on the feeling of genuine speculation. This attentive seriousness sets us up for the big turn. Here's the rest of the poem:

I'm here to tell you I come from
a place where hanging used to happen:

it happened in the trees, by God,
it happens even now in air,

the air the mouth lets loose; I hear
a hanging all the time. It leaves

a sadness in the voice; we speak,
and wait for history to catch up

with us. It's slow, but then, that lets
you hear it coming; you hear it now

before you speak, that sadness in
your voice, the part of you that wants

to last, to hang or dip, to hold
the word for just a little more—

my people, this is an elegy
to you, the sadness in your voice. (89–90)

The amplitude of these eight couplets, the oratorical plunge into southern melancholy and collective guilt, not only stands in contrast to the microscopic attention of the opening but also relies on that contrast for support. The scrutiny attempts to justify the high-mindedness.

This doesn't entirely succeed. It's hard to believe that the dip in a southern drawl really relates to lynching. It's not that the metaphor's wrong by nature, not that we need to test it against the findings of sociolinguistics. I just wish that Manning would apply some of the same salutary doubt he uses to pick apart syllables at the beginning of the poem to his own metaphor at the end. The turn comes less than halfway through. If there were one more swerve in the rhetorical structure, one more bolt of reinforcing skepticism, perhaps the somewhat showy metaphor would become a provisional truth, a plausible attitude of thought and feeling. The poem remains an impressive feat of sincerity in action: Manning's attention to the actual texture of speech parallels his desire to address historical truths while staying true to the protean variability of the present ("It did, it did, but now"). The flaw comes when speechifying takes the place of such searching.

Elizabeth Arnold's "Civilization," from her book of the same name, establishes a metaphor similar to Manning's. The poem's dated "September 2001." It seems to me one of the few that address that catastrophe with original insight:

The British journalist's voice was spent as she said
(unenthusiastically, the interview now over), "Thanks,"

with the eager young insatiable American official
turning, then, to other matters. But the voice

—a European's, flat, well schooled in the world's
hope-pulverizing particle storm's gifts of disappointment — stayed,

the syllable's slight elongation something on the order of
the querulous sendings of frail human wonderings out

into the void, as if the waning of her voice spoke
all of history's ups and downs, a honeycomb's packed maze of cells

whose lights shine through their tiny paper membranes
too thin not to be available to being torn,

light leaking from a world cracked open,
sky seen through the pavement I walk down. (2006, 39)

Arnold's drama of confidence and uncertainty informs the very
texture of her lines. Consider her penchant for condensation, for
phrases like "hope-pulverizing particle storm's gift of disappointment," or the appropriately attenuated "sendings of frail human
wonderings out." Thickening the rhythm of the line as the sentence
itself snakes forward, these phrases make the verse movement appear consubstantial with the movement of intelligence through matter. Their slight jumbling of syntax and idiom has a similar result.
Maybe no one would ever say "sendings of frail human wonderings
out," but this is why it works: the phrase captures consciousness
stitching together the constituent pieces of perception. Whatever
wobble there is balances against and intensifies the urgency of the
occasion, the necessity of speaking at a moment of global violence.
Arnold avoids grandiosity, though, by turning to the seemingly
mundane and private image of the patches of sky reflected on pavement, in a passage that, in one final turn, swivels from the ordinary
to the cataclysmic as it precisely depicts a "world cracked open."

Arnold's speed, her skill for dwelling upon each image no longer
than need be as she collects and distributes the energies of her sentences, seems to me part and parcel of her sincerity. As her conviction and skepticism cycle onward—achieving precision through
variability, like a compass needle—she offers what might be called a
kinetics of truthfulness. Such movement also points to what makes
Arnold so American. I don't mean to stick a toy flag in her poem;

after all, it's one in which the very word *American* seems nearly synonymous with *naive*. But Arnold's forward-plunging effort at speech appears tinged with a different spirit. I have in mind that ranginess that D. H. Lawrence saw as escapist alienation, but also that William James celebrated when explaining that his brand of American pragmatism was nothing more than "an attitude of orientation . . . . *The attitude of looking away from first things, principles, 'categories,' supposed necessities; and of looking toward last things, fruits, consequences, facts*" (1987, 510).

Perhaps it's Robert Frost, that poet who managed to write both as the American public man and as the guide who only has at heart our getting lost, who gave the most helpful definition of sincerity. It's one far subtler than that of his advocate Louis Untermeyer, and it's a conception of poetic speech that in stressing movement bears direct relation to the practice of contemporary poets like Manning and Arnold. In one of his notebooks, Frost writes: "There is such a thing as sincerity. It is hard to define but it is probably nothing more than your highest liveliness escaping from a succession of dead selves. Miraculously. It is the same with illusions. Any belief you sink into when you should be leaving it behind is an illusion. Reality is the cold feeling on the end of the trout's nose" (2006, 456–57). Sincerity for Frost is not simply "being yourself" or "telling it like it is." It happens "miraculously," not by command of the will. The force that breaks through the "succession of dead selves" is not a set identity so much as an action, discernible precisely because of its kinetic movement: "liveliness." And illusion is not wrong because it fails to measure up to some Platonic ideal but simply because it happens not to work. It's no accident that Frost jumps here from defining sincerity to defining reality. The creaturely alertness that he suggests runs beneath truth-telling is the same with which we sense our way through the stuff of experience, the sheer material we half perceive and half create. The blend of conviction and uncertainty that informs the alertness described by Frost offers in microcosm the union of form and freedom required for any true act of creation. In such a situation, "form" proves more surprising than traditional conventions to be observed, just as "freedom" becomes more crucial than "freedom *to*" or "freedom *from*": it is an engage-ment with necessity and consequence. What's at stake is the search for an order that will preserve the liveliness of the search itself. It may flow through irony, earnestness, absurdity, disguise, and even wrong conclusions, but it doesn't take these as positions. We'll know the sincere poem from the way it moves.

Acknowledgments

Thanks to the editors of the publications in which these chapters and subchapters first appeared, sometimes in earlier versions:

Blackbird: "Larry Levis"
Boston Globe: "*Old War*"
Diode: "*World Tree*"
Harvard Review: "C. K. Williams"
New York Times: "*Emblems of the Passing World*"
Parnassus: "James Wright's Classicism"
P. N. Review: "Lorine Niedecker," "George Oppen," and
    "Palpable Fact: James Schuyler and Immediacy"
Poetry: "*Poets of the Civil War*," "Sincerity and Its Discontents,"
    "*Up to Speed*," and "*War and the 'Iliad'*"
Poetry Northwest: "The Wolf, the Hog, the Snake, Not Wanting
    in Me"
Raritan: "*The Epistles of Horace*"
Yale Review: "James McMichael," "John Koethe," "Louise Glück,"
    and "Mah Wallah-Woe"

"John Berryman's Acoustics" first appeared in *John Berryman: Centenary Essays*, edited by Philip Coleman and Peter Campion (Oxford: Peter Lang, 2017). "Larry Levis" began as a talk delivered on September 23, 2010, at Levis: A Celebration, at Virginia Commonwealth University.

Works Cited

Anderson, Perry. 1998. *The Origins of Postmodernity*. New York: Verso.

Antin, David. 1972. *Talking*. London: Dalkey Archive.

Antin, David. 1976. *Talking at the Boundaries*. New York: New Directions.

Antin, David. 2005. *i never knew what time it was*. Berkeley: University of California Press.

Antin, David. 2011. *Radical Coherency: Selected Essays on Art and Literature, 1966 to 2005*. Chicago: University of Chicago Press.

Arendt, Hannah. 1958. *Between Past and Future*. London: Penguin Books.

Armantrout, Rae. 2004. *Up to Speed*. Middletown, CT: Wesleyan University Press.

Arnold, Elizabeth. 2006. *Civilization*. Chicago: Flood Editions.

Ashbery, John. 1986. *Selected Poems*. London: Penguin Books.

Auden, W. H. 1976. *Collected Poems*. London: Faber and Faber.

Baldwin, James. 1955. *Notes of a Native Son*. Boston: Beacon.

Bellow, Saul. 2010. *Letters*. Edited by Benjamin Taylor. New York: Viking.

Bernstein, Charles, and Bruce Andrews. 1984. *The L=A=N=G=U=A=G=E Book*. Carbondale: Southern Illinois University Press.

Berryman, John. 1969. *The Dream Songs*. New York: Farrar, Straus, and Giroux.

Berryman, John. 1976. *The Freedom of the Poet*. New York: Farrar, Straus, and Giroux.

Berryman, John. 1989. *Collected Poems 1937–1971*. Edited by Charles Thornbury. New York: Farrar, Straus, and Giroux.

Berryman, John. 2004. *Selected Poems*. Edited by Kevin Young. New York: Library of America.

Bishop, Elizabeth. 2008. *Poems, Prose, and Letters*. Edited by Lloyd Schwartz. New York: Library of America.

Blackmur, R. P. 1936. "The Instincts of Bard," review of *A Further Range* by Robert Frost. *The Nation*, June.

Blackmur, R. P. 1952. *Language as Gesture*. New York: Columbia University Press.

Chapman, Danielle. 2005. "Bad Habits." *Poetry*, January.

Cockburn, Alexander. 1996. *The Golden Age Is in Us: Journeys and Encounters, 1987–1994*. New York: Verso.

Corn, Wanda M. 1999. *The Great American Thing: Modern Art and National Identity, 1915–1935*. Berkeley: University of California Press.

Dangerfield, George. 1965. *The Awakening of American Nationalism*. New York: Harper and Row.

Davie, Donald. 2000. *Two Ways Out of Whitman*. Edited by Doreen Davie. London: Carcanet.

Di Piero, W. S. 2004. "Fat." *Poetry*, October.

Dickinson, Emily. 1960. *The Complete Poems of Emily Dickinson*. Edited by Thomas H. Johnson. Boston: Little, Brown.

Dijkstra, Bram. 1969. *The Hieroglyphics of a New Speech: Cubism, Stieglitz, and the Early Poetry of William Carlos Williams*. Princeton, NJ: Princeton University Press.

Eliot, T. S. 1962. *The Complete Poems and Plays, 1909–1950*. New York: Harcourt.

Eliot, T. S. 1975. *Selected Prose of T. S. Eliot*. Edited by Frank Kermode. New York: Harcourt.

Eisenhower, Dwight David. January 17, 1961. "Farewell Address." Accessed July 31, 2016. http: courscsa.matrix.msu.edu/~hst306/documents/indust.html.

Evans, Walker. 1980. "The Reappearance of Photography." In *Classic Essays on Photography*, edited by Alan Trachtenberg. Sedgwick, ME: Leete's Island Books. (Originally published in *Hound and Horn* 5, no. 1 [1931].)

Fisher, Philip. 1999. *Still the New World: American Literature in a Culture of Creative Destruction*. Cambridge, MA: Harvard University Press.

Fitts, Dudley. 1936. Review of *A Further Range* by Robert Frost. *New England Quarterly* 9, no. 3 (September).

Foster, Jeanne. 2001. "The First Workshop: A Memoir of James Wright." *American Poetry Review* 30, no. 4 (July).

Frost, Robert. 1963. *The Letters of Robert Frost to Louis Untermeyer*. Edited by Louis Untermeyer. New York: Holt, Rhinehart and Winston.

Frost, Robert. 1964. *Selected Letters of Robert Frost.* Edited by Lawrence Thompson. New York: Holt, Rinehart and Winston.

Frost, Robert. 1995. *Collected Poems, Prose, and Plays of Robert Frost.* Edited by Richard Poirier and Mark Richardson. New York: Library of America.

Frost, Robert. 2006. *The Notebooks of Robert Frost.* Edited by Robert Faggen. Cambridge, MA: Harvard University Press.

Gay, John. 1923. *Poems.* Boston: Small, Maynard.

Glück, Louise. 1995. *Proofs and Theories: Essays on Poetry.* New York: Ecco.

Glück, Louise. 2012. *Poems 1962–2012.* New York: Farrar, Straus and Giroux.

Hejinian, Lyn. 1980. *My Life.* Providence, RI: Burning Deck.

Hoagland, Tony. 2006. *Real Sofistikashun.* Minneapolis: Graywolf.

Hoagland, Tony. 2010. *Unincorporated Persons in the Late Honda Dynasty.* Minneapolis: Graywolf.

Hofstadter, Richard. 1963. *Anti-intellectualism in American Life.* New York: Vintage.

Horace. 2001. *The Epistles of Horace.* Translated by David Ferry. New York: Farrar, Straus and Giroux.

Hughes, Langston. 1993. *The Big Sea: An Autobiography.* New York: Hill and Wang.

Hughes, Langston. 1994. "The Negro Artist and the Racial Mountain." In *Within the Circle: An Anthology of African American Literary Criticism from the Harlem Renaissance to the Present,* edited by Angelyn Mitchell. Durham, NC: Duke University Press. (Originally published in *The Nation,* June 23, 1926.)

Hughes, Langston. 1995. *The Collected Poems of Langston Hughes.* Edited by Arnold Rampersad and David Roessel. New York: Vintage.

Humphries, Rolfe. 1936. "A Further Shirking," review of *A Further Range* by Robert Frost. *New Masses,* August.

James, William. 1987. *Writings 1902–1910.* Edited by Bruce Kuklick. New York: Library of America.

Jameson, Fredric. 1996. *The Seeds of Time.* New York: Columbia University Press.

Kaplan, Justin. 1980. *Walt Whitman: A Life.* New York: Simon and Schuster.

Keats, John. 1988. *The Complete Poems.* Edited by John Barnard. London: Penguin Books.

Kirsch, Adam. 2015. *Emblems of the Passing World: Poems after Photographs by August Sander*. New York: Other.

Koethe, John. 2000. *Poetry at One Remove: Essays*. Ann Arbor: University of Michigan Press.

Koethe, John. 2006. *Sally's Hair*. New York: HarperCollins.

Lawrence, D. H. 1968. *Studies in Classic American Literature*. New York: Viking.

Lefebvre, Henri. 2014. *Critique of Everyday Life*. New York: Verso.

Lenin, Vladimir Ilyich. 1987. *Essential Works of Lenin*. Edited by Henry M. Christman. New York: Dover Books.

Levis, Larry. 2003. *The Selected Levis*. Rev. ed. Edited by David St. John. Pittsburgh: University of Pittsburgh Press.

Levis, Larry. 2004. "After the Obsession with Some Beloved Figure: An Interview with Larry Levis," by Leslie Kelen. In *A Condition of the Spirit: The Life and Work of Larry Levis*, edited by Christopher Buckley and Alexander Long. Spokane: Eastern Washington University Press. (Originally published in *Antioch Review* 48, no. 3 [Summer 1990].)

Lowell, Robert. 2003. *Collected Poems*. Edited by Frank Bidart and David Gewanter. New York: Farrar, Straus and Giroux.

Lowell, Robert. 2006. *Selected Poems*. Edited by Frank Bidart. New York: Farrar, Straus and Giroux.

Lukács, Georg. 1971. *The Theory of the Novel*. Translated by Anna Bostock. Boston: MIT Press.

Mandel, Ernest. 1978. *Late Capitalism*. Translated by Ernest Mandel. New York: Verso. (Originally published in German as *Der Spätkapitalismus*. Berlin: Suhrkamp Verlag, 1972.)

Manning, Maurice. 2010. *The Common Man*. Boston: Houghton Mifflin Harcourt.

Marx, Karl, and Friedrich Engels. 2011. *The Communist Manifesto*. Translated by Samuel Moore, edited by Marshall Berman. London: Penguin Books.

McLuhan, Marshall. 2005. *The Medium Is the Message*. Edited by W. Terrence Gordon. Berkeley, CA: Ginko.

McMichael, James. 1996. *The World at Large*. Chicago: University of Chicago Press.

McMichael, James. 2006. *Capacity*. New York: Farrar, Straus and Giroux.

Melville, Herman. 2005. "Inscription." In *Poets of the Civil War*, edited by J. D. McClatchy. New York: Library of America.

Moss, Thylias. 2004. *Slave Moth*. New York: Persea Books.

Mullen, Harryette. 2006. *Recyclopedia: Trimmings, S*PeRM**K*T, and Muse and Drudge*. Minneapolis: Graywolf.

Niedecker, Lorine. 2002. *Collected Works*. Edited by Jenny Lynn Penberthy. Berkeley: University of California Press.

O'Hara, Frank. 1964. *Lunch Poems*. San Francisco: City Lights.

O'Hara, Frank. 1971. *The Collected Poems of Frank O'Hara*. Edited by Donald Allen. New York: Alfred A. Knopf.

Olson, Charles. 1997. *Collected Prose*. Edited by Donald Allen and Benjamin Friedlander. Berkeley: University of California Press.

Oppen, George. 2002. *New Collected Poems*. Edited by Michael Davidson. New York: New Directions.

Oxford English Dictionary. 2018. http: https://public-oed-com.

Pardlo, Gregory. 2010. "Revisiting the Racial Mountain." *Pen America*, accessed April 13, 2017, https://pen.org/revisiting-the-racial -mountain/.

Pinsky, Robert. 1996. *The Figured Wheel: New and Collected Poems, 1966– 1996*. New York: Farrar, Straus and Giroux.

Pinsky, Robert. 2002. *Democracy, Culture and the Voice of Poetry*. Princeton, NJ: Princeton University Press.

Pinsky, Robert. 2007. *Gulf Music*. New York: Farrar, Straus and Giroux.

Pound, Ezra. 1968. *Literary Essays*. New York: New Directions.

Pound, Ezra. 1974. *Gaudier-Brzeska: A Memoir*. New York: New Directions.

Pound, Ezra. 1990. *Personae*. Edited by Lea Baechler and A. Walton Litz. New York: New Directions.

Pound, Ezra. 1995. *The Cantos of Ezra Pound*. New York: New Directions.

Pound, Ezra, and Marcella Spann. 1964. *From Confucius to Cummings*. New York: New Directions.

Ransom, John Crowe. 1984. *Selected Essays*. Edited by Thomas Daniel Young and John Hindle. Baton Rouge: Louisiana State University Press.

Riley, Atsuro. 2010. *Romey's Order*. Chicago: University of Chicago Press.

Rilke, Rainer Maria. 2018. "Some Reflections on Dolls." In *On Dolls*, edited by Kenneth Gross. London: Notting Hill Editions.

Roethke, Theodore. 1968. *Selected Letters*. Edited by Ralph J. Mills Jr. Seattle: University of Washington Press.

Rosenthal, M. L. 1991. *Our Life in Poetry: Selected Essays and Reviews*. New York: Persea.

Schuyler, James. 1993. *Collected Poems*. New York: Farrar, Straus, and Giroux.

Schuyler, James. 1998. *Selected Art Writings*. Edited by Simon Pettet. Santa Rosa, CA: Black Sparrow.

Shapiro, Alan. 1993. *In Praise of the Impure: Poetry and the Ethical Imagination; Essays, 1980–1991*. Evanston, IL: Northwestern University Press.

Shapiro, Alan. 2008. *Old War*. Boston: Houghton Mifflin.

Sleigh, Tom. 2007. *Space Walk*. Boston: Houghton Mifflin.

Stevens, Wallace. 1997. *Collected Poetry and Prose of Wallace Stevens*. Edited by Frank Kermode and Joan Richardson. New York: Library of America.

Stitt, Peter, and Frank Graziano. 1990. *James Wright: The Heart of Light*. Ann Arbor: University of Michigan Press.

Toomer, Jean. 2011. *Cane*. New York: Liveright.

Trilling, Lionel. 1972. *Sincerity and Authenticity*. Cambridge, MA: Harvard University Press.

Untermeyer, Louis, 1919. *Modern American Poetry*. New York: Harcourt.

Weil, Simone, and Rachel Bespaloff. 2005. *War and the "Iliad."* Translated by Mary McCarthy, edited by Christopher Benfey. New York: New York Review Books.

Whitman, Walt. 1982. *Poetry and Prose*. Edited by Justin Kaplan. New York: Literary Classics of the United States.

Williams, C. K. 2006. *Collected Poems*. New York: Farrar, Straus and Giroux.

Williams, William Carlos. 1986. *The Collected Poems of William Carlos Williams*, vol. 1, *1909–1939*. Edited by A. Walton Litz and Christopher MacGowan. New York: New Directions.

Williams, William Carlos. 1988. *The Collected Poems of William Carlos Williams*, vol. 2, *1939–1962*. Edited by Christopher MacGowan. New York: New Directions.

Wilson, Edmund. 2007. *Literary Essays and Reviews of the 1920s and 30s*. Edited by Lewis Dabney. New York: Library of America.

Wojahn, David. 2006. *Interrogation Palace: New and Selected Poems 1982–2004*. Pittsburgh: University of Pittsburgh Press.

Wojahn, David. 2011. *World Tree*. Pittsburgh: University of Pittsburgh Press.

Wojahn, David. 2015. *From the Valley of Making: Essays on the Craft of Poetry*. Ann Arbor: University of Michigan Press.

Wordsworth, William. 2011. *The Major Works*. Edited by Stephen Gill. Oxford: Oxford University Press.

Wright, James. 1990. *Above the River: The Complete Poems*. New York: Farrar, Straus, and Giroux.

Wright, James. 2005a. *Selected Poems*. Edited by Anne Wright. New York: Farrar, Straus, and Giroux.

Wright, James. 2005b. *A Wild Perfection: The Selected Letters of James Wright*. Edited by Anne Wright, Jonathan Blunk, and Saundra Rose Maley. New York: Farrar, Straus, and Giroux.

Yagoda, Ben. 2009. *Memoir: A History*. New York: Riverhead Books.

Yeats, W. B. 1983. *The Collected Works*, vol. 1, *The Poems*. Edited by Richard J. Finneran. New York: Macmillan.

Index of Names

Adams, John, 31, 73–74
Allen, Donald, 109, 131
Ammons, A. R., 144
Anderson, Perry, 132
Andrews, Bruce, 195
Antin, David, 126–37, 153
Arendt, Hannah, 28–29, 71
Armantrout, Rae, 195–97
Arnold, Elizabeth, 244
Arnold, Matthew, 14
Ashbery, John, 103–4, 110, 126, 138–39
Auden, W. H., 13, 28, 86, 108, 168, 202, 234

Bacall, Lauren, 27
Baldwin, James, 84
Baraka, Amiri, 162
Bartlett, John, 80
Baudelaire, Charles, 14, 30, 118
Bellow, Saul, 77
Benjamin, Walter, 30
Bennett, Arnold, 31
Berchtold, Leopold, 33–34, 39
Bernstein, Charles, 195
Berryman, John, 71–84
Bespaloff, Rachel, 179–200
Bidart, Frank, 101, 113–14, 118, 126
Bishop, Elizabeth, 87, 181

Blackmur, R. P., 12
Bly, Robert, 86, 100
Bogart, Humphrey, 27, 77
Bonaparte, Napoléon, 114
Breton, André, 56
Bridwell, E. Nelson, 4
Browning, Robert, 32
Burton, Richard, 141

Catullus, 101
Cervantes, Miguel de, 83
Chapman, Danielle, 229
Cockburn, Alexander, v
Coleman, Philip, 71
Coleridge, Samuel Taylor, 50, 169
Corn, Wanda M., 38
Coughlin, Charles, 53
Crane, Hart, 30, 80
Creeley, Robert, 230
Cullen, Countee, 217

Dangerfield, George, 16
Davidson, Michael, 61, 103
Davie, Donald, 70, 71, 80
De Forest, John W., 193
Demuth, Charles, 37
Dickey, James, 86
Dickinson, Emily, 4–6, 39, 193, 227–28

Dijkstra, Bram, 37
Di Piero, W. S., 207
Duchamp, Marcel, 38

Eisenhower, Dwight David, 77, 83
Eliade, Mircea, 190
Eliot, T. S., 13, 19, 30, 63, 80, 114, 118, 126, 131, 147, 152, 228
Ellison, Ralph, 76
Emerson, Ralph Waldo, 21, 104, 144, 208, 211
Engels, Friedrich, 68, 143
Evans, Walker, 191

Faulkner, William, 157, 193
Ferry, David, 199–205
Fisher, Philip, 209
Ford, Henry, 40–42
Foster, Jeanne, 96
Frost, Robert, 7, 9–13, 19–27, 80, 155, 201, 246

Gay, John, 201
Gibbons, Reginald, 200
Ginsberg, Allen, 87, 107, 113
Glück, Louise, 148–53, 228–29
Guest, Barbara, 104

Hall, Donald, 86–87
Hardy, Thomas, 93–94
Hartley, Marsden, 37
Hass, Robert, 235
Hawthorne, Nathaniel, 22
Hazlitt, William, 41
Hejinian, Lyn, 197
Hemingway, Ernest, 27, 32
Hoagland, Tony, 230–41
Hofstadter, Richard, 16
Homer, 29, 31–32, 69, 180, 187, 192, 199
Horace, 94, 199–206, 234
Hughes, Langston, 217–24
Humphries, Rolfe, 12
Huston, John, 27

Jackson, Andrew, 16
James, William, 20, 246
Jameson, Fredric, 132
Jarrell, Randall, 126
Jefferson, Thomas, 21, 26, 73–74

Kafka, Franz, 78
Kaplan, Justin, 208
Keats, John, 41, 49, 184
Kennedy, John F., 58–59
Kirsch, Adam, 191–93
Koch, Kenneth, 104
Koestenbaum, Wayne, 103
Koethe, John, 137–42, 146, 148, 153

Lansky, Meyer, 27
Lawrence, D. H., 6, 226–27, 242, 246
Lefebvre, Henri, 30, 56
Lenin, Vladimir Ilyich, v, 3, 8, 69, 186
Lennon, John, 186
Lentricchia, Frank, 20
Levine, Philip, 104
Levis, Larry, 166–75
Lichtenstein, Roy, 132, 136
Lowell, Robert, 7, 13, 28, 71, 87, 113–27, 129, 131–32, 137–38, 152–54, 188
Luciano, Charles "Lucky," 27
Lukács, Georg, 53, 56–57, 124–25, 137, 147, 152
Lupino, Ida, 77

Malatesta, Sigismundo, 34
Mandel, Ernest, 67
Manning, Maurice, 243–44, 246
Marcu, Valeriu, v, 3, 8
Marx, Karl, 28, 44, 53, 61, 64, 68–69
McAlmon, Robert, 40
McClatchy, J. D., 193
McLuhan, Marshall, 72–75
McMichael, James, 142–48, 153
Melville, Herman, 22, 194
Mills, Clark, 16
Milton, John, 129, 193

Moss, Thylias, 222–25
Mullen, Harryette, 196–99

Nelson, Maggie, 105
Niedecker, Lorine, 50–62, 66, 69, 70,
    125, 154

O'Hara, Frank, 104, 199, 202, 204
Olson, Charles, 113, 230
Ovid, 12, 22, 29, 31–32

Pardlo, Gregory, 218
Perl, Jed, 103
Pinsky, Robert, 101, 154–65
Plath, Sylvia, 154, 160
Poirier, Richard, 20
Pope, Alexander, 205, 234
Porter, Fairfield, 105–7, 109
Pound, Ezra, 29–36, 40, 46, 50, 55–58,
    60–61, 63, 69–70, 80, 94, 131, 145,
    162, 228, 230
Powell, Jim, 200
Pritchett, V. S., 115

Ransom, John Crowe, 91, 95
Riley, Atsuro, 238–41
Rilke, Rainer Maria, 133, 135, 168
Robinson, Edward G., 27
Robinson, Edwin Arlington, 22
Roethke, Theodore, 86
Roosevelt, Franklin Delano, 27
Rosenthal, M. L., 79, 113
Russell, Bertrand, 16

Saint-Gaudens, Augustus, 119–20
Sander, August, 191–93
Sappho, 195, 200, 204
Schuyler, James, 103–9, 138
Schwartz, Delmore, 126
Scott, Walter, 193
Shakespeare, William, 40–41, 47, 86,
    100, 121, 196
Shapiro, Alan, 144, 181–86
Shaw, Robert Gould, 119
Sheeler, Charles, 38, 40–44, 47

Sleigh, Tom, 213–15
Smart, Christopher, 172, 174
Stalin, Josef, 12, 42, 69, 187
Stein, Gertrude, 104, 197
Stevens, Wallace, vii, 9–19, 23–27, 141
Stieglitz, Alfred, 37
Strand, Mark, 87
Swinburne, Algernon Charles, 80–81

Tate, Allen, 131
Tennyson, Alfred, 80–81
Toomer, Jean, 218–22, 224–25
Trilling, Lionel, 11, 155, 191, 226
Trotsky, Leon, 42

Untermeyer, Louis, 227–28, 246

Vendler, Helen, 103
Virgil, 18, 200

Weber, Max, 22
Weil, Simone, 179–83, 186, 189, 195, 199
Whitman, Walt, 14, 18, 66, 68, 74, 86,
    104, 127, 132, 174, 193, 208–15, 227
Wilkie, Wendell, 27
Williams, C. K., 100, 235–38
Williams, William Carlos, 30–51, 55–
    56, 59, 66, 67–70, 96, 102, 131, 196
Williamson, Alan, 96, 101, 146
Wilson, Edmund, 40
Wiman, Christian, 103
Winters, Anne, 101
Winters, Yvor, 86
Wojahn, David, 96, 186–90, 207
Wordsworth, William, 23, 138, 153, 169,
    228, 229, 234
Wright, James, 85–102, 104
Wyatt, Thomas, 182

Yagoda, Ben, 115
Yeats, W. B., 34, 75, 80, 86, 101, 157
Young, Kevin, 76

Zukofsky, Louis, 51